INADVERTENT EXPANSION

INADVERTENT EXPANSION

How Peripheral Agents Shape
World Politics

Nicholas D. Anderson

CORNELL UNIVERSITY PRESS **ITHACA AND LONDON**

First published 2024 by Cornell University Press

Library of Congress Cataloging-in-Publication Data

Names: Anderson, Nicholas D. (Nicholas Duncan), author.
Title: Inadvertent expansion : how peripheral agents shape world politics / Nicholas D. Anderson.
Description: Ithaca : Cornell University Press, 2024. | Includes bibliographical references and index.
Identifiers: LCCN 2024020244 (print) | LCCN 2024020245 (ebook) | ISBN 9781501779473 (hardcover) | ISBN 9781501779497 (epub) | ISBN 9781501779480 (pdf)
Subjects: LCSH: Imperialism—History—19th century. | Imperialism—History—20th century. | Colonization—History—19th century. | Colonization—History—20th century. | World politics—19th century. | World politics—20th century.
Classification: LCC JC359 .A624 2024 (print) | LCC JC359 (ebook) | DDC 325/.3209034—dc23/eng/20240718
LC record available at https://lccn.loc.gov/2024020244
LC ebook record available at https://lccn.loc.gov/2024020245

Dedicated to the memory of my adviser and friend,
Nuno P. Monteiro (1971–2021)

Contents

Figures and Tables

Figures

Tables

Acknowledgments

This is a book about the ways in which leaders can lose complete control over important segments of the states and empires they are purportedly in charge of, producing foreign policy outcomes they had not intended at all. Funnily enough, the process by which this book came about, to some extent, reflects this basic theoretical insight. I did not initially set out to write a largely historical book. And I did not intend to write a book focused on empire. But a historical book focused, at least in part, on empire is what I ended up with.

I came to the topic for this book as, I think, many scholars of international relations do: by reading the work of the late Robert Jervis. In what I would argue is his greatest book, *System Effects*, Jervis speculates in one very brief section that territorial expansion might be subject to positive feedback effects, with expansion itself helping generate the conditions that drive future instances of expansion, which, in turn, generate still further expansion, and so on.[1] This 130-word section of his 300-page book began an intellectual and personal journey that would lead through various cities, libraries, university departments, academic conferences, and hundreds, if not thousands, of books, articles, and diplomatic documents.

This book has been more years in the making than I care to admit. This means, not only that I have gotten older but that I have accumulated an unusually large number of debts along the way. It began at Yale University, where I was fortunate to be a part of the department of political science. My mentors and colleagues at Yale provided much-needed constructive criticism, encouragement, support, and friendship that helped get this book off the ground. These include Dave Allison, Consuelo Amat, Jonathon Baron, Tyler Bowen, Matthew Cebul, Suparna Chaudhry, Alex Debs, Mike Goldfien, Stephen Herzog, Susan Hyde, Adria Lawrence, Jason Lyall, Guatam Nair, Will Nomikos, Maggie Peters, Lauren Pinson, Chris Price, Didac Queralt, Hari Ramesh, James Scott, Ian Shapiro, and Dana Stuster. A turning point in the book's development occurred as the result of a series of challenging and constructive conversations with Dan Altman, Richard Maass, Dan Nexon, and, especially, Keir Lieber and Josh Shifrinson. I also spent two years in the University of California, Berkeley's political science department, and benefited from the warm hospitality and helpful advice of Ron Hassner, Aila Matanock, and Paul Pierson. At Harvard University Kennedy School's Belfer Center for Science and International Affairs, I had many useful exchanges on various aspects of the book with Paul Behringer, Dan Jacobs, Tyler Jost, Sean Lynn-Jones, Steve Miller, and Steve Walt. Since coming to the Elliott School at the George Washington University, I have also had many fruitful exchanges on the book with many graduate students, visitors, fellows, and faculty, including Neha Ansari, Andrew Bowen, Dani Gilbert, Alex Kirss, Kendrick Kuo, Do Young Lee, Alex Lennon, Harris Mylonas, and Jo Spear. I have also been fortunate to have some of the very best in the business read and comment on various parts and at various stages of this book, including Gary Bass, David Edelstein, Tanisha Fazal, Eugene Gholz, Stacie Goddard, Kyle Haynes, Lindsay Hundley, Min Kim, Sarah Kreps, Matthew Kroenig, Melissa Lee, Sojeong Lee, Paul MacDonald, John Mearsheimer, Rachel Metz, Asfandyar Mir, Didac Queralt, Sebastian Rosato, Madison Schramm, John Schuessler, Travis Sharp, William Spaniel, Andrew Szarejko, and Dani Villa. Special thanks go to Mariya Grinberg and Jack Snyder, who read and commented on more versions of this manuscript, at more stages of its development, than they probably wanted to. I also owe thanks to Léa Glaezner for help checking my French translations. And I owe a great deal to Victor Cha, Alex Downes, Charlie Glaser, and Daryl Press, who have been an incredibly important part of my academic, professional, and personal development over many years.

I spent an inordinate amount of time in various libraries over the course of this book and benefited immensely from the hard-working staff at Sterling Memorial Library at Yale, Widener Library at Harvard, Gelman Library at George Washington, the Library of Congress, and the UC Berkeley library system. Various aspects of this project have also benefited from many presentations over the years, including at George Washington, Harvard, Yale, the IR Theory Colloquium (virtual), and various annual meetings of the American Political Science Association and the International Studies Association. Thanks also go to Kelly Sandefer and Beehive Mapping, who created the beautiful campaign maps that accompany the case studies in the book. I am grateful to the journal *International Security* for permission to use portions of my earlier article, "Push and Pull on the Periphery: Inadvertent Expansion in World Politics," *International Security* 47, no. 3 (Winter 2022–23): 136–173, throughout this book. It has also been a great pleasure working with Jacqulyn Teoh and the amazing editorial staff at Cornell University Press. And I am deeply appreciative of two anonymous reviewers, who offered incredibly constructive feedback on every chapter of the book. And I would like to acknowledge Barry Posen's truly great book *Inadvertent Escalation: Conventional War and Nuclear Risks* as the inspiration for this book's title.

Tragically, two of my mentors passed away before this book was published. Frances M. Rosenbluth was a consistent source of guidance and support from my very early days in graduate school. I was drawn to Frances as a mentor because of her wide-ranging interests, the tough questions she asked, her constant reminders to keep the big picture in mind, and her incredible personal warmth. We also shared a love of Japan, its history, and its politics. She was an icon in our department at Yale and in the broader field of political science. Frances was diagnosed with an aggressive form of brain cancer and died in November 2021 at the age of 63, leaving behind her partner, Ian, and her sons, Ben, John, and Will. And Nuno P. Monteiro was a model mentor from my very first days at Yale. Challenging, dedicated, responsive, and kind—always pushing me to ask big questions but to fit the answers into article- or book-sized packages, and to dig deeper and to get to the theoretical core of whatever problem was in front of me. He had insatiable curiosity, a magnetic personality, an irrepressible sense of humor, and a rare generosity of spirit. Nuno died of a heart attack in May 2021 at the age of 50, leaving behind his wife Audrey, and his children Sebastian and Ava. I have dedicated this book to his memory.

The most important thanks go to my family: my parents-in-law, Kyong-ja and Adam; my siblings, Em and Ben; my sister-in-law, Jen; my nieces and nephews, Victoria, Charlotte, Joey, and Charlie; and my parents, Carol and Duncan. Thank you for a lifetime of unconditional love, support, and understanding. The other result of having spent so many years on this book is that my life has changed dramatically in the meantime: I got married and had two kids along the way. Our kids—Murphy and Perry—themselves reflect the academic journey we have been on, being born in Berkeley, CA, and in Cambridge, MA (respectively), a mere 360-days apart. Their curiosity, energy, humor, passion, and love are a constant and much-needed reminder of what is really important in life—and what is not. And my most important thanks go to my partner, Babs. For the late-night pep talks, for your patience during all the inane discussions of international relations theory, research design, and imperial Japanese history and for all of the support, encouragement, understanding, laughter, and love—I cannot thank you enough. I do not think I would have gotten through it without you.

INADVERTENT EXPANSION

consciousness,
  intention

Introduction

> Colonies can be conquered by accident. This may at first appear
> unlikely when we contemplate the immense colonial empires that
> Europe once possessed—such elaborate constructions must surely
> be the product of a policy, of a design, of economic calculation.
> But if you believe that, you may well be deceiving yourself.
>
> —Douglas Porch, 1982

In late 1842, Sir Charles James Napier, a major general of the British East India Company, decided—without authorization—to seize Sind (now Sindh, Pakistan) for the British Empire. The rapidly aging yet still rashly defiant major general had independently decided that the ruling authorities in the region were tyrannical and untrustworthy and, as such, posed an unacceptable threat to the empire.[1] As he wrote ominously in a journal entry that year, "We have no right to seize Scinde; yet we shall do so, and a very advantageous, useful, humane piece of rascality it will be."[2]

With an army of three thousand, Napier began a march on Hyderabad in late January the very next year.[3] On February 18, his troops attacked the joint armies of the local authorities at Miani. Despite being outnumbered nearly four-to-one, the East India Company's forces achieved a decisive victory; only 63 of Napier's men were killed and 193 wounded while the other side suffered as many as 6,000 casualties.[4] Napier then continued on to Hyderabad, quickly deposed and exiled local leaders, and declared Sind to be under British control.[5] He was then widely reported to have informed his superiors of the acquisition by sending a one-word message in Latin: "*Peccavi*," or "I have sinned."[6]

When news of the conquest arrived back in London, it shocked and infuriated officials. The East India Company's council of directors, livid, passed a resolution condemning Napier's actions and calling for the return of the territories.[7] Prime Minister Robert Peel privately referred to Napier's actions as "unconscionable folly" and said the whole affair was "disgraceful to the character of this country."[8] Publicly, however, the prime minister and his cabinet were more circumspect in their response.[9] Though they would never have approved the Sind conquest beforehand, they were hard pressed to call for its reversal now that British blood had been spilled.[10] As the cabinet member William Gladstone later recalled, the cabinet was "powerless, inasmuch as the mischief of retaining it was less than the mischief of abandoning it, and it remains an accomplished fact."[11] They also recognized that the difficulty of communication had been a key problem hampering central control—this was still the pretelegraph era, after all, as the first telegraph line between Britain and India would only be operational in 1870.[12] In Peel's words, "Time—distance—the course of events may have so fettered our discretion that we had no alternative but to maintain the occupation of Scinde."[13] Moreover, from London's perspective, the geopolitical risk associated with retaining Sind was minimal—the local authorities had been decisively defeated, and no other powerful state had significant imperial or territorial interests in the area. And so it was that during the British Empire's acquisition of a territory the size of New York State containing nearly two million inhabitants, the central government in London had virtually no knowledge of, or control over, the process, whatsoever.[14]

This is a book about inadvertent expansion in world politics. It addresses a number of puzzles and questions that are raised by the escapades of Napier and by others, like them. First, *how common* are such inadvertent forms of territorial expansion as the British experienced in Sind? Was it—as much existing international relations theory would lead us to believe—a one-off? Was it an unexpected blip amid the broader and more predictable patterns of great power politics, attributable to the contingency of real-world international relations and the "messiness" of history? Or is inadvertent expansion a regular feature of the history of great power politics, displaying patterns of behavior and a regularity of occurrence that suggest it is a general phenomenon befitting its own theory?

Second, *why* do frontier actors such as Napier launch these unauthorized expansionist bids? Under what broad conditions are they most able and most willing to use political intrigue or military force to independently claim foreign territory? What are their expectations about how their actions will be received by their superiors back home, and how does this influence their decisions? And what roles are played by the vast distances involved, the vagaries of rudimentary technology, and the challenges associated with controlling such peripheral actors from the capital?

Third, *why* do the leaders in the capital, such as Prime Minister Peel, accept these independent territorial claims in some cases, but not others? Why, in some cases, do we see leaders accepting territories when they are reluctant to do so and when the territories in question have little intrinsic economic or strategic value? Why, in other cases, do we see leaders turning away territories in which they are deeply interested, and when the territories have significant economic or strategic value? How does the process of unauthorized expansion itself shape how leaders view these opportunities for territorial gain? And what role is played by the broader security environment surrounding these territorial claims?

Territorial Expansion in International Relations

Inadvertent expansion is a little-explored phenomenon in the study of territorial expansion. In debates over what explains the tendency for great powers to expand territorially, answers generally focus on the gains of conquest, anarchy and the search for security, the offensive or defensive nature of technology or geography, commitment problems and the presence of "buffer states," state institutional capacity, and the revisionist intentions of leaders.[15] However, despite their great variety and value, all of these arguments share a common tendency: that of seeing expansion as a largely strategic activity, dependent upon decisions made by leaders in the capitals of powerful states. A clear example of this sort of thinking can be found in Robert Gilpin's *War and Change in World Politics*, in which he argues that "a state will seek to change the system through territorial, political, and economic expansion until the marginal costs of further change are equal to or greater than the marginal benefits."[16] Another example comes from John Mearsheimer, who, in laying out his theory of offensive realism, explicitly assumes that states are "rational actors" and argues that "conquering and controlling territory" is their "paramount political objective."[17] Tanisha Fazal similarly points to the "strong incentives" states have "to take over the buffer states that lie between themselves and their opponents."[18] And Dan Altman, focusing on modern conquest, unpacks the "calculated risk" that leaders engage in when making forcible territorial gains.[19] In short, a centralized and strategic conception of territorial expansion pervades much of the existing literature.

Other theories of territorial expansion de-emphasize its strategic nature, focusing instead on the biases associated with domestic political regime type, the influence of financial and capitalist elites, leader psychology, status seeking, domestic political logrolling and nationalist mythmaking, xenophobia, and a "cult of the offensive" in military doctrine and strategy.[20] In these theories, the motives driving expansion render the activity less than entirely strategic or rational from the perspective of the state or empire as a whole. Yet, they still conceive of expansion to be rooted in decisions made by the leaders in the capital. For instance, Bruce Bueno de Mesquita and his coauthors argue that "leaders of small winning-coalition systems"—in effect, autocrats—will be "more inclined to seek territorial expansion" than their large winning-coalition counterparts.[21] Similarly, Jeffrey Taliaferro argues that when "leaders perceive themselves as facing losses relative to their expectation level, the pursuit of relatively risky strategies in the periphery becomes more likely."[22] Thus, even many of the nonunitary and nonrational theories of territorial expansion tend to explain expansion decisions with reference to state leaders.

There are two recent exceptions to these broader trends in the literature. The first is research by Peter Krause and Ehud Eiran on territorial expansion by small nonstate groups and organizations—what they refer to as "radical flank groups."[23] Krause and Eiran argue that modern constraints on territorial expansion by states are not equally binding on nonstate actors and, in fact, can be used to their advantage. They test their arguments by focusing on Israeli settlement of the West Bank, from 1967 to the present, and find that, in fact, these radical flank groups established a majority of all settlements in this period. The second exception is research by Paul MacDonald on "autonomous expansion" in colonial empires.[24] MacDonald argues that the unique governance structures of colonial empires—with chains of delegation running from the capital, to the imperial proconsul, to the local intermediary—predispose these empires to expand autonomously from metropolitan leadership. Using examples from the history of the British in India and sub-Saharan Africa, he shows that various forms of instability in these hierarchical governance structures can prompt a number of forms of autonomous expansion.

These works represent important advances in the study of inadvertent expansion, and the arguments I present in this book share theoretical affinities with them. Nonetheless, they leave several questions unanswered. For instance, Krause and Eiran's work does not account for variation, such as when and where "radical flanks" are more or less likely to claim territory and when leaders in the capital are more or less likely to accept or reject it. MacDonald's arguments are limited to circumstances of organized European imperialism—situations where there are formal proconsul positions as well as local imperial officials—and do not apply to inadvertent expansion observed beyond such circumstances. The theory this book presents builds on the insights of these works to better explain variation in the behaviors and decisions of actors in the periphery and the metropole not only in cases involving formal imperialism but also in those involving the extension of state territory, wartime expansion, and the like. In doing so, I offer a more comprehensive explanation of periphery-driven expansion in world politics that deepens our understanding of how great power territorial expansion occurs.

The Argument in Brief

Inadvertent expansion is territorial expansion that is planned and executed by actors on the periphery of a state or empire without the authorization of central leadership in the capital. The process of inadvertent expansion unfolds in two basic steps—"unauthorized peripheral expansion" and "subsequent central authorization." In the first step, state or nonstate actors on the geographic periphery of states and empires plan, execute, and, in most cases, fully carry out instances of territorial expansion without the aid, authorization, or foreknowledge of leaders at home in the capital. This might consist of the military or colonial army engaging in armed conquest, diplomats or colonial officials annexing territory, or merchants and other private actors seizing territory. Whatever the case may be, the crucial point at this stage is that the leaders in the capital with responsibility for national or imperial security policy are *not* involved in the planning, authorization, or execution of the expansion.

I argue that this first step is largely the result of inadequate central control over the periphery. It is a manifestation of what is known as a "principal-agent problem"—a situation in which one actor (the principal) delegates decision-making authority to another actor (the agent), yet the agent makes decisions that differ from those the principal would make if it were on the ground making decisions itself. In this first stage of unauthorized peripheral expansion, the principal is the central leadership of the state or empire, and the agent is a state or nonstate actor on the periphery, and the problem is that the agent has just acquired foreign territory without the necessary permission or authority to do so.

Principal-agent problems are exacerbated by a lack of central control over the periphery, typically in the form of the ability to monitor the behavior of peripheral agents. When leaders in the capital have difficulty monitoring, and thereby controlling, their peripheral agents, unauthorized peripheral expansion is more likely to occur. In contrast, when leaders in the capital are better able to monitor and control their peripheral agents, unauthorized peripheral expansion is less likely to occur. In the history of great power territorial expansion, the ability to monitor and control the periphery is crucially determined by the state of transportation and communications technology, with rudimentary technology hindering central control and advanced technology enabling it. However, this is not the only determinant. In a number of important cases, weak civilian control over the military can hamper civilian or central control to the point that unauthorized peripheral expansion becomes more likely. In short, we should expect the incidence of unauthorized peripheral expansion to vary inversely with the amount of central control over the periphery: when central control is weaker, we should see more, and when it is stronger, we should see less.

In the second step of the process of inadvertent expansion, which I refer to as subsequent central authorization, the peripheral agents present to their principals in the capital the partly or wholly acquired territory as a fait accompli. This initiates a deliberative process in the capital that results in a decision among central leaders to either reject the fait accompli, leaving their peripheral agents to fend for themselves, or accept the fait accompli, completing the process of inadvertent expansion.

It is important to recognize that the very act of unauthorized peripheral expansion changes "the facts on the ground" and thereby alters the strategic calculus of the leaders in the capital. It places constraints on the leaders' ability to promptly reject the territorial claim for three basic reasons. First, unauthorized peripheral expansion has the effect of sinking the costs of territorial acquisition, since these costs cannot be recovered once incurred. Second, unauthorized peripheral expansion tends to generate domestic political pressure on the leaders in the capital to support their own agents and nationals. And third, unauthorized peripheral expansion tends to engage the national honor and prestige of leaders in the capital in ways they simply were not engaged before, making withdrawal significantly more difficult. Thus, for reasons of sunk costs, domestic political pressure, and national honor, leaders are often constrained in their ability to reject the territorial claims of their wayward agents.

However, despite these constraints, leaders in the capital still have one other crucial consideration: the geopolitical risk associated with acquiring the territory in question. When leaders expect few significant geopolitical risks associated with acceptance of the fait accompli, they are significantly more likely to subsequently authorize the acquisition. In contrast, when leaders expect significant geopolitical risk associated with acceptance of the fait accompli—such as crippling economic isolation, a severe interstate crisis, or the possibility of a major war with a regional power or rival great power—they will be far less likely to authorize the acquisition.

In sum, inadvertent expansion is most likely to occur when leaders in the capital lack adequate control over their peripheral agents and when there are few geopolitical risks associated with acceptance. To put it simply, inadvertent expansion is most likely in low-control, low-stakes contexts. Even in cases where the leaders do not positively "want" the territory in question, the constraints imposed by unauthorized peripheral expansion are often enough to force their hands and encourage subsequent central authorization, leading to inadvertent expansion.

To be absolutely clear, the fact that any individual case of territorial expansion is inadvertent in no way absolves the governments in question of moral responsibility for the associated horrors of conquest and empire. First, as the case studies in this book demonstrate, inadvertent expansion is no more humane than its intentional counterpart. Second, to have unconstrained actors on the periphery basically presupposes the existence of an empire, and the construction of such empires typically involves significant amounts of intentional territorial expansion by the capital. In other words, the path to instances of inadvertent expansion is usually forged by many past intentional expansion decisions. And third, state and imperial leaders do have agency in these cases, since they are the ones who make the ultimate determination as to whether to reject or retain the territories in question. Thus, describing territorial expansion as inadvertent does not make it any more justifiable. The aim of this book is not to excuse territorial expansion or empire by uncovering its inadvertence but instead to understand and explain this important and underappreciated process in the history of great power politics.

Importance and Contributions

Inadvertent expansion is a surprisingly common phenomenon. Far from being an unusual and highly contingent outcome—a curiosity to be pondered by historians of particular empires in particular time periods—it was, in fact, a regular feature of great power politics right up to the 1930s. As the findings of chapter 2 show, nearly one-in-four instances of territorial expansion among great powers between 1816 and 2014 are inadvertent in nature. It is experienced by all but two (Austria-Hungary, China) of the nine great powers during that period. It occurs regularly over the course of more than a century, from as early as 1818 to as late as 1932 and in all regions of the world. Indeed, a wide variety of territories were acquired in this manner, from remote islands in the South Pacific, to topographically forbidding central African kingdoms, to densely populated regions of East and Southeast Asia (see figure 0.1). In short, inadvertent expansion is a regular feature in the modern history of great power politics.

This book makes three central contributions to the literature on territorial expansion and to international relations theory more broadly. First, it articulates the concept of inadvertent expansion, a phenomenon that has been largely ignored in the international relations literature. While the idea of periphery-driven territorial expansion is far from entirely new—particularly in the history of empire and some theoretical work on imperialism—it has yet to insert itself into the core debates over the causes and processes of territorial expansion in international relations scholarship. While a few scholars have recognized that territorial expansion can vary in terms of its process or the form it takes, very few have discussed the radically decentralized nature of inadvertent expansion. By recognizing the phenomenon of inadvertent expansion, clearly conceptualizing it in terms of its basic steps and attributes, and observing it across dozens of cases, this book thus furthers our understanding of varieties of territorial expansion and how states and empires come to be.

Second, I present a new theory of inadvertent expansion. Although the phenomenon of inadvertent expansion has gotten considerable attention in impe-

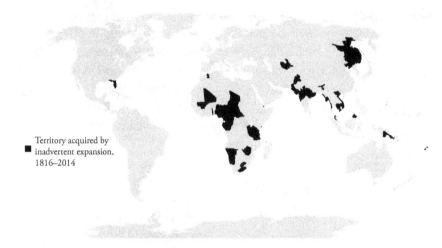

Territory acquired by
inadvertent expansion,
1816–2014

FIGURE 0.1. Territory acquired by inadvertent expansion, 1816–2014. Territorial acquisition areas are approximate, not exact. Map created using MapChart.net, 2022.

rial history, with many articles and books devoted to instances or campaigns of inadvertent expansion, few scholars, whether in history or international relations, have tried to explain it comprehensively across space and time. Drawing on diverse bodies of literature—including imperial history, the principal-agent theory, behavioral economics, and international relations—I construct a theory that applies to a broader set of cases and a longer swath of time than existing explanations for periphery-driven territorial expansion.

Third, I conduct the first-ever comprehensive accounting of inadvertent expansion in the modern history of great power politics. I present data comprising 258 observations of territorial expansion by the great powers since 1816, each of which is coded with respect to whether its expansion was inadvertent or intentional in nature. This allows me to show broad patterns of inadvertent expansion across great powers, regions, and historical eras, and it provides a wide variety of historically rich cases with which to illustrate how inadvertent expansion works in practice.

Understanding inadvertent expansion may seem like merely a matter of historical interest. After all, if rudimentary technology stands as one of the reasons why inadvertent expansion occurred, then advances in technology would appear to make this form of expansion obsolete. Yet, as I discuss further in the book's conclusion, inadvertent expansion has contemporary relevance in a number of important ways. First, the disappearance of great power inadvertent expansion likely played some role in contributing to the broader decline of territorial expansion we have observed since 1945, helping shape the world we inhabit today. Second, inadvertent expansion has not completely gone away. There are a number of contemporary cases of the militaries of smaller states in developing world contexts claiming territory, seemingly without government authorization. And third, while no great power has experienced inadvertent expansion for many years, the mechanisms that drove it forward—sunk costs, domestic politics, and honor concerns—may still motivate other inadvertent foreign policies, such as conflicts, crises, even wars.

Road Map

The pages that follow present a theory of inadvertent expansion then test and illustrate it in the modern history of great power politics. I begin, in chapter 1, by laying out my theory of inadvertent expansion in two parts. The first part covers the unauthorized peripheral expansion stage of inadvertent expansion, drawing on principal-agent theory to explain when we should expect this phenomenon to be more or less common. The second part covers the subsequent central authorization stage of inadvertent expansion, showing how forces such as sunk costs, domestic politics, international honor, and geopolitical risk can encourage or discourage acceptance of the fait accompli. I close this chapter with a detailed discussion of the research design, the methods employed, and the case selection criteria that guide the empirical chapters that follow.

In chapter 2, I present the broad patterns of inadvertent expansion among great powers. I introduce new data on great power expansion between 1816 and 2014, showing how inadvertent expansion varies (or does not) across a wide variety of important factors. I also support the two central claims of my theory: that a lack of central control over the periphery and conditions of low geopolitical risk are associated with more inadvertent expansions. Using a linear probability model and the great power expansion data, I show that territorial expansion is significantly more likely to be inadvertent than intentional when the territory in question lacks a connection to the global telegraph network as well as under conditions of relatively low geopolitical risk.

Chapters 3–7 present a series of paired comparative case studies of successful and failed inadvertent expansion in the modern history of great power politics. These cases show how the explanatory variables and outcomes vary in ways expected by the theory. They cover a variety of great power actors, regional contexts, and historical time periods, and, as I detail further in chapter 1, they were selected to conduct controlled comparisons, illustrate the mechanisms of the theory, and demonstrate its generalizability.

In brief, chapter 3 presents two US cases, the acquisition of Florida and the nonacquisition of the Republic of Texas. Chapters 4 and 5 each examine two cases involving the Russian Empire and the French Empire. Whereas the former looks at Russia's acquisition of parts of the Khanate of Kokand and its nonacquisition of the Ili region, the latter looks at France's initial nonacquisition of the kingdom of Tonkin, and its ultimate acquisition of Tonkin. Chapter 6 presents the only cross–great power comparison in the book, examining Japan's acquisition of Manchuria and Italy's nonacquisition of the port city of Fiume. Chapter 7 looks at Germany's acquisition of what is now Tanzania and its nonacquisition of what is now Kenya and Uganda. The book's conclusion then reviews the arguments and central findings, discusses the contemporary relevance of the theory, and presents its most important theoretical and policy implications.

A THEORY OF INADVERTENT EXPANSION

We seem, as it were, to have conquered and peopled half the world in a fit of absence of mind.

—John Robert Seeley, 1883

A comprehensive understanding of inadvertent expansion requires answering a few basic questions. First, under what conditions are inadvertent expansion opportunities most likely to arise? More concretely, under what conditions are actors on the periphery likely to present leaders in the capital with faits accomplis in the form of unauthorized territorial claims and acquisitions? Second, what explains variation in central leaders' decisions when faced with these faits accomplis? Or, more plainly, why do leaders in the capital subsequently authorize this peripheral expansion and accept the territory in some cases, but not others?

The theory presented in this chapter addresses both questions, and, with a variety of illustrative examples, I lay out three primary arguments. First, inadvertent expansion opportunities are most likely to arise when leaders in the capital have limited control over their agents on the periphery of the state or empire. Second, the very act of these peripheral agents engaging in unauthorized expansion creates incentives for leaders in the capital to retain their territorial acquisitions as a result of sunk costs, domestic political pressure, and the engagement of national honor. And third, the geopolitical risk associated with acquiring the territory in question is a crucial factor determining when leaders accept, and when they reject, the territorial fait accompli presented by their peripheral agents.

Expansion: Intentional and Inadvertent

The broad outcome this book seeks to explain, or dependent variable, is "expansion," which I define narrowly as the coercive acquisition of foreign territory that is intended to be long term or permanent for the expanding state. Expansion, as used here, includes the gain of territory through armed conquest or political annexation. This definition excludes largely voluntary transfers of territory, such as when states engage in treaty-based territorial exchange or the adjustment of shared borders.[1] It also excludes purchases or leases of territory that do not include an important coercive component, such as when the United States purchased Alaska from Russia in 1867, as well as various forms of "domestic expansion," such as territorial expropriation, ethnic cleansing, counterinsurgency, and other pacification campaigns.[2] Finally, it excludes forcible acquisitions of territory that are intended to be temporary or provisional in nature, such as military occupations or, in its modern guise, "neotrusteeship."[3]

The definition of expansion this book employs differs from others that are more broadly conceptualized. Fareed Zakaria, for instance, understands the term to include not only imperialism but also "an activist foreign policy that ranges from attention to international events to increases in diplomatic legations to participation in great power diplomacy."[4] The problem with such an inclusive definition is its conceptual clarity and precision: it becomes so broad as to lose much of its meaning.[5] A more circumscribed definition, such as the one employed here, mitigates this problem.

Expansion is related to, but distinct from, a number of concepts in international relations scholarship with which it is often conflated. For instance, expansion is not identical with "imperialism," since expansion can also consist of the extension of a state's national borders, and, it only covers the initial acquisition of foreign territory, not its ongoing administration.[6] Expansion is also not the same thing as "war," but it often includes the use of force and regularly precipitates or follows from the occurrence of war.[7] Expansion is not identical to "power-maximization," as this concept refers not merely to extended territorial control but also to a variety of other policies intended to increase the relative economic and military capabilities of a state.[8] Finally, expansion is distinct from the somewhat opaque concept of "rise," which most often refers to the secular increase in economic and military capabilities of one state relative to others.[9]

Most international relations scholarship tends to treat expansion as if it were a singular phenomenon: the largely strategic and leader-directed extension of the state's territorial domain. But this is not always the case. For instance, Colin Elman draws a distinction between what he refers to as "manual and automatic expansion," the former consisting of "conscious bids for hegemony" and, the lat-

ter, "incremental, localized attempts to expand, with a view to immediate opportunities . . . [not] with the deliberate purpose of becoming the dominant state
in the international system."[10] Similarly, Randall Schweller argues that "we must
distinguish between aggressive and nonaggressive expansion and between safe
and risky expansion. All states . . . can be expected to engage in nonaggressive
expansion as well as cheap, relatively safe expansion on the periphery."[11] These
are welcome distinctions, to be sure. But because the concepts are not thoroughly
developed, we are not given much of an indication of when to expect one form
over the other.[12] And, more importantly for our purposes, both forms remain
largely leader centric.

The primary distinction I draw is between what I refer to as "intentional expansion" and "inadvertent expansion." Intentional expansion is territorial expansion
that is planned and ordered by the central leadership of a state or empire and
is executed in accordance with those plans. Thorough planning for expansion
by state leaders will include *where* it will take place, *when* it will take place, *how
much* territory to acquire, and *how* it will be acquired. Intentional expansion is
exemplified in many cases of territorial expansion that are well known in the
historical record and in international relations scholarship, such as the German
conquest of Poland in 1939 and Japan's conquest of much of Southeast Asia in
1941–42.

In contrast, inadvertent expansion is territorial expansion that is planned and
executed by actors on the periphery of a state or empire without the authorization
of central leadership in the capital. A case of territorial expansion is inadvertent if
the peripheral actor who carries it out lacks prior orders, permission, or authority
from their superiors in the capital or, in some cases, acts against direct orders to
the contrary. Inadvertent expansion is exemplified by the case that opened this
book—the British conquest of Sind in 1843—as well as those that populate later
chapters (among many others).

It is important to note that this idea of inadvertent expansion is not entirely
new, particularly in the history of empire. In summarizing this literature, Michael
Doyle refers to a whole category of theories as "peri-centric," which root the
sources of imperialism in the periphery.[13] In the history of the British Empire,
this includes foundational works by John Gallagher and Ronald Robinson on the
"Imperialism of Free Trade" and informal empire, John Galbraith on the "turbulent frontier" and the "man on the spot," and David Fieldhouse on "colonial
sub-imperialism."[14] A number of historians have also taken a more interactionist
view of the relationship between center and periphery in producing imperialism,
such as Robinson, John Darwin, and Ronald Hyam.[15]

In international relations, specifically, only Paul MacDonald has sought to
articulate a concept similar to inadvertent expansion, which he calls "autono-

mous expansion." MacDonald defines autonomous expansion as the "political expansion of overseas empires without prior authorization or approval from officials in the metropole."[16] This is virtually equivalent to inadvertent expansion, but I do not adopt MacDonald's terminology for two reasons. First, the term "autonomous" has a number of meanings, including self-governing, independent, and operating without human control—none of which exactly capture what occurs in cases of inadvertent expansion.[17] And having multiple meanings associated with the term can hinder conceptual clarity, leading readers to ask, "autonomous *in what sense*?" Second, if the term "autonomous" applies to any party in these cases, it is to the actors on the periphery, as they are the ones acting autonomously, without direction from the center. Yet what is just as interesting about inadvertent expansion is how little control those in power, the leaders in the capital, often have over the process. In contrast, the term "inadvertent" has fewer meanings, being defined as "not resulting from or achieved through deliberate planning" and geared toward the actors in the center, which I would argue thus makes it a more fitting term for the phenomenon.[18]

Principals, Agents, and Peripheral Expansion

Inadvertent expansion is a regular feature of the modern history of great power politics, occurring dozens of times over the course of more than a century. However, despite the variety of actors involved, regions in which it has occurred, temporal contexts, and territories acquired, instances of inadvertent expansion at a basic level tend to follow a common two-step sequence: "unauthorized peripheral expansion" and "subsequent central authorization."

In the first step of unauthorized peripheral expansion, actors on the geographic periphery of a state or empire plan, execute, and, in many cases, fully carry out an instance of territorial expansion without the authorization of the leaders at home in the capital.[19] These actors on the periphery consist of a variety of state and nonstate actors including members of the national military, colonial armies, imperial officials, members of private-chartered companies, merchants, and explorers. The leaders in the capital whose authorization would normally be required to engage in territorial conquest or annexation include the head of state or government—such as the president, prime minister, autocrat, or monarch—and the key members of his or her cabinet primarily responsible for national or imperial security policy, including the defense, foreign, and colonial ministers.

Unauthorized peripheral expansion can take the form of a military or colonial army engaging in armed conquest, such as when French colonial forces invaded German Cameroon in the opening months of World War I, without orders from

Paris.[20] It can also take the form of diplomatic or colonial officials annexing territory, such as when Sir Stamford Raffles acquired Singapore on behalf of the British Empire in 1819, without prior authorization from London.[21] It can also consist of members of private-chartered companies and other economic actors seizing territory for economic gain, such as the German trader Adolph Lüderitz annexing territory without government authorization in what would become Germany's first overseas colony of South-West Africa (now Namibia).[22] Despite their many differences, what these forms of peripheral expansion share in common is that they were *not* specifically ordered or authorized by leaders at home in the capital.

The first question that needs addressing, then, is under what conditions peripheral actors are more likely to claim foreign territory without authorization. In short, what explains unauthorized peripheral expansion? The best way to understand unauthorized peripheral expansion is as a particular manifestation of what is known as a "principal-agent problem."[23] Whenever one actor, known as the "principal," delegates some decision-making authority to another actor, known as the "agent," the possibility for principal-agent problems arises. In the theory of inadvertent expansion, the principals are leaders in the capital and the agents, peripheral actors.[24] In almost all cases of unauthorized peripheral expansion, these agents are either state actors—such as members of the military, diplomatic, or colonial apparatus—or nonstate actors who are operating under government orders and support. In these cases, the delegation of authority is direct and fairly explicit.[25] Yet every act of delegation entails potential losses in terms of agency or control on the part of the principal, and this is where problems can arise.

There are two jointly necessary conditions for principal-agent problems to occur. The first of these involves information asymmetries in favor of the agent. Agents will typically possess, or have greater access to, information that is, or would be, of value to the principal. This can be due to the agent's proximity to the task at hand or expertise in a given issue area or the significant costs associated with monitoring the agent's behavior. In cases of inadvertent expansion, these information asymmetries can be particularly severe. Many cases involve relatively few people communicating over vast distances, often using nineteenth-century transportation and communications technology. For instance, in 1850, when the explorer Gennadii Nevelskoi unilaterally annexed the Amur Basin to the Russian Empire, it took at least five months to get a reply to a message sent from Saint Petersburg.[26] Similarly, in 1852, when Commodore George Lambert independently sparked the Second Anglo-Burmese War, leading to the British conquest of lower Burma, it took approximately four months to get a reply to a message sent from London.[27] These conditions greatly exacerbated information asymmetries in favor of peripheral agents and hampered central control by leaders in the capital. As the British colonial secretary Michael Hicks Beach told a colleague, shortly before his peripheral agent independently conquered Zululand in 1879, "I cannot really control him without a telegraph."[28]

However, the information asymmetries common in cases of inadvertent expansion are not simply a matter of vast distances and slow communications. Even distance-demolishing technologies such as the telegraph would not solve all problems in this regard—though, as I show in chapter 2, they make a profound difference. First, even as telegraph cables were rapidly connected to coastal regions throughout the world in the late nineteenth century, communication with the interior of many regions remained difficult to establish. Second, leaders in the capital still relied upon their peripheral agents to send information from the frontier, allowing these agents a great deal of artistic license in how they dealt with the facts.[29] As one historian of the Russian Empire in Central Asia notes, the "real power which local officers wielded . . . [lay] in their monopoly of information. It was extremely difficult to resist the arguments for action which these officers pressed when the only information available came from them too."[30] And third, even when specific orders could get through to them in time, peripheral agents without representatives from the capital peering over their shoulders always had the option of turning a blind eye. As the famed counterinsurgent of French Algeria Thomas Robert Bugeaud once declared, "In the face of the enemy, one must never accept any precise instructions or plans imposed from above. . . . One should burn instructions so as to avoid the temptation of reading them."[31]

The second necessary condition for principal-agent problems to occur is a divergence of preferences between principal and agent. In delegating, the principal wants the agent to act exactly as the principal would if it were making the decisions itself, while agents will be tempted to make their own decisions, at least some of the time. There are many reasons why preferences can diverge in delegated-agency relations, including agent self-interest, barriers to communication, varied perceptions, differing risk orientations, and divergent structural conditions facing principal and agent. In cases of inadvertent expansion, the most important driver of preference divergence is the differing positions and associated perceptions of the leaders in the capital and their peripheral agents. And the most important issue on which preferences diverge is on national or imperial security policy, with peripheral agents often wanting to act quickly and aggressively and leaders in the capital often preferring to act slowly and cautiously.

These differences can be neatly summed up with the ideas of the "view from the capital" and the "view from the frontier." In cases of inadvertent expansion, the view from the capital is that which is typically held by leaders in the capital. Their responsibilities are broad, being concerned with the interests of the state or empire as a whole. Their areas of concern are often global, including not only the territory at issue but also adjacent territories, other important regional actors, relationships with the other great powers, and, of course, domestic politics at home. And the leaders' distance from the frontier means that their sense of urgency to act in response to any given contingency there is generally lower than that of the peripheral agents. From the perspective of the capital, the daily fluctuations of threats and opportunities present on the periphery are seen as distant and abstract.

The view from the frontier, in contrast, is that which is typically held by peripheral agents in cases of inadvertent expansion. Their responsibilities are relatively narrow, being concerned, at most, with a portion of the state or empire. Their areas of concern are often local, being essentially limited to the territory at issue and, perhaps, some surrounding areas. And their proximity to the frontier means that their sense of urgency to act in any given contingency is often much higher than that of the leaders back in the capital. The threats and opportunities these peripheral agents regularly face—though often mild when considering the security of the state or empire as a whole—are, for them, immediate and very real. Thus, viewing a given problem from the capital or from the frontier can lead to highly divergent perceptions and to corresponding differences in policy preferences.

This difference between the view from the capital and the view from the frontier is well articulated in a letter from the governor-general of India, Lord Ellenborough, to Queen Victoria, justifying the recent conquest of Sind. "Your Majesty will not have failed to observe," Ellenborough wrote in October 1843,

> how very different a position the British Government stands in Europe from that which it is placed in India. In Europe peace is maintained by the balance of power amongst several states. In India all balance has been overthrown by our preponderance, and to exist we must continue to be supreme. The necessity of our position may often render necessary here measures wholly unsuited to the state of things which prevails in Europe. The least appearance of weakness or of hesitation would lead to a general combination of all against a foreign, and necessarily an unpopular, Government.[32]

Thus, a combination of information asymmetries and preference divergence will tend to produce principal-agent problems. The most important among these, for our purposes, is what is known as "moral hazard."[33] Given that the agent is acting at the behest of the principal, and given that it is generally the principal who is responsible for the outcomes in question, the agent may feel emboldened to make riskier, less responsible choices than it otherwise would, potentially creating significant problems for the principal. When it comes to inadvertent expansion, the most important manifestation of moral hazard is unauthorized peripheral expansion. Since these peripheral agents are representatives of a powerful state back home—or, at the very least, claim to be acting in its name—they will often have a well-founded expectation that they will be supported by leaders in the capital, regardless of whether their actions were authorized or not.

Now, at least in theory, leaders in the capital should not be totally powerless in the face of these usurpations of authority from the periphery. According to principal-agent theory, there are a number of ways principals can mitigate the risk of wayward agents.[34] However, each of these is complicated by the challenging context of globe-spanning empires. The first possible solution is screening: leaders can presumably screen and select peripheral actors who are more likely to be obedient. The problem here, however, is of "multiple agents."[35] There are a small number of principals but, in the case of major empires, a vast number of agency positions to be filled. The idea that each and every agent can be adequately screened—and that each and every position will have multiple eligible potential candidates—is simply not realistic. And this is especially true for the rugged, distant, and often unprestigious posts on the far-flung edges of many nineteenth- and early twentieth-century states and empires.[36] A second potential solution is sanction: leaders can threaten punishment for disobedient agents and promise reward for those who follow their orders. The problem here, as I discuss later, is political. Elites in the capital and the broader public often rally in favor of these wayward peripheral actors, largely insulating them from significant punishment. A third possible solution is monitoring: leaders can more closely monitor their agents and thereby directly exert control over their behavior. But as noted, with vast distances and mostly nineteenth-century transportation and communication technology, monitoring is prohibitively costly and, therefore, effectively impossible.

Unauthorized peripheral expansion, then, is the first step in the process of inadvertent expansion. But what motivates peripheral agents to engage in unauthorized peripheral expansion in the first place? In some cases, the territory in question has intrinsic strategic or economic value, and an irresistible window of opportunity presents itself.[37] In others, the agents are genuinely threatened by actors on the other side of the frontier and expand for defensive reasons.[38] Peripheral agents may also have more bureaucratic or parochial interests, such as promotion within the military or advancement in their organizations.[39] Finally, some may simply want the glory and prestige that is so often historically associated with territorial conquest.[40] The strength and relevance of these motivations vary widely—both across peripheries and across time—as personnel and circumstances change.

Whatever their individual motivations may be, the crucial permissive factor enabling unauthorized peripheral expansion is the degree of control leaders in the capital have over these peripheral agents. When leaders in the capital have only limited control over their peripheral agents, unauthorized peripheral expansion is more likely. In contrast, when leaders in the capital have significant control over their peripheral agents, unauthorized peripheral expansion is much less likely. In line with principal-agent theory, "control" results from the ability to monitor the agents' behavior, often coming in the form of advanced transportation and communications technology. However, there are other ways in which central control can break down. For instance, in cases of weak civilian oversight of the military, control by leaders in the capital over their peripheral agents can be severely hampered.[41]

In sum, unauthorized peripheral expansion is most likely when control by leaders in the capital over their agents on the periphery is relatively low. It is a principal-agent problem driven by a combination of information asymmetries favoring peripheral agents, a divergence of preferences between the capital and the periphery, and moral hazard on the part of peripheral agents. This is the first step in the process of inadvertent expansion.

Peripheral Pulls

The second step of inadvertent expansion consists of subsequent central authorization.[42] After claiming territory without authorization, the actors on the periphery present the leaders in the capital with their acquisitions as a fait accompli.[43] In some cases, they directly contact their metropolitan bosses to notify them of their gains. In other cases, news filters back to the capital more indirectly through other channels. In either case, knowledge of the acquisition among leaders in the capital initiates a deliberative process on whether to reject or accept the fait accompli. If leaders in the capital decide to reject the fait accompli, then they effectively cut these peripheral actors loose, instructing them to return the acquired territories or fend for themselves. In contrast, if the leaders decide to accept the fait accompli, as they have in dozens of cases in the modern era, the territory then becomes part of the state or empire, thereby completing the process of inadvertent expansion.

The key question that needs addressing for this second step, then, is why leaders in the capital accept these faits accomplis in some cases, but not in others. More simply, what explains subsequent central authorization? Before getting into what explains variation in leader decision-making, it is important to note that, for leaders facing these faits accomplis, there are important constraints on their freedom of choice. Across numerous cases of inadvertent expansion, leaders appear to reluctantly come up with arguments for retaining these territories ex post such that it is difficult to imagine they would marshal in favor of their acquisition ex ante. The primary reason for this is that, by engaging in unauthorized expansion, the peripheral agents change "the facts on the ground," altering the strategic calculus of the leaders in the capital. And for three central reasons, these changed facts place constraints on these leaders, which can make returning the territory to its previous occupants surprisingly difficult.

First, unauthorized peripheral expansion will often sink the costs of territorial acquisition for leaders in the capital.[44] Sunk costs are costs that have already been incurred and, therefore, cannot be recovered.[45] In cases of inadvertent expansion, by the time leaders in the capital become aware of what is transpiring on the periphery, their agents have already used state or imperial resources to partially or wholly conquer the territory or negotiate its annexation. If we think of the costs of territorial expansion as being a combination of current "acquisition costs" and future "governance costs," unauthorized peripheral expansion often sinks a good portion, if not all, of the first half of the equation. Once expended, these costs—often paid in both treasure *and* blood—are not recoverable, and this will often encourage authorization of the territorial fait accompli.[46] For many leaders, the prospect of giving up newly acquired territories will appear as a missed opportunity and, given the irrecoverable costs incurred, a wasted one. The existence of these sunk costs tends to strengthen the arguments of proexpansion hawks in the capital and to weaken the arguments of cost- or risk-conscious doves, pushing the leaders toward acceptance.

Second, unauthorized peripheral expansion also tends to generate domestic political pressure on leaders in the capital to support their own agents and nationals, regardless of "who started it" or how unscrupulous they may have been.[47] This sometimes comes in the form of political, military, and imperial elites in and around the capital putting pressure on the leadership to look after their subordinates or nationals. These effects can also be powerfully felt from the opposition in government. In cases where the leadership is opposed to an acquisition, but powerful political opponents are supportive, leaders will often keep their opposition quiet out of a fear of looking unpatriotic or being accused of "siding with the enemy."[48] In still other cases, the state or empire's domestic public at large becomes aware of events on the periphery, rallies in favor of their conationals, and puts pressure on the government to support them as well. These kinds of pressures, both elite level and public, narrow the options of leaders and make ordering a prompt withdrawal from the territory difficult.

To be clear, this kind of pressure does not always materialize. In certain cases, the public is largely disengaged from events on the frontier. In others, some may even be opposed to the acceptance of the fait accompli. Yet, in most cases, both political elites and the public pressure leaders to support their conationals, and even the expectation of this kind of pressure among leaders can be enough to make them think twice about rejecting the fait accompli. It is simply very politically difficult for leaders to deny their own citizens aid in times of need. As David Landes puts it, "Imperialism was in large measure built on the *fait accompli* . . . with the state almost always ready to pull its nationals' chestnuts out of the fire."[49]

Third, unauthorized peripheral expansion engages the prestige, honor, and reputation of leaders in the capital, and the state or empire as a whole, in ways they simply were not engaged before.[50] This can make relinquishing the territory and retrenching appear prohibitively difficult from the perspective of leaders in the capital.[51] It is not that leaders see territorial expansion as invariably prestige or status enhancing—though, in some cases they do. Rather, it is that they often fear that backing down and rejecting the territorial fait accompli is status diminishing. These concerns are particularly potent in the colonial context, where great powers often have other territorial holdings in the area and feel that their continued control rests heavily upon the maintenance of a reputation for resolve in the face of a challenge.[52] As Czar Nicholas I of Russia remarked upon learning of the unauthorized annexation of the Amur Basin, "Where once the Russian flag has been raised, never shall it be lowered."[53]

Thus, for reasons of sunk costs, domestic political pressure, and the engagement of national honor, leaders in the capital will often feel powerfully bound to accept their peripheral agents' territorial faits accomplis. Peripheral agents often know this and will use these very same forces to manipulate leaders in the capital, further constraining them toward acceptance. For instance, they can help gin up domestic political support in favor of their cause through means such as waging press campaigns, engaging in pamphleteering, sending allied individuals and organizations on speaking tours, and directly lobbying members of the great power's government. Some of their strategies are incredibly shrewd. In the process of his unauthorized acquisition of what would become Rhodesia in 1890, for example, Cecil Rhodes made a point of recruiting young men from influential families for his expeditions, so that the government in London would feel extra pressure to intervene on their behalf if needed.[54] Peripheral agents also make regular reference to concerns of national honor and prestige in their communications with the capital to make these concerns salient. These communications include, as examples, arguments that backing down would weaken the great power's authority in the region and elsewhere, that it would only invite attack and encourage dissension, that the locals "respect only force," that the other great powers "are watching," and, more generally, that there is a need to support the great power's important political and social mission and to defend the "honor of the flag."[55] And the knowledge among peripheral agents that these incentives exist, and of their ability to manipulate them, only feeds the moral hazard that leads them to engage in unauthorized peripheral expansion in the first place.

Unauthorized peripheral expansion can also generate incentives for leaders in the capital to reject the territorial fait accompli, largely out of a desire to rein in rogue peripheral agents and to reassert central control.[56] However, this incentive often pales in comparison with the stronger domestic political pressures and honor concerns that leaders feel bound by, particularly in cases of successful peripheral expansion, when sunk cost concerns will also be powerfully felt. Once the important segments of the elite and public become aware of what has transpired on the frontier and rally to the peripheral agents' cause, it becomes very politically difficult for leaders in the capital to censure or punish their agents in any way. This, as noted earlier, explains why peripheral agents who engage in unauthorized peripheral expansion are so often not only not punished but *rewarded* for their insubordination. But, perhaps more importantly, these are often deeply embarrassing experiences for leaders in the capital, threatening to make them look weak, incompetent, and out of control in front of their political opponents, their populace, and the world at large. A quick and tidy acceptance— along with an effort to cover the inadvertence up—is often a more appealing alternative than engaging in a long, drawn out, and very public process of rejection and retrenchment.[57]

Geopolitical Risk and Central Authorization

With so many incentives pushing leaders in the capital toward acceptance of the fait accompli, it would seem that there is little reason then for them to reject it. Nonetheless, there are a number of instances in which they decided to rebuff their peripheral agents and to refrain from subsequently authorizing the acquisition. The historical record of inadvertent expansion shows a number of different motivations for these decisions. When the British colonial secretary Lord Glenelg rejected his agents' claims of the Transkei region of South Africa in 1835, it was a combination of the perceived worthlessness of the territory and popular revulsion at the inhumane treatment of the locals that led to its relinquishment.[58] When French leaders rejected their peripheral agent Joseph Galliéni after his unilateral annexation of Senegal in 1881, it was due to the unacceptable terms of the annexation treaty he had negotiated.[59] And when the United States refused to accept Hawaii in 1893 after a coup orchestrated, in part, by its own local consular official, the primary reason was that it occurred in the context of a leadership transition in which the incoming president, Grover Cleveland, was utterly uninterested in the territory.[60] Thus, like any important decision in world politics, leaders are influenced by a variety of factors.

However, what stands out as the most important factor weighing on the minds of leaders in the capital when deciding whether to accept or reject a fait accompli is the amount of geopolitical risk associated with doing so. The prospect of significant geopolitical repercussions is often enough to discourage leaders from authorizing their peripheral agents' deeds. And the absence of these potential risks will usually clear the way for the constraints imposed by sunk costs, domestic politics, or national honor to take hold and for leaders to accept the fait accompli and engage in inadvertent expansion. Geopolitical risk is understood here as an objective condition rather than a purely perceptual variable. This is not to say that leaders do not periodically get it wrong, either over- or underestimating the geopolitical risk of a given circumstance. It is also not to say that objectively risky circumstances do not occasionally fail to materialize, because they definitely do. Yet the theory assumes that most leaders will accurately assess the geopolitical risk associated with territorial expansion most of the time. While this is not the sole motivation driving decisions to accept or reject agents' unauthorized claims, the quantitative evidence and the historical case studies this book examines show that it is the most important determinant of this decision.

There are three key kinds of geopolitical risk that give leaders pause and lead them to rethink the option of accepting the fait accompli. The first is the prospect of crippling international economic isolation. If leaders think that authorizing peripheral expansion will lead to international trade sanctions, substantial foreign economic disinvestment, or being cut off from other forms of international economic exchange, they will be far less likely to accept the fait accompli. The second is the prospect of armed conflict with a local regional power. The possibility of becoming embroiled in a war with a distant regional power—even one that is significantly inferior to the great power in question—will often give leaders pause. The third, and perhaps the gravest, risk is the prospect of encroaching on the interests of another great power to the point of risking a major crisis or even war. Leaders will be highly reluctant to accept the offerings of their peripheral agents when the consequences could be this grave. In contrast, the absence of geopolitical risk clears the way for sunk costs, domestic political pressure, and national honor concerns to take hold, and leaders under these conditions will be significantly more likely to accept the fait accompli.

A skeptical reader might point out, however, that the leaders of powerful states have regularly risked economic isolation and war for territorial gain.[61] We need look no further than the United States' annexation of Texas in 1845, which sparked the Mexican-American War, as well as the expansion of Japan and Germany in the late 1930s, to see that leaders can be highly risk acceptant when pursuing territorial gains. What makes inadvertent expansion different? The key difference between inadvertent expansion and intentional expansion in this regard is, quite simply, planning and preparation by the state's leaders. Territorial expansion is among the least certain and highest-risk foreign policy initiatives a state can undertake. While it can promise the acquisition of strategic territory and valuable resources, it also risks overburdening the state with obligations, getting bogged down in a long and costly pacification campaign, and impinging upon the interests of other great powers. Thus, when it comes to intentional expansion, leaders will generally carefully consider where to expand, when to do so, how much territory to take, and how to do so. And leaders will time and conduct their campaigns in ways that aim to minimize adverse consequences or, at the very least, to prepare themselves to weather them. In contrast, inadvertent expansion is thrust upon leaders in the capital unwittingly. They have had no control over what territory was taken, when it was taken, how much was taken, and the mode by which it was taken. And they have also had little opportunity to try to avoid adverse consequences or to dig in and bear them. Given these differences, leaders will usually be hard pressed to face significant risks for policies that they have had no control over.

It is worth highlighting that the two forces present at this second stage of subsequent central authorization push in opposite directions. On the one hand, leaders will often feel constrained to accept the territory due to sunk acquisition costs, domestic political pressure, and honor concerns. On the other hand, leaders may face severe geopolitical risk associated with doing so, discouraging them from accepting the fait accompli. The confluence of these countervailing forces can periodically put leaders in a deeply unenviable position. On the one hand, they may face a nationalistic public rallying for acceptance, an opposition in government urging them to defend the national honor, and, in extreme cases, the risk of a coup or even assassination for appearing to look weak. On the other hand, leaders may face the risk of crippling economic isolation, conflict with a regional power thousands of kilometers from home, or a territorial dispute with another great power, possibly escalating to all-out war.

This veritable minefield of decision-making for leaders in the capital is what I refer to as the "dilemma of inadvertent expansion." Thankfully for the leaders involved, these situations are relatively rare. In most cases, leaders in the capital are presented with territorial faits accomplis by their peripheral agents with few significant risks associated with acceptance, and acceptance is the result. In other cases, metropolitan leaders do face substantial risks associated with acceptance, yet the public is not fully engaged or there is minimal interest at the elite level, giving leaders a safe off-ramp to reject the fait accompli. However, in some cases, these two potent forces come together, requiring leaders to weigh the costs and

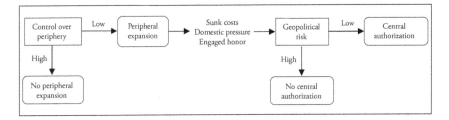

FIGURE 1.1.   Theory of inadvertent expansion.

risks associated with making one decision or the other. Even in these difficult circumstances, considerations of geopolitical risk tend to predominate. But they are, nonetheless, remarkably challenging positions for leaders to find themselves in—with their political positions, and even their lives, at stake.

To sum up the theory in its entirety: inadvertent expansion, the outcome or dependent variable this book seeks to explain, occurs in two basic steps—unauthorized peripheral expansion and subsequent central authorization. The most important explanatory variable for unauthorized peripheral expansion is the degree of control leaders in the capital have over their agents on the periphery, with less control being associated with an increased likelihood of unauthorized peripheral expansion. Once this occurs, the very act of unauthorized peripheral expansion tends to constrain leaders in the capital toward acceptance of the territory being offered due to sunk territorial acquisition costs, the emergence of domestic political pressure, and the engagement of national honor. Yet, at the second step of subsequent central authorization, leaders in the capital also need to consider the degree of geopolitical risk associated with acquiring the territory, with lower perceived risk being associated with an increased likelihood of authorization. Thus, we should expect to observe most inadvertent expansion when leaders in the capital both have relatively low control over their peripheral agents and perceive few geopolitical risks associated with expansion into a given territory. Figure 1.1 illustrates the theory.

Research Design and Methods

Defining the relevant counterfactual of inadvertent expansion is not entirely straightforward.[62] If the outcome of interest is inadvertent expansion, is the relevant counterfactual intentional expansion, with the most important variation being between forms of expansion? Is it nonexpansion, with the most important variation being whether peripheral expansion occurs or not? Or is it *failed* inadvertent expansion—essentially, unauthorized peripheral expansion with leaders in the capital rejecting the fait accompli at the subsequent central authorization stage? A further complication is that some of these counterfactuals, particularly failed inadvertent expansion, are not easily observable in the empirical record. For most historians and in most histories, as I discuss in chapter 2, these are essentially "non-events," and are, therefore, less likely to appear in the historical record. Thus, given the subject matter of this book, defining and observing the relevant counterfactual poses serious challenges.

This book settles on examining two counterfactuals. The first, which I consider in chapter 2, is variation between forms of expansion: intentional and inadvertent. This helps deal with the problem of the low observability of failed inadvertent expansion and illustrates what is unique and distinctive about inadvertent expansion within the broader universe of cases of territorial expansion by the great powers. The second counterfactual, which I examine in chapters 3–7, is variation between successful inadvertent expansion and failed inadvertent expansion—that is, variation between cases where leaders accept or reject the territorial fait accompli. This is much closer to the important variation explained by the theory and clarifies what explains leaders' choices when faced with similar inadvertent expansion opportunities.

This is a mixed-methods study of inadvertent expansion, making use of both quantitative and qualitative methods. The quantitative component, located in chapter 2, presents and analyzes data on all instances of great power territorial expansion from 1816 to 2014. Each territorial expansion observation is coded as to whether it is intentional or inadvertent, and this variation provides the primary basis for comparison. The purpose of the quantitative component is threefold: first, to demonstrate the generality of the phenomenon of inadvertent expansion by presenting the universe of post-1815 cases; second, to present basic descriptive statistics regarding inadvertent expansion and to highlight some of the broad patterns the phenomenon displays over space and time; and third, to analyze the data using statistical modeling techniques to show support for some of the claims made in the theory of inadvertent expansion laid out earlier. What the quantitative analysis mainly shows is what is *distinctive* about cases of inadvertent expansion within the broader universe of great power territorial expansion observations.

The qualitative component, presented in chapters 3–7, consists of a series of paired theory-testing case studies of successful and failed inadvertent expansion by great powers between 1818 and 1932.[63] Each of these chapters pairs a "positive" case of successful inadvertent expansion (where unauthorized peripheral expansion leads to subsequent central authorization by the capital) with a "negative" case of failed inadvertent expansion (where peripheral expansion ultimately leads to rejection of the fait accompli by the capital). Including cases of both successful and failed inadvertent expansion helps mitigate the risk of selection bias that might result from including only one or the other.[64]

These historical cases rely on the comparative method and process tracing. The inclusion of paired cases allows me to engage in a controlled comparison across cases.[65] Through comparing cases of successful inadvertent expansion with cases of failed inadvertent expansion, I show that, in each case, the outcomes covary with the key explanatory variables highlighted by the theory. In each case, I also engage in process tracing.[66] Each case study presents ground level evidence of the argument and its causal mechanisms at work to show that the outcomes are produced for the *reasons* specified by the theory.[67] While this qualitative component thus provides evidence for all parts of the theory, its primary value is in addressing the question of why leaders in the capital agree to accept the territorial fait accompli of their peripheral agents in some cases, but not others.

Finally, a few words on scope conditions and case selection. This book focuses on acts of territorial expansion carried out by great powers from 1816 to the present. This is not to suggest that minor powers have never engaged or do not engage in inadvertent expansion, as they most certainly have and do.[68] But, as I detail in chapter 2, I limit the empirical scope to great powers because they have carried out most of the territorial expansion, their expansion is most consequential, and the historical record for these actors is most complete. I also limit my temporal scope to the post-Napoleonic (1816–) international system. This is similarly not intended to suggest that inadvertent expansion is a strictly modern phenomenon. In fact, given the importance of weak central control over the periphery to inadvertent expansion, it is likely to be more common the farther back we go in time. However, for reasons of empirical tractability and to build off of existing data collection efforts, I focus only on the post-1815 period.

The book includes ten cases, with at least one from each of the great powers that experienced successful or failed inadvertent expansion: France, Germany, Italy, Japan, Russia, the United States, and the brief introductory example of the United Kingdom.[69] The inclusion of this many cases both increases the representativeness of the sample selected and helps illustrate the generalizability of the theory.[70] In the book's online appendix (https://doi.org/10.7910/DVN/JBGNNH), I include the results of a balance test between the cases selected and the broader population of inadvertent expansion observations, which shows that the sample of cases selected is relatively well balanced on most important variables.[71]

The chapters' cases span over a century of history, from the United States in Florida in 1818 to Japan in Manchuria in 1932. They occur in five of six major world regions, including the Western Hemisphere, South and Central Asia, the Asia-Pacific, Europe, and sub-Saharan Africa. The cases also show considerable variation in terms of the great power's domestic political regime type, including the reasonably democratic regime of late nineteenth-century France, the mixed-regime of the early nineteenth-century United States, and the harshly autocratic regime of mid-nineteenth-century Russia. Moreover, they include great powers with continental orientations, such as the Russian Empire, as well as maritime orientation, such as the Japanese Empire. The cases also span great powers that differ in terms of their relative power, such as late nineteenth-century Germany, which was then the most powerful continental European state, as well as "barely great" interwar Italy and Japan. Finally, there is variation across the cases as to whether the expansion itself is an extension of state borders, as in the case of Russia in Central Asia, or the growth of overseas empires, as in the cases of France in Tonkin or Germany in East Africa. All of this variation should increase our confidence that the theory, and the phenomenon of inadvertent expansion more broadly, is not simply the product of a particular actor or a particular context.[72]

Chapters 3–7 each consists of a pair of highly comparable cases that were selected and paired to facilitate controlled comparison and to highlight important aspects of the theory.[73] For instance, chapter 3 includes a pair of US cases in which it is the same great power, operating in the same region, in roughly the same time period, but with varying levels of geopolitical risk leading to divergent outcomes. What is notable about these US cases is that it is also the very same individual—Andrew Jackson—who is the peripheral agent in one case (Florida) but the leader in the capital in the other (Texas). Having Jackson figure so prominently in both cases also well illustrates the notion of the "view from the frontier" and the "view from the capital," showing how it manifests in the very same individual in both key positions.

Chapter 4 consists of a pair of Russian cases in which it is the same great power, operating in the same region, and with the cases separated by only five years, yet with divergent outcomes. Both Russian cases feature nearly all of the very same leaders in the capital across the two cases, who, due to varying geopolitical risk, found reason to make different authorization decisions across the two cases. Similarly, chapter 5 includes a pair of French cases that also involve the same great power, operating in the same region, and separated by only a decade, yet with varying outcomes. These cases, however, deal with the very same territorial entity (Tonkin) and involve an almost-identical process of peripheral expansion yet, also for reasons of geopolitical risk, have differing outcomes. Chapter 5 is presented as a pair of comparative cases but, in other ways, can also be seen as a single longitudinal case.[74]

Chapter 6 involves the only cross–great power comparison, presenting one Japan case and one Italy case. These two cases are very well matched on many important factors such as relative power, time period, domestic political regime type, and the proximity of the expansion to their respective capitals. The confluence of domestic political pressure and geopolitical risk in the Japan and Italy cases also powerfully illustrates the dilemma of inadvertent expansion.

Chapter 7 includes a pair of German cases involving the same great power, operating in the same region, separated by only five years, but with varied outcomes for reasons of geopolitical risk. These two cases involve the very same peripheral agent, whose fait accompli is accepted in one but rejected in the other. The German cases also present a unique inferential opportunity in the form of a timely change of leadership in Berlin: the fall of Bismarck in March 1890. This transition shows, first, how reluctant leaders can be pressured to accept territorial claims for domestic political reasons, whereas enthusiastic leaders can be discouraged by geopolitical conditions. It also shows how different leaders with *very* different orientations toward empire can be similarly influenced by their expectations of geopolitical risk. Table 1.1 sums up the variations across these cases.

Overall, the careful pairing of the qualitative cases provides inferential leverage by controlling, to some extent, for any idiosyncrasies associated with individual great powers, time periods, regions, territorial entities, leaders in the capital, and/or peripheral agents across cases. This helps control for a number of potential confounders by effectively holding many factors constant. It is also worth noting that, while the quantitative data presented in chapter 2 includes both armed conquest and political annexation, the qualitative component is primarily focused on conquest, with only a single chapter—Germany in East Africa (chap. 7)—including cases of annexation. This is partly because these cases tend to be the most consequential but primarily in order to facilitate cross-case comparison.

TABLE 1.1 Case study summary

	GREAT POWER	TERRITORY (YEARS)	OUTCOME	UNIQUE FEATURE OF CROSS-CASE COMPARISON
Chapter 3	United States	Florida (1818–19)	Acquisition	Same individual in different key position
		Texas (1836–37)	Nonacquisition	
Chapter 4	Russia	Kokand (1864–66)	Acquisition	Same leadership in capital
		Ili region (1871–81)	Nonacquisition	
Chapter 5	France	Tonkin (1873–74)	Nonacquisition	Same territory and nearly identical process of expansion
		Tonkin (1882–83)	Acquisition	
Chapter 6	Japan	Manchuria (1931–32)	Acquisition	Modern communications technology
	Italy	Fiume (1919–20)	Nonacquisition	
Chapter 7	Germany	Contemporary Tanzania (1884–85)	Acquisition	Same peripheral agent
		Contemporary Kenya/ Uganda (1889–90)	Nonacquisition	

In sum, the chapters were structured and the cases selected to enable a "most similar" comparison *within* each chapter, and a "most different" comparison *across* the chapters. The within-chapter comparisons increase our confidence that the variation in outcomes is explained by the factors specified by the theory, and the across-chapter comparisons help demonstrate the generalizability of the theory.[75] What remains is to examine the theory in light of this abundance of quantitative and qualitative evidence. It is to this task that I now turn for the rest of the book.

PATTERNS OF INADVERTENT EXPANSION, 1816–2014

This chapter discusses the broad patterns of intentional and inadvertent expansion over the course of the past two centuries. The purpose of this chapter is threefold. First, to give the reader a sense of the generality of the phenomenon of inadvertent expansion by presenting the entire universe of cases. Drawing on data from 1816 to the present, I show inadvertent expansion to be a surprisingly common occurrence in the history of great power politics, occurring in almost one-in-four cases of great power territorial expansion. A second purpose is to both present basic descriptive statistics regarding inadvertent expansion and illuminate some of the broad patterns the phenomenon displays over space and time. The data collected show that inadvertent expansion exhibits considerable variation by great power actor, time period, region, and many other factors. The third purpose of the chapter is to statistically analyze the data to test some of the central claims made in the theory of inadvertent expansion presented in chapter 1. The analysis suggests that great power territorial expansion is more likely to be inadvertent than intentional under conditions of relatively low control by the capital over the periphery and geopolitical risk. Overall, the chapter shows what is distinctive about inadvertent expansion within the broader universe of great power territorial expansion observations.

Inadvertent Expansion Data

To get a better understanding of the conditions under which inadvertent expansion occurs, I compiled and collected data on territorial expansion by the great powers from 1816 to the present. I made use of a wide variety of sources in collecting the data, including existing data on the topic, encyclopedias, historical dictionaries and chronologies, historical surveys, in-depth histories, and even primary source documents when necessary.[1]

The most detailed and comprehensive existing data on territorial expansion is the Correlates of War's (COW) "Territorial Change" data, collected by Jaroslav Tir, Philip Schafer, Paul F. Diehl, and Gary Goertz.[2] Despite the immense value and important contributions of the territorial change data, I did not simply take it "off the shelf" and rely on it for two reasons. First, it was sometimes a challenge to identify each and every observation of expansion in the data.[3] This poses problems in studying inadvertent expansion, since each individual observation must be carefully examined to uncover whether the initiative originated in the capital or on the periphery. And second, in the course of researching, I came across a number of observations that, as best as I could tell, are not included in the territorial change data.[4] The data presented here, therefore, provide a more complete picture of the history of great power territorial expansion.

The unit of analysis for the data is the successful great power expansion observation. So, for example, despite the fact that it unfolded over several months, the US invasion of Florida in 1818 is still considered a single observation. In chapter 1, I defined expansion as the coercive acquisition of foreign territory that is intended to be long term or permanent for the expanding state. In accordance with this definition, expansion observations had to meet five criteria to be included in the data. First, the expansion observations had to be coercive in nature. Thus, voluntary purchases, transfers, and trades of territory are not included in the data.[5] Second, the territory acquired had to be foreign at the time of acquisition. Various forms of domestic expansion—such as expropriation, counterinsurgency campaigns, and territorial pacification—are, therefore, not included in the data.[6] Third, the territory had to be inhabited or claimed by another political entity. Genuine terra nullius claims are not included in the data.[7] Fourth, the territorial acquisition had to be non-temporary, at least in its intent. Cases of temporary military occupation are not included in the data.[8] Finally, the expansion observation had to be successfully carried out to its full fruition. Cases where expansion was attempted but not successfully completed are not included in the data.[9]

As this fifth and final criterion makes clear, the quantitative data do not include "negative," or failed, cases of great power territorial expansion. The primary reason negative cases are excluded is that they are not easily observable in the historical record.[10] When it comes to intentional expansion, failed or negative cases are incredibly difficult to distinguish from interstate war, brief military occupations, and other temporary armed incursions on foreign territory.

To make these distinctions, one would need to have a fairly solid understanding of state leaders' plans and intentions before each and every armed incursion on foreign territory by each of the great powers over the course of two centuries—a tall order, to be sure. When it comes to inadvertent expansion, failed or negative cases are difficult to distinguish from militarized territorial disputes and often do not show up in the historical record in a meaningful way at all. What typically occurs in these cases is a peripheral agent claims or conquers a piece of foreign territory and then is either ignored or quickly (and often quietly) rebuffed by leaders in the capital. Events such as these are often simply not notable enough to show up in most histories or even in many published collections of government documents. Compared to cases that ultimately lead to new territory being gained, these negative cases are far more difficult to observe and far less likely to be a prominent part of recorded history. Therefore, generating a representative sample of such negative cases, let alone the entire universe of them, is likely to be prohibitively difficult for a single book by a single scholar.

On the one hand, the exclusion of failed or negative cases of territorial expansion in the quantitative data obviously introduces the risk of "selection bias," since the cases in which expansion succeeds may differ in important ways from those where it fails and, therefore, may not be representative of the phenomenon as a whole.[11] On the other hand, the data collection effort for this book was already substantial, involving traversing the histories of nine great powers over the course of, in some cases, two hundred years. And, given the difficulties of observing "attempted" or failed expansion, as discussed earlier, I think this is simply a problem to be aware of, and in light of which the results should be interpreted, not one that can be readily solved.[12] Five failed or negative cases of inadvertent expansion—where faits accomplis were presented by peripheral actors but rejected by leaders in the capital—are given detailed qualitative examination in chapters 3–7.

I have restricted the empirical scope of the data to the great powers from 1816 to the present. I use the COW's State System Membership data on "Major Powers" to indicate the identity and the tenure of the great powers, with a few modifications.[13] I have limited my focus to the great powers for three central reasons. First, the great powers do most of the territorial expansion. According to the territorial change data, great powers account for 76 percent of all cases of successful conquest and annexation globally from 1816 to 2014. Second, territorial expansion by the great powers tends to be more consequential. As just one possible indicator of "consequence," the territorial change data suggest that great power expansion accounts for 79 percent of the territorial area gained and 62 percent of the population gained through conquest and annexation globally since 1816.[14] And third, the empirical record is most complete for the great powers, and reliably coding expansion as inadvertent or intentional often requires a great deal of in-depth historical research.

Altogether, I compiled and collected data on 258 cases of territorial expansion by the great powers between 1816 and 2014. For each observation, I include a set of variables with basic information about the event in question. For the purpose of this book, the most important of these is *inadvertent*—a dichotomous variable indicating whether the expansion observation is inadvertent or not (and, therefore, implicitly "intentional"). As outlined in chapter 1, I consider an expansion observation to be inadvertent when it is planned and executed by actors on the periphery, without the authorization of leaders in the capital. My basic coding procedure for each observation was to seek out information on who specifically ordered the territorial acquisition in question. When I found evidence in the historical record that the acquisition was ordered or authorized in advance by leaders in the capital—the chief executive or key members of the security apparatus, including the foreign minister, defense minister, or colonial minister—I considered the observation intentional.[15] When I found a primary source or at least two secondary sources indicating that the territory was acquired without orders or prior authorization of any of these leaders in the capital, I coded the observation as inadvertent.[16]

For three reasons, who ordered a given territorial acquisition is often a surprisingly difficult piece of information to unearth. First, in writing on territorial expansion and empire in both history and political science, *causes* and *consequences* tend to be emphasized at the expense of *process*.[17] That is, scholars usually focus on *why* a piece of territory was acquired, or *how it was governed* after acquisition, but the actual *process* of acquisition gets far less attention. A second issue is the widespread personification of the state or empire, which is also common in both history and political science.[18] Frequent references to "Russia," "Japan," or "the British Empire" acquiring various territories obscure the nature of the specific actors involved as well as the authorities under which they were operating. Relatedly, many scholars operate with implicit (or explicit) rational and unitary assumptions of the state, which can encourage post hoc reasoning and reliance on "revealed preferences"—they acquired the territory, so they *must have* wanted to. Third, the historical record on a good number of these cases is incredibly thin. Cases of inadvertent expansion, in particular, are often less dramatic than their intentional counterparts and, therefore, tend to receive considerably less attention in historical research. Furthermore, as noted in chapter 1, the leaders who experience inadvertent expansion often have incentives to cover up these episodes, so as to not appear incompetent or out of control, and may suppress, distort, or even destroy records of events. It seems likely, therefore, that inadvertent expansion is even more common than I have been able to uncover here. In short, coding expansion observations as either intentional or inadvertent is both time consuming and challenging.[19]

Besides whether the expansion was inadvertent, each observation includes the *year* and *month* in which it took place, the gaining great power (*gainer*), the territorial *entity* acquired, and the *region* in which the observation occurred.[20] I define regions broadly, dividing the world into just six major regions: the Western Hemisphere, Europe, sub-Saharan Africa, the Middle East and North Africa, South and Central Asia, and the Asia Pacific. I also include variables that indicate whether the territorial entity was acquired via armed *conquest* or political *annexation*. Following the territorial change data, and in line with international legal definitions, I consider expansion to be annexation when territory is acquired primarily through diplomacy, and I consider expansion to be conquest when territory is acquired primarily through the use of military force.[21]

The theory presented in chapter 1 argues that inadvertent expansion should be more likely when leaders in the capital have limited control over their peripheral agents and in situations that involve relatively low levels of geopolitical risk. To capture the concept of control over the periphery, I include the variable *telegraph*, which is a dichotomous variable indicating whether the territorial entity acquired was connected to the global telegraph network at the time of acquisition.[22] The idea here is that, if there was a telegraph station in the territory at the time of acquisition, this would allow leaders in the great power's capital to rapidly communicate with any of their agents in and around the territory and thereby better monitor and potentially control their behavior.[23] Another variable included to get at the concept of control is *extra_regional*, a dichotomous variable indicating whether the territorial entity acquired is outside of the great power's own region. The idea here is that, all else being equal, agents within a great power's own region are easier to control than those in other regions. A third, more granular, measure that I include along these lines is the *distance* of the entity acquired from the great power's capital.[24] This, again, is on the assumption that, all else being equal, agents in more distant territories should be more difficult to control than those in more proximate territories.

I also include two variables meant to capture the second factor: geopolitical risk. While, according to the theory of inadvertent expansion, this factor mainly influences the second step of subsequent central authorization, it is worth seeing if there are broad differences between intentional and inadvertent expansion with respect to geopolitical risk. Building off of arguments made by Colin Elman and Randall Schweller, I construct the dichotomous variable *risk*.[25] I consider territorial expansion to be risky when it is: (1) onto the territory of another great power, (2) onto territory adjacent to another great power's national borders,

(3) onto the territory of a political entity allied with another great power, (4) in violation of a prior agreement with another great power on the territorial integrity of the entity in question, and/or (5) onto the territory of a regional power—a relatively powerful state that does not meet the typical threshold of great power status. I use the Alliance Treaty Obligation and Provision data, as well as the Correlates of War's Formal Alliances data, as measures of formal alliances.[26] Examples of the kind of states that are considered regional powers are Mexico, Austria (post-1918), Spain, Romania, the Ottoman Empire, Egypt, China (pre-1949), and Taiwan (post-1949). A related variable that I include is the dichotomous variable *conflict*, which indicates whether the expansion observation is part of a broader conflict. I consider expansion to be part of a broader conflict when it is undertaken during, and as part of, a broader war, or when it takes place in the immediate aftermath, and as a direct result of, a broader war. I consider wars as being those conflicts included in the Correlates of War's "Inter-state," "Intra-state," and "Extra-state" war data.[27]

I also include a number of variables that can be thought of as controls for other plausible explanations for inadvertent expansion. First, and as noted earlier, I include the dichotomous variable *annexation*. Given that political annexations generally require fewer resources and are less difficult to organize than armed conquest, it is possible that inadvertent expansion is more likely to occur via annexation. Second, I include a measure of the capacity of the state's institutions. It seems plausible that states with weak institutions may be more likely to experience inadvertent expansion, since they have smaller central state apparatuses and less capacity to monitor their agents at any distance from the capital. For this, I include the great power's "information capacity" (*info_capacity*), an annual index that measures the state's ability to collect and process reliable information about its population and territory.[28] Third, I include a number of regime type variables. The dichotomous variable *democracy* indicates whether the expanding great power has a Polity score of six or greater at the time of acquisition.[29] There is an enormous literature in international relations pointing to the unique foreign policy behavior of democratic states. And it is at least plausible that, allowing more individual liberty for their citizens and being more subject to popular pressures, democracies may be more likely to experience inadvertent expansion. I also include an *autocracy* indicator for the expanding great power, its simple *polity* score, and its "Varieties of Democracy" polyarchy score (*vdem_polyarchy*), a common alternative regime type measure.[30] Fourth, I include the great power's Composite Index of National Capabilities score (*gainer_cinc*), a standard measure of relative power.[31] Again, many theories in international relations point to relative power as an important explanatory factor for a variety of foreign policy outcomes, so it is accounted for here.

Descriptive Statistics

The data collected show inadvertent expansion to be a surprisingly common phenomenon.[32] Of the 251 cases of great power territorial expansion that I have coded as either intentional or inadvertent, a total of 55—or 22 percent—are inadvertent. This point, I think, deserves emphasis: in the modern history of great power politics, nearly one-in-four cases of territorial expansion are the result of decisions made by actors without the authority to make them. Thus, in almost a quarter of cases of territorial expansion by the great powers, there is a sharp disconnect between the intentions of the leaders in charge and the state apparatuses that they are purportedly in charge of. And the kinds of territories acquired in this manner run the gamut, from tiny islands in the South Pacific—such as France's annexation of Tahiti in 1842—to large swaths of territory containing tens of millions of people—such as Japan's conquest of Manchuria in 1932. All cases of inadvertent expansion are listed in table 2.1.

Besides being a common occurrence, the data on inadvertent expansion show some other interesting patterns. First, there are cases of inadvertent expansion as early as 1818 and as late as 1932, though, notably, it tends to occur in earlier years than intentional expansion. As shown in figure 2.1, inadvertent expansion is a regular occurrence throughout the nineteenth century and into the early twentieth century, with a small cluster of observations during World War I. Intentional expansion, in contrast, is more common throughout and sees increases during the late nineteenth-century "scramble" for empire and during the two world wars. Second, a majority of the great powers experience inadvertent expansion, though they vary considerably in the extent to which they do. As indicated in table 2.1, France, the United Kingdom, and Russia experienced a considerable amount of inadvertent expansion. Japan, Germany, and the United States, by contrast, experienced moderate-to-low amounts of inadvertent expansion. And great powers such as Austria, Italy, and China have seen no successful cases of inadvertent expansion at all.[33] Third, inadvertent expansion occurs in all world regions, though some regions experience a lot more than others. As suggested by the cases listed in table 2.1, South and Central Asia, sub-Saharan Africa, and the Asia Pacific see significant amounts of inadvertent expansion, whereas the Western Hemisphere, the Middle East and North Africa, and Europe see little to none.

In sum, inadvertent expansion occurs in nearly one-in-four cases of great power territorial expansion, a wide variety of territories have been acquired in this manner, it covers over a century of history, it is experienced by a majority of the great powers, and it occurs in all world regions. It is, therefore, a general phenomenon—a regular occurrence in the history of great power politics.

TABLE 2.1 Cases of inadvertent expansion

GREAT POWER	DATE (YEAR/ MONTH)	TERRITORY	GREAT POWER	DATE (YEAR/ MONTH)	TERRITORY
France	1840	Nosy Be	Russia	1850/8	Amur Region
	1841/4	Mayotte Island		1852/ summer	Ussuri Region
	1842/8	Tahiti		1864/9	Chimkent
	1843/6	Coastal Gabon		1865/6	Tashkent
	1860/9	Senegal (part)		1866/5	Khujand
	1862/3	Obock		1868/6	Khanate of Bukhara
	1863/8	Cambodia		1876/2	Khanate of Kokand
	1867/6	Western Cochinchina			
	1880/6	Gabon	United Kingdom	1818/6	Maratha Empire
	1880/9	Congo		1819/2	Singapore
	1883/2	Southern French Sudan		1825/12	Upper Burma
	1883/8	Annam		1842/4	Chatham Islands
	1883/8	Tonkin		1843/3	Sind
	1893/4	Northern French Sudan		1846/2	Eastern Punjab
	1894/8	Ubangi-Shari		1847/12	Xhosa Territory
	1900/4	Chad		1848/2	Orange River Territory
	1904/6	Eastern Morocco		1849/3	Punjab
	1914/8	Togoland		1852/12	Lower Burma
	1916/1	Cameroon		1857/3	Keeling (Cocos) Islands
				1874/4	Western Peninsular Malaya
Germany	1884/4	South-West Africa		1874/9	Fiji
	1884/7	Togoland		1878/7	Xhosa Territory
	1885/5	East Africa		1879/9	Zulu Kingdom
	1885/5	Wituland		1884/11	Papua
				1888/5	North Borneo
Japan	1914/10	Caroline Islands		1890/9	Rhodesia
	1914/10	Mariana Islands		1900/3	Nigeria
	1914/10	Marshall Islands		1914/8	Togoland
	1932/2	Manchuria			
			United States	1818/5	Florida

However, the questions that primarily concern this book are when and why it occurs. Throughout this book, I have argued that two factors are central to the process: the degree of control leaders in the capital have over their peripheral agents, and the geopolitical risk associated with acquisition. The key variables here are *telegraph* and *risk*. If the theory of inadvertent expansion is correct, with

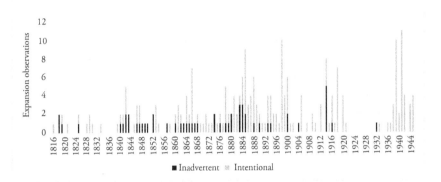

FIGURE 2.1.   Intentional and inadvertent expansion by year, 1816–1945. Data after 1945 are not included in the figure because there are so few (four) observations. These are China's conquests of Tibet in 1950, the Dachen Islands in 1955, the Paracel Islands in 1974, and Russia's conquest of Crimea in 2014.

respect to the telegraph, expansion should be *less* likely to be inadvertent in cases where there *is* a telegraph station in the territory at the time of acquisition and *more* likely to be inadvertent in cases where there *is not* a telegraph station in the territory at the time of acquisition. With respect to risk, expansion should be *less* likely to be inadvertent in cases that *are* risky and *more* likely to be inadvertent in cases that *are not* risky. Figure 2.2 presents two difference-in-proportions comparisons.

As the figure clearly shows, these theoretical expectations appear to be borne out. Starting with *telegraph*, on the left-hand side, 8 percent of expansion observations are inadvertent in cases where there *is* a telegraph station in the territory at the time of acquisition. In contrast, 38 percent of observations are inadvertent in cases where there *is not* a telegraph station in the territory at the time of acquisition—a large and highly statistically significant difference. A similar pattern is evident with respect to *risk*, on the figure's right-hand side. Nine percent of expansion observations are inadvertent in cases that *do* involve considerable risk, whereas 32 percent of observations are inadvertent in cases that *do not* involve much risk—again, a large and statistically significant difference.

The average differences in value between intentional and inadvertent expansion for all the remaining variables are presented in table 2.2. As is clear, some variables see much greater differences than others across the two types of expansion. Variables such as *year*, *extra_regional*, *distance*, and *conflict* show considerable differences between intentional and inadvertent expansion. Based on these

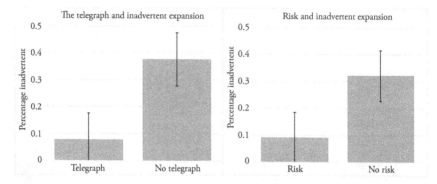

FIGURE 2.2. The telegraph, risk, and inadvertent expansion. Error bars indicate 95 percent confidence intervals. Significance testing conducted using bivariate linear regression analysis with robust standard errors clustered on the great power. See online appendix for full details. (https://doi.org/10.7910/DVN/JBGNNH)

TABLE 2.2 Intentional and inadvertent expansion by variable

VARIABLE	RANGE	AVG. (INTENTIONAL)	AVG. (INADVERTENT)	DIFFERENCE	N
Year*	1816–2014	1896	1874	−22	251
Telegraph	0/1	0.62	0.18	−0.44	251
Risk	0/1	0.52	0.18	−0.34	251
Annexation	0/1	0.40	0.45	+0.05	251
Extra_regional	0/1	0.55	0.78	+0.23	251
Distance (km)	201–19,137	5,519	7,040	+1,521	251
Conflict	0/1	0.56	0.38	−0.18	251
Info_capacity	0.21–0.61	0.53	0.51	−0.02	250
Polity	(−10)–10	0.46	0.75	+0.29	251
Democracy	0/1	0.36	0.31	−0.05	251
Autocracy	0/1	0.26	0.20	−0.06	251
Vdem_polyarchy	0.02–0.71	0.29	0.31	+0.02	251
Gainer_cinc	0.02–0.38	0.14	0.16	+0.02	251

* Median reported

figures, it appears that inadvertent expansion is *more* likely: in earlier years, when the territorial entity is outside the great power's home region, and at a greater distance from the great power's capital. It appears that inadvertent expansion is *less* likely, in contrast, when the expansion is part of a broader conflict. For the remaining variables, there appears to be little difference between the two forms of expansion: *annexation, info_capacity,* the regime type variables (*polity, democ-*

racy, autocracy, and *vdem_polyarchy*), and *gainer_cinc* scores show little to no meaningful difference between cases of inadvertent expansion and intentional expansion. Inadvertent expansion, it seems, is no more likely to take the form of annexation than conquest. Great powers with weak and strong institutions are equally likely to engage in inadvertent expansion. Democracies and autocracies alike seem to expand both intentionally and inadvertently. And relatively powerful as well as relatively weak great powers have a similar record with respect to both types of expansion.

Analysis

These comparisons are certainly interesting, and even enlightening. But with the evidence presented so far, it is difficult to tell which factors most distinguish inadvertent and intentional expansion. Because some of these measures may be correlated with each other, and many are likely correlated with time, it is necessary to observe the independent relationship of each while controlling for the others. This is the task I turn to now.

As noted earlier, the unit of analysis is the great power territorial expansion observation and the outcome of interest is *inadvertent*, a dichotomous variable indicating whether the expansion was inadvertent or not. Thus, the variation being analyzed here is between successful forms of expansion: inadvertent and intentional. In an ideal world, we would have data that include all cases of successful intentional and inadvertent expansion *as well as* all cases of failed intentional and inadvertent expansion. This would provide a more complete picture of the broad conditions under which inadvertent expansion opportunities arise as well as when leaders either accept and or reject the fait accompli. However, as discussed in chapter 1, cases of failed inadvertent expansion are not easily observable in the historical record, making comprehensive collection difficult. As a result, this quantitative analysis examines variation between forms of expansion. The qualitative case studies in the chapters that follow take up the question of variation between acceptance and rejection of the fait accompli.

The primary explanatory variables I include are *telegraph* and *risk*. One concern with the telegraph measure may be that it is simply a proxy for the passage of time. Because the telegraph emerged in Europe and North America the mid-nineteenth century and gradually spread across the globe in the decades that followed, any apparent relationship between the telegraph and inadvertent expansion may simply be due to some other variable that is also correlated with time. To try to deal with this concern, I include the *year* in which the expansion observation occurred as a control variable. Another concern with the telegraph measure may be that it is simply a proxy for distance, since territories that are closer are likely to be telegraphically connected to the capital sooner than those that are more distant. To try to deal with this concern, I include *distance* as a control variable in the analysis. As for geopolitical risk, one concern may be that it is simply picking up the difference between peacetime and wartime territorial expansion. To try to address this concern, I include *conflict* as a control variable. As more general controls for other plausible explanations, I include *annexation, info_capacity, democracy,* and *gainer_cinc.* The analysis is conducted using a linear probability model. In all cases, robust standard errors are reported to account for error heteroskedasticity. Table 2.3 presents the results.

As the results make clear, both the telegraph and geopolitical risk appear to be correlated with expansion being inadvertent rather than intentional, even when accounting for other factors, such as time, distance, the form of expansion, state institutional capacity, regime type, and relative power. Even with these controls, observations of territorial expansion are 23 percent less likely to be inadvertent when there is a *telegraph* in the territory acquired at the time of acquisition. Simi-

TABLE 2.3   Linear probability analysis of inadvertent expansion

	DEPENDENT VARIABLE: INADVERTENT
Telegraph	−0.234***
	(0.074)
Risk	−0.140**
	(0.055)
Year	−0.001*
	(0.001)
Distance	−0.00000
	(0.00001)
Conflict	0.026
	(0.067)
Annexation	−0.092
	(0.062)
Info_capacity	0.147
	(0.286)
Democracy	−0.026
	(0.059)
Gainer_cinc	−0.289
	(0.348)
Observations	250

Note: $*p < 0.1$; $**p < 0.05$; $***p < 0.01$

larly, when the expansion observation involves considerable *risk*, it appears to be 14 percent less likely to be inadvertent, even when controlling for these other factors. Both of these measures are statistically significant at conventional levels, and none of the other variables reaches statistical significance.

As a whole, the analysis suggests that two factors are most importantly associated with expansion being inadvertent rather than intentional. The first is the absence of a connection to the global telegraph network in the territorial entity acquired at the time of acquisition. The second is the geopolitical risk associated with the expansion observation in question. The great power's state capacity, form of expansion, regime type, and relative power, notably, do not seem to be correlated with expansion being intentional or inadvertent.

I ran a number of tests to see how robust these results are to alternative model specifications and variable inclusions. The full results are available in the online appendix (https://doi.org/10.7910/DVN/JBGNNH), though I briefly describe the procedures and findings here. First, I reran the analysis using logistic regression rather than a linear probability model. The results are unchanged. Second, I reran the analysis including *extra_regional* rather than *distance* as the distance control. The results are, again, unchanged, and *extra_regional* is not statistically significant. Third, instead of using *democracy* as the great power's regime-type measure, I reran the analysis including an *autocracy* indicator, a simple *polity* score, and a Varieties of Democracy Polyarchy score (*vdem_polyarchy*) for electoral democracy. The results are unchanged, and none of the alternative regime-type measures reach conventional levels of statistical significance. Fourth, I reran the analysis with dichotomous variables controlling for each of the great powers, one by one, to see if the results are driven by any particular great power actor. The results are unchanged, and the statistical significance of *risk* even increases when controlling for the United Kingdom, Italy, or Japan. Fifth, and finally, I reran the analysis with dichotomous variables controlling for each region in which expansion takes place, one by one, to see if the results are driven by any particular region. The results are mostly unchanged, with an important exception: *risk* loses its statistical significance when controlling for sub-Saharan African expansion. This suggests that the cases in sub-Saharan Africa play a statistically influential role in low-risk conditions being associated with inadvertent territorial expansion. However, given that sub-Saharan African cases account for nearly half of all cases of inadvertent expansion (24/55 or 44 percent), this may not be entirely surprising.[34] Overall, the results are quite robust to alternative models and variables. The presence or absence of rapid modern communications in the form of a telegraph station, as well as relatively low geopolitical risk, are strongly associated with whether territorial expansion is inadvertent or intentional.

Discussion

These results provide strong, though only partial, support for the theory of inadvertent expansion presented in chapter 1. First, the argument that inadvertent expansion is more likely when leaders in the capital lack adequate control over their agents on the periphery is supported by the analysis. The strongest predictor of when expansion is inadvertent rather than intentional is the absence of a globally connected telegraph station in the territorial entity acquired at the time of acquisition. The presence of such a station is associated with a 30 percent reduction in the probability of expansion being inadvertent (see figure 2.2), and this relationship holds even when controlling for a variety of other plausible explanatory factors. As the evidence from this chapter suggests and as is illustrated in the historical case studies in the chapters ahead, the inability of leaders in the capital to rapidly and reliably communicate with, and thereby monitor, their agents on the periphery plays a crucial role in the ability for peripheral agents to spring territorial faits accomplis upon them—what I refer to as unauthorized peripheral expansion.

Second, the argument that inadvertent expansion is more likely when there is little significant geopolitical risk associated with territorial acquisition is also supported by the analysis. The only other significant predictor of when expansion is inadvertent rather than intentional is the absence of geopolitical risk. The presence of such risk is associated with a 23 percent reduction in the probability of expansion being inadvertent (see figure 2.2), and this result holds even when controlling for other explanatory variables. As these results indicate, and as is further supported in the qualitative chapters that follow, the presence of geopolitical risk will discourage leaders in the capital from accepting the territorial faits accomplis presented by their peripheral agents—what I refer to as subsequent central authorization.

Other possible explanatory factors—including whether expansion takes the form of annexation, the distance of the territory from the capital, whether it occurs in peacetime, the expanding great power's state institutional capacity, its regime type, or its relative power—were not supported in the analysis.

This chapter has provided a macroscopic perspective of the phenomenon of inadvertent expansion in world politics. In it, I introduced and analyzed data on great power territorial expansion from 1816 to 2014. The chapter presented two central findings. First, inadvertent expansion is a surprisingly general phenomenon. Far from being an occasional and obscure "accident of history," it has been a regular feature of the modern history of great power politics. It occurs in nearly one-in-four cases of great power territorial expansion, spanning over one hundred years, from the early nineteenth century to well into the twentieth century. It is successfully carried out by six different great powers, from the sprawling British Empire to the late-modernizing Imperial Japan. And a wide variety of territories have been acquired in this manner, from small remote islands in the South Pacific, to topographically forbidding central African kingdoms, to densely populated regions of East and Southeast Asia.

Second, the most important conditions under which inadvertent expansion is likely to occur are when the capital lacks sufficient control over its agents on the periphery and when the acquisition in question involves little geopolitical risk. Expansion into territorial entities that were not connected to the global telegraph network at the time of acquisition is significantly more likely to be inadvertent than expansion into territories that were connected. Similarly, expansion in conditions involving little geopolitical risk is significantly more likely to be inadvertent than expansion in conditions involving considerable risk. Other plausible factors do not appear to be related to whether expansion is intentional or inadvertent. What this chapter has primarily accomplished is to uncover what is *distinctive* about inadvertent expansion within the broader universe of cases of territorial expansion, and this distinctiveness has been shown to be consistent with the theory of inadvertent expansion presented in chapter 1.

However, two caveats are necessary in closing. First, a lack of rapid communications technology is neither a necessary nor a sufficient condition for inadvertent expansion. There are ten cases in the data of inadvertent expansion into territories that *are* connected to the global telegraph network, showing that it can occur under conditions of modern communications technology.[35] And there are seventy-five cases in the data of intentional expansion in the absence of a proximate telegraph station, indicating that great powers can still readily direct territorial expansion from the capital, even without the aid of rapid modern communications. This also applies to geopolitical risk. There are eleven cases of inadvertent expansion in conditions that are objectively risky, showing that the existence of geopolitical risk is not a foolproof guarantee of expansion being intentional.[36] And there are seven cases of inadvertent expansion that are both into territories with a global telegraph network connection *and* that involve considerable geopolitical risk.[37] However, what the evidence presented in this chapter does suggest is that relatively low peripheral control by the capital and low geopolitical risk seem to make inadvertent expansion significantly more likely.

The second caveat is that, as mentioned earlier, the structure of the data and the variation examined in the analysis are not ideal for testing the theory of inadvertent expansion as it is presented in chapter 1. The ideal data would include not only all cases of successful intentional and inadvertent expansion but also all cases of *unsuccessful* intentional and inadvertent expansion. This would give us a much better sense of the universe of cases of inadvertent expansion *opportunities*—helping us deal with problems of selection bias—and allow us to quantitatively examine the variation between acceptances and rejections of the fait accompli by leaders in the capital. Difficulties of observation and data collection rule this possibility out. However, it is possible to examine variation between successful and failed inadvertent expansion on a smaller sample of cases and in a more focused and detailed way. Conducting such an examination is the task of the remainder of this book.

INADVERTENT EXPANSION IN THE AMERICAN SOUTH

The United States

The occupation of these places in Spanish Florida by the commander of American forces was not by virtue of any orders received by him from this Government to that effect.

—John Quincy Adams, 1818

This chapter examines inadvertent expansion as it occurred in two cases from the antebellum United States of America. The first case examines the United States' acquisition of Florida from 1818–19. The second case presents the United States' nonacquisition of the Republic of Texas in 1836–37. The purpose of these cases is twofold. First, this chapter presents the book's first pair of comparative theory-testing case studies, illustrating how varying perceptions of geopolitical risk produced divergent outcomes, leading to successful expansion in Florida but failed expansion in Texas. Florida and Texas are a useful comparison in that they hold many factors fixed—the same great power, operating in the same region and in the same era—while the outcomes vary across the two cases. Second, this chapter powerfully illustrates the differences between what I referred to in chapter 1 as the "view from the capital" and the "view from the frontier," in that the *very same individual* inhabits both positions—and adopts the associated perspectives—across the two cases. In the case of Florida in 1818, the peripheral agent driving the unauthorized conquest is Andrew Jackson, then a major general in the US Army. By the time the United States has an opportunity to acquire Texas in 1836, Jackson is, of course, president of the United States—the leader in the capital with the most authority to either accept or reject the territorial fait accompli. Jackson's boldness, in the case of Florida, and his reticence, in the case of Texas, are striking indications of how vastly different an individual's perceptions can be depending upon the position they inhabit.

Jackson Enters the "Wolf's Den": The United States in Spanish Florida, 1818–19

The United States acquired the Spanish imperial provinces of East and West Florida (now Florida) between January 1818 and February 1819, over the course of the First Seminole War (1817–18). The conquest of these provinces was carried out by Andrew Jackson, then a major general in the US Army, overstepping the bounds imposed by his superiors in Washington. The theory of inadvertent expansion makes four arguments that are borne out in this case. First, that peripheral expansion is a manifestation of a principal-agent problem, driven by diverse preferences between capital and periphery and information asymmetries favoring the latter. In the case of Florida, the vast distances under pretelegraph technology made controlling frontier agents such as Jackson very difficult for Washington. Second, that the acquisition of a given territory, in part or in whole, will often place constraints on leaders in the capital that make it difficult to readily relinquish the new possession. In the case at hand, Jackson's invasion sunk the costs of eventual acquisition by the United States, and his powerful domestic political supporters made backing down extremely difficult for leaders in Washington. Third, that the confluence of pressures to accept the territorial fait accompli and the potential geopolitical risks associated with doing so will create a dilemma for leaders in the capital. In the Florida case, domestic support for Jackson would run up against the risk of potential conflict with Spain, and even the United Kingdom, presenting leaders in Washington with a distressing dilemma. And fourth, that a lack of geopolitical risk associated with acquisition will encourage leaders in the capital to accept the territorial fait accompli, resulting in subsequent central authorization. In the case of Florida, once it became clear to the United States that both the Spanish had little appetite for war and the British were not coming to their aid, they partially withdrew and then pressed Spain hard for the complete cession of Florida, resulting in its acquisition through the Transcontinental Treaty of February 1819.

Historical Background

On the eve of the invasion, in early 1818, Florida had been a backwater province of Spain's vast New World empire for most of the past three hundred years, predating the founding of the Jamestown settlement by more than a century. While it was fairly large, at nearly 152,000 km², it lacked the natural resources of other Spanish imperial holdings—such as gold, silver, and sugar—and was, therefore, sparsely populated and only lightly defended.[1] It had been divided into East and West Florida during a brief interregnum of British rule (1763–83), and the vast majority of the population of twenty thousand lived in the two provincial capitals of St. Augustine (East) and Pensacola (West).[2] Its only neighbor, of course, was the growing American juggernaut, whose population had soared from 3.9 million in 1790 up to over 9 million by 1818.[3] The United States had acquired an enormous swath of what was very recently Spanish territory with the Louisiana Purchase, of 1803, and had been chipping away at Spanish West Florida since 1810, taking approximately half of that province in the process.

Anglo-American settler encroachment on Native American lands helped spark a civil war within the Creek Confederacy, in which the United States became deeply involved.[4] The August 1814 settlement of this war in favor of the United States led to the expulsion of the Red Sticks Creeks from the Mississippi Territory and the expropriation of approximately 93,000 km² of tribal lands.[5] Many of the Red Sticks fled across the southern border with Spanish Florida, where they connected with other Native American tribes—becoming collectively known as the Seminoles—and launched attacks on the Georgia, Mississippi, and Alabama border regions.

The primary agent of the Red Sticks' expulsion was Major General Andrew Jackson. Jackson was the commander of the Southern Division of the US Army, effectively in charge of the defense of the southern half of the United States. During the Creek War (1813–14) and the War of 1812 (1812–15), he became a national celebrity with his spectacular victories at the Battles of Horseshoe Bend and New Orleans.[6] Jackson was the key actor on America's southeastern frontier who would independently launch the conquest of Florida. The US president at the time was James Monroe, the secretary of war was John C. Calhoun, and the position of secretary of state was held by John Quincy Adams. They were the key leaders in the US capital who would be dragged unwittingly into the conquest of all of Spanish Florida.

The Seminole War, which would be the occasion for the conquest of Florida, began with yet another expulsion.[7] In November 1817, US forces attacked the Creek village of Fowltown after it had refused orders to vacate, and the Creeks retaliated by ambushing a US Army transport boat on the Apalachicola River, killing several civilians on board.[8] News of the attack shocked and infuriated officials from the frontier to the capital. Andrew Jackson, who was monitoring events from the Southern Division headquarters in Nashville, Tennessee, wrote on December 16 that it was time "that the wolf be struck in his den."[9] The Seminole War had begun.

Washington and the Florida Frontier

Washington faced serious principal-agent problems with respect to its peripheral agents in the South, such as Jackson. These were due to information asymmetries favoring those on the periphery and a divergence of preferences between leaders in the capital and their peripheral agents. First, as a result of the highly rudimentary transportation and communications technology of the time, there were stark information asymmetries in favor of the periphery. This was still the prerail and pretelegraph era, and it took approximately one month for a letter to travel from Washington to Spanish Florida on horseback, meaning that it would take at least sixty days to receive a reply.[10] Long travel times from the capital to the frontier meant that the administration in Washington was at the informational mercy of its peripheral agents and had to rely heavily on the official reports they sent back.

Second, there was a divergence of preferences between leaders in Washington and their agents on the Spanish frontier. Both sides, ultimately, wanted the Floridas for the United States, indeed Washington had been in negotiations with Madrid over them since the beginning of the War of 1812.[11] Yet, they differed as to when and how the Floridas should be achieved. Leaders in the capital felt that time was on their side, and they were certain that acquiring the Floridas could, ultimately, be achieved through diplomacy and negotiation with Spain, without the need to risk war to acquire them immediately. Their agents on the periphery, and particularly Major General Jackson, however, were considerably less cautious in their approach. Jackson felt that, so long as the Floridas were in Spanish hands, and so long as the Seminoles were able to effectively have sanctuary there, the United States' southern frontier would see no peace or stability.

Florida

Given these preferences in Washington, when the Seminole War broke out, the orders to the Southern Division of the Army were clear: if needed, they could enter Spanish territory in pursuit of the Seminoles, but under no circumstances were they to take territory or attack a Spanish fort. As Secretary of War John Calhoun wrote to the commander of US forces in the war, Major General Edmund Gaines, on December 16, 1817, you should "consider yourself at liberty to march across the Florida line, and to attack them from within its limits, should it be found necessary, *unless they should shelter themselves under a Spanish post*. In the last event, you will immediately notify this Department."[12] Jackson, of course, saw things differently. After seeing Gaines's orders, he penned a letter to Monroe, on January 6, 1818, arguing that "the whole of East Florida [should be] seized." Jackson added: "This can be done without implicating the Government; let it be signified to me through any channel . . . that the possession of the Floridas would be desirable to the United States, and in sixty days it will be accomplished."[13]

Jackson never received a response to this letter. In fact, when it arrived in Washington, President Monroe was seriously ill and bedridden, and he happened to be without a secretary. The letter was apparently briefly skimmed by Calhoun and Treasury Secretary William Crawford, only to end up in a pile of Monroe's other papers, not to be seen by the president until there was a congressional investigation of the Seminole War a full year later.[14] What Jackson had not been aware of when he wrote the letter was that General Gaines was to be diverted to another theater and that Jackson himself would be appointed as commander of US forces in the Seminole War. Secretary Calhoun wrote to Jackson on December 26, 1817, that he should "repair, with as little delay as practicable, to Fort Scott, and assume the immediate command of the forces in that section" and that he should "adopt the necessary measures to terminate [the] conflict"—though this order would not arrive in Nashville until January 11, 1818—five days after Jackson had sent his provocative letter to the president.[15]

While Calhoun's new orders did not explicitly place the same limitations on Jackson that had been placed on Gaines with regard to respecting Spanish sovereignty, it is clear from his January 6 letter that Jackson had seen Gaines's orders. And, on January 30, 1818, President Monroe wrote to Calhoun, asking him to instruct Jackson "not to attack any post occupied by Spanish troops, from the possibility, that it might bring the allied powers upon us," though, for reasons that remain unknown, it seems this order was never transmitted to Jackson.[16] Calhoun later claimed, with substantial justification, that he had assumed "that the orders in this case to Genl Gains [sic] are obligatory on Genl Jackson," adding that "there is no military principle better established."[17] In any case, the administration seems to have believed that its instructions for Jackson were clear. As President Monroe assured Congress on March 25, 1818, over two months after Jackson had departed for Florida, "Orders have been given to the general in command not to enter Florida, unless it be in pursuit of the enemy, and, in that case, to respect the Spanish authority wherever it is maintained."[18]

Upon receipt of his orders, Jackson quickly readied his force of eleven hundred and prepared for the 775 km journey southbound to the Florida frontier in Georgia, reporting to Calhoun on January 20, 1818, that they were ready "to inflict speedy and merited chastisement on the deluded Seminoles."[19] Conditions would prove difficult on the forty-six-day journey, with heavy rains, flooded and washed-out roads, multiple crossings of swollen rivers, and ration and supply shortages.[20] Jackson's forces crossed the border into Spanish Florida around March 13, and, on March 16, they arrived at the ruins of the old British fort at Prospect Bluff (also known as "Negro Fort"), where he ordered it rebuilt and renamed Fort Gadsden, after his aide-de-camp. This was a first territorial claim Jackson was not supposed to make.

After ten day's rest and resupply, Jackson and his forces left Fort Gadsden on March 26 headed for St. Marks, a Spanish fort approximately 110 km to the east. Jackson had written to Calhoun the previous day, reporting that he had "no doubt

but that St. Marks is in possession of the Indians" and that he would "take possession of the garrison as a depot for my supplies."[21] On his way, Jackson was reinforced
on April 1 by Tennessee militia members as well as two thousand Creek allies,
bringing his total forces to nearly five thousand.[22] With this larger force, Jackson
engaged in what historian and Jackson biographer Robert Remini has referred to
as a "thoroughgoing campaign of terror," killing and capturing Seminoles, seizing their cattle and foodstuffs, and burning their villages to the ground.[23] A few
days later, Jackson proudly reported to Calhoun that the "duty was executed to my
satisfaction; nearly three hundred houses were consumed."[24] Jackson's forces then
took the fort of St. Marks without resistance, on April 7, justifying the conquest
to the Spanish commandant there on "the immutable principle of self-defence."[25]
With this, his second unauthorized territorial acquisition had been carried out.

Jackson and his forces then headed east for Bowlegs Town, a Seminole village
160 km from St. Marks on the Suwannee River. Jackson's forces razed the town
when they arrived on April 16, and in skirmishes in and around the town they
killed forty-nine Seminole warriors and took over one hundred men, women,
and children prisoner.[26] At St. Marks and then in Bowlegs Town, Jackson happened upon and arrested two British nationals on the dubious charge of instigat-
ing the war and aiding the Seminoles.[27] Jackson then returned to St. Marks, put
his two British captives on trial, and had them executed on the morning of April
29, 1818—one being shot, and the other being hung from the yardarm of his own
ship.[28] In reporting these events to Calhoun, Jackson wrote on May 5: "I hope
the execution of these two unprincipled villains will prove an awful example to
the world, and convince the Government of Great Britain, as well as her subjects,
that certain (if slow) retribution awaits these unchristian wretches, who, by false
promises, delude and excite an Indian tribe to all the horrid deeds of savage war."[29]

However, Jackson's work in Florida was not quite complete. He claimed to
have received intelligence that as many as five hundred Seminole warriors had
congregated in the capital of Spanish West Florida, Pensacola, some 275 km west
of Fort Gadsden.[30] On May 10, Jackson gathered a force of approximately twelve
hundred and set out across the Apalachicola River for Pensacola.[31] Two weeks
later, on May 24, Jackson's forces took the city without resistance, with Jackson
warning the governor before storming the city that "the blood which may be shed
by a useless resistance on your part to my demand will rest on your head."[32] After
taking Fort Barrancas on May 28, a Spanish fort just 10 km outside Pensacola,
Jackson issued a proclamation appointing a US territorial governor, seizing the
royal archives, and establishing tax collection procedures, while shipping the
Spanish governor and garrison off to Havana, Cuba.[33] As Jackson would report
to Calhoun on June 2, 1818, the articles of capitulation "amount to a complete
cession to the United States of that portion of the Floridas."[34] (See figure 3.1.)

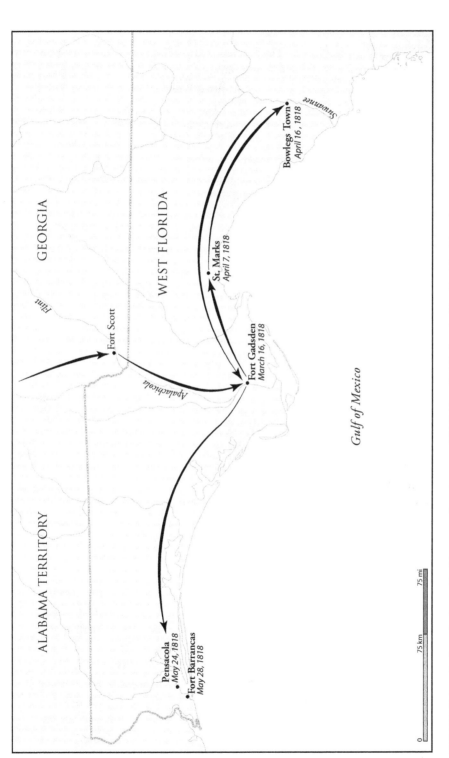

FIGURE 3.1. Andrew Jackson Florida campaign, January 1818–May 1818. Created by Beehive Mapping.

With much of Spanish Florida under the control of his forces, Jackson finally saw his job as complete—though he was always ready for more. As he prepared to head back to Nashville on June 2, he wrote to President Monroe, telling him that with some minor reinforcements, "I will insure you Cuba in a few days."[35] However, along with Jackson's brashness were notable undertones of diffidence. On "our Southern frontier, I have established peace and safety," Jackson wrote to the president, "and hope the government will never yield it[;] should my acts . . . be disapproved, I have this consolation[:] that I exercised my best exertions and Judgt. and that sound national policy will dictate holding Possession as long as we are a republick."[36] Andrew Jackson had, without orders, taken control of much of Spanish Florida in eighty days, and at a cost of just seven of his forces killed.[37] His fait accompli was complete. The question that now seemed to be on his mind was how the administration in Washington would react.

Washington Reacts

News of Jackson's exploits in Florida began to filter back to Washington through unofficial channels in late April and early May 1818. The first dispatches the administration received from Jackson directly were on May 4, reporting on his conquest of St. Marks. Though it was a clear violation of his orders, the administration's reaction to this first acquisition was fairly muted.[38] With the exception of Secretary of State Adams, who worried that Jackson was acting "without due regard to humanity," no one in Monroe's cabinet raised significant concerns.[39] For the time being, the administration was content to await further information from the frontier.

However, the Florida issue began to heat up in June. Once the Spanish learned of what was transpiring there, the minister to Washington Luis de Onís lodged a formal complaint on June 17, referring to Jackson's actions as "monstrous acts of hostility."[40] The following day, the president and his cabinet became aware of the storming of Pensacola and the execution of the two British subjects.[41] This was clearly a more serious turn of events, as not only had a major Spanish city been taken but Jackson risked bringing the United Kingdom into the conflict as well. As Secretary Adams noted in his diary that day, "This, and other events in this Indian war, makes so many difficulties for the administration."[42]

Matters would come to a head in July. On the seventh, Secretary of State Adams was awoken in the middle of the night by Minister Onís, demanding a meeting the following day.[43] There, he would deliver a second diplomatic protest, this time for the conquest of Pensacola, referring to Jackson's conduct as "excessive aggression, unexampled in the history of nations."[44] On July 9, Monroe received official documents from Jackson at his farm in Loudoun County, and he quickly prepared to return to the capital. The following day, in a letter to former president James Madison, Monroe foreshadowed the debate that would take place in his cabinet by pointing out that "there are serious difficulties in this business, on which ever side we view it."[45] The president arrived back in Washington on July 13, as Adams put it, "in the midst of the storm."[46]

The Monroe cabinet held six separate hours-long cabinet meetings from July 15 to July 21, 1818, to discuss the Florida crisis. The basic initial stance of most cabinet members was of opposition to Jackson's conduct in Florida. Yet, it would not be quite so simple. As it turned out, the very act of Jackson's conquering Spanish territory in Florida would make it extremely difficult to simply cut the major general loose and withdraw, and this was so for two reasons. First, Jackson's conquests sunk the costs of acquisition of these Spanish territories. The ease with which Jackson's forces acquired most of East and West Florida put Spain's inability to protect and defend these territories in stark relief. Secretary of State Adams, having been in negotiations with Spain over the Floridas from almost the time he took office in September 1817, was quick to grasp this and pushed for approval of Jackson's actions and retention of the territories on these grounds.[47] And Adams's position was not without foundation. The French minister, who was acting as something of an intermediary between the United States and Spain in negotiations, reported to Adams on July 10 that Spain was ready to cede the Floridas to the United States.[48] The following day, the Spanish minister Onís himself told Adams that they were willing to give up the Floridas "for nothing."[49] George Erving, the US minister to Spain, wrote to Washington on July 13, noting that Jackson's actions were forcing the hand of Madrid with respect to the Florida cession and broader border negotiations.[50] President Monroe, too, began to recognize this as the cabinet debate progressed. As he wrote in a letter to Andrew Jackson on July 19, the recent events in Florida "show the incompetency of Spain to maintain her authority" and that Jackson's actions "will furnish a strong inducement in Spain to cede the territory."[51] Thus, it was difficult to deny that Jackson's fait accompli had significantly strengthened the United States' hand in border negotiations with Spain, essentially overnight, making arguments for a blanket withdrawal more difficult to sustain.

Second, Jackson's unauthorized conquest helped generate significant domestic political pressure on the administration to support its own nationals, rather than siding with Spain. Jackson was the most popular military figure in the country—a veritable national celebrity—and the administration perceived significant domestic political costs associated with repudiating him.[52] And Jackson's notoriously fierce temper and his vengeful disposition likely only strengthened these perceptions.[53] Secretary of State Adams, again, came to this realization fairly early on in the debate. On July 16, Adams argued that to disavow the major general would create the appearance that the administration was trying "to put down Jackson in the public opinion; [and] that he would immediately resign, and turn the attack upon the Administration, and would carry a large portion of the public with him."[54] "It would be said," Adams argued in the cabinet debate of July 18, that "after having the benefit of his services, he was abandoned and sacrificed to the enemies of this country."[55] In the penultimate cabinet meeting, on July 20, Adams summed up his view more generally, noting that if one's own agent's actions were "dubious, it was better to err on the side of vigor than of weakness—on the side of our own officer, who had rendered the most eminent services to the nation, than on the side of our bitterest enemies, and against him."[56]

The rest of the administration would come around to this point of view.[57] Two months later, looking back on the cabinet debates, Secretary of War Calhoun noted in a letter to Senator Charles Tait that "from the popularity of the General, it was inexpedient to punish" Jackson.[58] Monroe, too, would ultimately agree, writing in a September 1818 letter to Virginia politician and friend George Hay that turning on Jackson would have created "internal feuds of the most pernicious character."[59] Monroe expanded on these views in a letter to former president Madison, some seven months after the cabinet debates: "Had Gen! Jackson been ordered to trial I have no doubt that the interior of the country would have been much agitated, if not convulsed, by appeals to sectional interests, by imputations of subserviency to the views of [Spain's King] Ferdinand, of hostility to the cause of the colonies, &c."[60] Thus, the administration perceived significant domestic political costs associated with cutting Jackson loose and disavowing his actions altogether.

However, there was also significant geopolitical risk involved in backing Jackson and retaining the Floridas. Secretary of War Calhoun and President Monroe held this view, seeing Jackson as having committed what amounted to an unauthorized act of war against Spain.[61] On July 13, Calhoun told Secretary of State Adams that he was "extremely dissatisfied with General Jackson's proceedings in Florida" and he thought that "we shall certainly have a Spanish war."[62] President Monroe agreed. As he noted in his July 19 letter to Andrew Jackson, if they retained Spanish Florida, it would not be "improbable that war would immediately follow. . . . The war would probably soon become general; and we do not foresee that we should have a single European power on our side. Why risk these consequences?"[63] In the view of Calhoun and Monroe, returning Spain's territory seemed the surest way to avoid war with Spain. As Calhoun argued in the cabinet meeting of July 20, by putting the responsibility squarely on Jackson's shoulders, the administration "would take away from Spain all pretext for war, and for resorting to the aid of other European powers."[64]

This combination of the expected domestic political costs associated with relinquishing the Floridas and the geopolitical risk associated with retaining them created a dilemma for the administration.[65] If they stood firm and kept the territories, the administration felt they risked war with Spain, and possibly even the United Kingdom. If they backed down and relinquished them, they risked severe domestic political consequences, potentially bringing down the administration itself. Secretary of State Adams summed up the administration's precarious position in a diary entry on July 21, 1818:

> The Administration were placed in a dilemma from which it is impossible to escape censure by some, and factious crimination by many. If they avow and approve Jackson's conduct, they incur the double responsibility of having commenced a war against Spain, and of warring in violation of the Constitution without the authority of Congress. If they disavow him, they must give offence to all his friends, encounter the shock of his popularity, and having the appearance of truckling to Spain. For all this I should be prepared.[66]

Washington Decides

To get out of this dilemma, the Monroe administration ultimately decided to split the difference, settling on a partial rebuke of Jackson as well as a partial withdrawal from Florida.[67] With respect to his decision on Jackson, the president decided to make it clear that the major general had acted without prior authorization, absolving the administration of complicity in his actions. Yet, Monroe also emphasized that Jackson was acting from principled motives and in the national interest, aiming to avoid the wrath of Jackson's domestic political supporters. The administration's policy on Florida would be published in an article, ghostwritten by Attorney General William Wirt, in the *Daily National Intelligencer* on July 27, 1818.[68] In it, the administration made clear that "in attacking the posts of St. Mark and Pensacola, with the fort of Barrancas, General Jackson . . . took these measures on his own responsibility." Yet, the article was quick to add that Jackson's "operations proceeded from motives of the purest patriotism."[69] This formulation—of Jackson having acted on his own accord but with noble intent—would be repeated in Monroe's letters to Jackson himself, communications with Congress, and diplomatic correspondence with Spain.[70]

With respect to Florida, the administration decided to conduct a partial withdrawal, planning to pull out of Pensacola expeditiously and Fort St. Marks only once Spain was prepared to garrison it sufficiently and retaining Fort Gadsden indefinitely.[71] There were three reasons the administration settled on a partial withdrawal. First, it is clear the administration wanted to avoid what was viewed as an unnecessary war with Spain. In a letter to former president Thomas Jefferson on July 22, 1818, Monroe explained that central to his Florida policy was to avoid "giving to Spain just cause of war."[72] The president repeated this rationale in later communications with Andrew Jackson and with James Madison, arguing that one of his primary goals in Florida had been "to deprive Spain and the allied powers of any just cause of war."[73] Thus, withdrawal from Pensacola was seen as an important way to avoid backing Spain into a corner from which war would be its only option.

However, the administration felt that St. Marks and Fort Gadsden could be safely retained without similar attendant risks. Secretary of State Adams had, again, suspected this early on, but it became clearer as the Florida crisis progressed.[74] It was obvious that Spain would not be clamoring for war with the United States.[75] For much of the past decade, it had been either fighting Napoleon in the Peninsular War (1807–14) at home or struggling to put down Latin American revolutionaries abroad.[76] At this point, Spain was clinging to its empire by its fingernails, and there was simply very little it could do to expel the United States from Florida. And, perhaps more importantly, it became clear that Britain had no intention of coming to Spain's aid.[77] The War of 1812 had ended only three years earlier, and no one wanted another North American war. Britain and the United States had also just recently signed an arms limitation treaty for the Great Lakes and were in the midst of negotiating their outstanding boundary issues. While the British press and public were outraged by the unlawful execution of two of their nationals, the British foreign secretary Lord Castlereagh refused to let the fate of the two adventurers disrupt the ongoing rapprochement with the United States.[78] As Castlereagh would inform the American minister to the United Kingdom Richard Rush on January 7, 1819, his government had decided that "the conduct of these individuals had been unjustifiable, and therefore not calling for the interference of Great Britain."[79] Thus, it turned out that the United States could hold onto some of Spain's territory, as there were few geopolitical risks associated with doing so.

The second reason the administration opted for a partial withdrawal is that there were important constitutional issues at stake.[80] According to Article I of the US Constitution, Congress, not the executive, is vested with the power to declare war. Thus, by attacking Spanish holdings in Florida, Jackson had potentially usurped the power of Congress and violated the Constitution. By retaining Pensacola in particular—as it was felt that the other conquests could be justified on the basis of self-defense—the administration risked having engaged in an extraconstitutional war. This argument, made by Secretary of War Calhoun from the beginning, clearly resonated with President Monroe and, despite some resistance, even Adams ultimately relented to it.[81] As the president explained to Jackson in his letter of July 19, "If the Executive refused to evacuate the posts, especially Pensacola, it would amount to a declaration of war, to which it is incompetent. It would be accused of usurping the authority of Congress, and giving a deep and fatal wound to the Constitution."[82] Thus, at least some withdrawal was seen as necessary.

The third and final reason the Monroe administration settled on a partial withdrawal from Florida had to do with coercive diplomacy. Over the course of the crisis, it became increasingly clear that Spain was in a highly vulnerable position. With the Americans in control of much of Florida, and Britain standing aside, Spanish leaders had few options beyond trying to strike the best deal with Washington they could.[83] A partial withdrawal would allow Spain to come to the negotiating table with its dignity intact, but it would also allow the United States to retain coercive leverage for the purpose of the negotiations.[84] As President Monroe explained in his same letter to Andrew Jackson on July 19, "If we hold the posts, her government cannot treat with honor, which, by withdrawing the troops, we afford her an opportunity to do."[85] From this position of advantage, the administration could then pressure—even browbeat—Spain into giving up the Floridas. For instance, the *Intelligencer* article of July 27 closed by pointing out Spain's "incompetency to maintain her authority in the Floridas" and advised that it would "be much wiser for her to cede those provinces at once."[86] Similarly, in a famously tough-worded letter of November 28, 1818, to the Spanish government, Adams wrote: "Spain must immediately make her election, either to place a force in Florida adequate at once to the protection of her territory, and to the fulfillment of her engagements, or to cede to the United States a province, of which she retains nothing but the nominal possession."[87] Spain would ultimately opt for the latter.

A congressional inquiry into the Seminole War opened in December 1818. It included a floor debate lasting nearly a month, at that point the longest single issue debated in Congress in the nation's history.[88] The high point was a three-hour speech delivered by the Speaker of the House of Representatives Henry Clay of Kentucky.[89] Warning of the longer-term risks of Jackson's military disobedience, Clay admonished his colleagues to: "Beware how you give a fatal sanction, in this infant period of our republic, scarcely yet two score years old, to military insubordination. Remember that Greece had her Alexander, Rome her Caesar, England her Cromwell, France her Bonaparte, and that if we would escape the rock on which they split, we must avoid their errors."[90] But, ultimately, it would make little difference. All resolutions condemning Jackson's actions would be defeated by wide margins.[91] Jackson was simply too popular, and his recent exploits in Florida made him only more so. He was mobbed by adoring admirers wherever he went and was bestowed honors and awards by civil society organizations and local governments throughout the country.[92] A future president was very much in the making.

On February 22, 1819, John Quincy Adams and Spanish minister Luis de Onís signed the Transcontinental Treaty, which not only ceded the Floridas to the United States but defined the US-Spanish border all the way to the Pacific.[93] Adams would write in his diary that night that the "acknowledgement of a definite line of boundary to the South Seas form a great epocha in our history."[94] Although ratification would be delayed on the Spanish side, the United States would finally take possession of Florida in February 1821, with none other than Andrew Jackson as its inaugural territorial governor.

As part of the Adams-Onís Treaty, the United States, notably, agreed to relinquish its claims to the Spanish imperial province of Texas. President Monroe's reluctance to add another slaveholding state to the Union was at the forefront of his mind in his decision to exclude the claim.[95] As the president wrote to Thomas Jefferson in May 1820, "It is evident that further acquisition of territory, to the West and South, involves difficulties, of an internal nature, which menace the Union itself."[96] But it would not take long for Texas to once again burst onto the national scene. As the Spanish Empire continued to crumble, Texas would present the next major opportunity for American territorial expansion.

Jackson Stands Aloof: The United States and Texas, 1836–37

The United States refrained from acquiring the independent Republic of Texas (now the state of Texas) between April 1836 and March 1837, in the aftermath of the Texas Revolution. The revolutionary overthrow of Mexican authority in Texas was independently planned and executed by recent American émigrés, led by a former US governor and member of congress.[97] The theory of inadvertent expansion makes two arguments that are borne out in this case. First, that once a territory is acquired, a number of constraints crop up that make relinquishment difficult. In the case of Texas, the revolution, and particularly the brutal crackdown by Mexican forces, led to widespread sympathy and support for the cause, especially in the American South. And second, that the expectation of significant geopolitical risk associated with acquiring the territory will discourage leaders in the capital from accepting it. In the case at hand, American leaders in the capital strongly suspected that annexing Texas would mean war with Mexico, an outcome they simply were not willing to risk. The United States' failure to accept the Texan fait accompli would mean that the erstwhile Mexican state would remain an independent republic for the following ten years, until it was annexed as the twenty-eighth state of the Union in 1845.

Historical Background

Within just six months of the February 1821 Adams-Onís Treaty having entered into force, Mexico declared its independence from Spain after a ten-year armed insurgency. Texas, a territory of 678,000 km^2 over which the United States had relinquished all claims, became part of the Republic of Mexico's northernmost state of Coahuila y Tejas in 1824.[98] Like the Spanish Empire before it, Mexico faced the problem of chronic underpopulation on its northern frontier.[99] To deal with this, the Mexican government encouraged immigration to Texas both by selling land at rates significantly lower than in the United States and by authorizing colonization agents (or empresarios) such as Stephen F. Austin to facilitate settlement from across the border. And the immigrants—and their slaves—poured in. Starting with a local population of roughly twenty-five hundred at independence, by 1835 approximately forty thousand Americans had settled in Texas, outnumbering the Mexican population by a factor of greater than ten to one.[100]

These demographic shifts alarmed Mexican officials, who began to make efforts to stem the flow of migrants, putting the government in Mexico City on a collision course with its new Texan inhabitants. In April 1830, the Mexican government passed a law banning immigration from the United States and the importation of slaves.[101] In 1832, the Mexican general Antonio López de Santa Anna launched a coup, resulting in the overthrow of the government in 1833 and the establishment of centralized authoritarian rule the following year.[102] Uprisings emerged in several Mexican states, only to be crushed by Santa Anna's forces. The migrant population in Texas chafed under the increasingly heavy hand extending from Mexico City. And, when the Mexican government imposed customs duties on Texan trade and sent its forces out to enforce its new edicts, matters reached a boiling point.[103]

Washington and the Texan Frontier

Among the migrants aggravated by the centralization of Mexican rule was Sam Houston. Born in Lexington, Virginia, Houston would serve as the state's governor and became a close personal friend of Andrew Jackson, having served under his command in the War of 1812.[104] Houston entered Texas at the suggestion of an old friend in December 1832, having been told that "there will be some fighting there next fall, and that a fine country will be gained without much bloodshed."[105] Within weeks of arriving, Houston was ushered into the elite of migrant Texan society. And within months he had begun plotting the overthrow of Mexican authority there. Sam Houston was the key peripheral actor who would attempt to drag the United States into the acquisition of Texas.

Monitoring events from Washington was Houston's friend and former commander, President Andrew Jackson. While President Jackson had able support in his Secretary of State John Forsyth and his Secretary of War Lewis Cass, he dominated foreign policy decision-making in the administration.[106] Jackson had long coveted Texas for the United States.[107] He thought that relinquishing American claims to Texas in the Adams-Onís Treaty had been a mistake, and almost from the time he took office as president in March 1829 he set out to acquire it.[108] As Jackson wrote to his friend John Overton in June 1829, "I have long since been aware of the importance of Texas to the United States, and of the real necessity of extending our boundary west of the Sabine. . . . I shall keep my eye on this object and the first propitious moment make the attempt to regain the Territory."[109] Working through his minister in Mexico, as well as his chargé d'affaires there, Jackson made a series of ham-handed attempts to purchase the northern state for as much as $5 million—all to no avail.[110]

However, this was as far as Jackson was willing to go. In fact, he specifically wanted to acquire Texas, as he put it, "without any just imputation of corruption on our part."[111] Everything had to be aboveboard. Hearing early rumors of his friend Houston's plans to claim Texas, Jackson referred to these as "deranged," part of a "wild scheme," and as the "mere effusions of a distempered brain."[112] If Jackson was to acquire Texas, he intended to do so through negotiation with the central government in Mexico City. "A revolt in Texas," Jackson told his chargé d'affaires in Mexico in February 1831, "may close the door forever to its advantageous settlement."[113]

Texas

But a revolt is precisely what would ultimately occur.[114] A small skirmish between American settlers and Mexican military authorities in the town of Gonzales in October 1835 sparked a more general armed uprising, determined to drive the Mexican army out of Texas.[115] The following month, the Texan revolutionaries created a provisional government, and named Sam Houston commander in chief of their armed forces.[116] By December, the revolutionary army had defeated all Mexican garrisons and was in control of the state. In response, the Mexican president Santa Anna ordered a two-pronged counteroffensive, one of which he led himself, to take the state back from the insurgent army. Santa Anna's armies slaughtered hundreds of Anglo-Texan revolutionaries after a two-week siege at the Alamo and the surrender at Goliad through February and early March 1836. As this was occurring, Anglo-Texan political leaders gathered on March 2, 1836, and officially declared the establishment of the independent Republic of Texas, drafting a constitution over the following two weeks. On April 15, 1836, former empresario and now-Texan revolutionary leader Stephen F. Austin sent President Jackson an impassioned plea for assistance, writing: "This people look to you, the guardians of their rights and interests and principles, will you, can you turn a deaf ear to the appeals of your fellow citizens in favor of *their* and *your* country men and friends, who are massacred, butchered, outraged in Texas at your very doors?"[117]

However, American assistance would not be necessary. In their final push to drive the revolutionaries out of Texas, Santa Anna's army was decisively defeated by Sam Houston's forces on April 21, 1836, at San Jacinto, and Santa Anna himself was taken prisoner. With this victory, the Texas Revolution was over. In September, elections were held, and the constitution and the matter of annexation to the United States were put to referendum. Sam Houston was elected president of the Republic of Texas in a landslide, the constitution was approved, and the voters supported annexation to the United States by 3,277 to 91.[118] The question now was how leaders in Washington would respond.

Washington Reacts

The sparking of the Texas Revolution, and the bloody battles that followed, constrained American leaders in two ways that made simply rejecting the Texan fait accompli difficult. First, the costs of acquiring Texas had been sunk. The revolution was over; the Texans had prevailed and made their intentions unmistakably clear. The actual on-the-ground costs associated with acquiring Texas had already been paid by the Anglo-Texan forces. All President Jackson had to do was agree to the request for annexation that was before him. And in light of Jackson's demonstrated desire to acquire Texas for the United States, along with his close personal friendship with Sam Houston, the successful revolution presented a golden opportunity for the administration.

Second, there was significant public support for the Texas revolutionaries in the United States. The outbreak of the revolution was accompanied by a flood of money and supplies across the Louisiana border in support of the Anglo-Texan insurgents. Young men from across the American South streamed across the border by the thousands to enlist and fight for the Texan cause.[119] The national and regional press were strongly sympathetic with the rebels, portraying events in Texas in a sensationalist manner.[120] Politicians from both the south and the west put pressure on the Jackson administration, urging them to recognize Texan independence and prepare the way for annexation.[121] Aiming to take advantage of this groundswell of support, the Texas government dispatched a number of commissioners to Washington, over the course of 1836, who lobbied members of Congress and the administration for recognition and annexation.[122] This broad public support is hardly surprising. After all, most of the revolutionaries were Americans, at least until very recently, and some, such as Sam Houston, had important ties to the US political elite. And the idea of a scrappy burgeoning republic casting off the yoke of distant tyranny to declare its independence clearly appealed to American sensibilities.

However, not all of the American public supported annexation. For Texas at this time had a slave population of roughly five thousand, having been brought in by the American settlers.[123] And the Texas Revolution was taking place in the wake of the Missouri Compromise of 1820, as well as the more recent Nullification Crisis of 1832–33, both of which exposed and exacerbated the important sectional conflicts between free and slaveholding states.[124] Abolitionists, Whig Party members, and northerners more generally were strongly opposed to the annexation of Texas, horrified at the prospect of adding a large slaveholding territory to the Union.[125] While the opposition was initially quiet and on the fringes of political debate, it would grow in volume and importance as the months passed.[126] So, while there were reasons to accept the Texan fait accompli, there were also reasons for caution.

Besides the simmering political opposition, there was also potentially significant geopolitical risk involved in annexing the newly independent republic. For one, Mexico, with a newly installed leader, seemed to be intent on taking Texas back from the revolutionaries by force. As the local US minister in Mexico City reported to Secretary of State Forsyth on May 19, 1836, less than a month after the Battle of San Jacinto, the Mexican "national congress has resolved to prosecute the war against Texas with the utmost vigor." The minister added that "the alleged reason for entertaining such questions is the supposed interference of the United States in the war of Texas."[127] In June, the American minister reported to Washington that "men in the streets in this capital are almost daily impressed and enrolled in the army in large numbers with the avowed intention of reducing that province to unconditional submission."[128] Similar observations were reported back to the capital in August and October.[129]

There was also at least some concern over the possibility of Mexico gaining the support of a European great power, such as the United Kingdom, in taking back the renegade state. On June 25, 1836, the US minister in Mexico reported to Forsyth that the "application of this government to Great Britain for aid to restore her authority in Texas is a question of great magnitude."[130] Mexico was apparently using its opposition to slavery in Texas as a means to try to elicit British aid.[131] And there was clearly concern over this in Washington. For instance, in August 1836 the acting secretary of state urged his minister in Mexico to "be vigilant as to the movements of the Mexican Government towards obtaining foreign aid for the subjugation of Texas, and give early information thereof to the Department."[132] Thus, while Mexico would be ultimately disappointed in its efforts to enlist British support, the possibility clearly weighed on the minds of policy makers in Washington.[133]

Washington Decides

Facing a combination of enthusiastic, though nonunanimous, domestic political support, as well as considerable geopolitical risk, President Jackson would in the end opt for a rejection of the Texans' fait accompli. Despite the president's considerable personal sympathy for the cause, and his own decades-long friendship with Houston, the downside risks seemed too great to consider annexation at this moment. Instead, the administration adopted a neutral stance in the Texas-Mexico conflict and refused to get involved until it had been settled between the two parties.[134] Jackson had earlier foreshadowed this position in his annual message to Congress of December 1835.[135] However, his position became unmistakably clear when, in reacting to Austin's request for assistance of April 15, 1836, Jackson coolly wrote: "The Texians[,] before they took the step to declare themselves Independent, which has aroused and united all mexico against them[,] ought to have pondered well, it was a rash and premature act[;] our nutrality must be faithfully maintained."[136] This position, which would be repeatedly referred to as one of "strict neutrality," defined the Jackson administration's response throughout the course of the crisis.[137]

The Jackson administration had a number of motivations when deciding to reject the Texan fait accompli. To the extent that there is a conventional wisdom on this matter, it is that concerns over the domestic political repercussions of annexation, particularly with regard to Texas's slaveholder status, scared the Jackson administration off.[138] These fears were particularly acute, the argument goes, in the context of an impending federal election in November 1836, where Jackson hoped his vice president, Martin Van Buren, would be elected president.[139] There is a lot of evidence to support this argument, and it was clearly an important part of what guided the president's decision-making. In a December 5, 1836, message to Congress, Jackson made reference to the "reconcilement of various and conflicting interests" as a prerequisite for the annexation of Texas.[140] And, using almost identical language, Secretary of State Forsyth reportedly told a Texan commissioner in early January 1837 that "various conflicting sectional interests in Congress would have to be reconciled before annexation would be agreed to."[141]

However, for three reasons, this "sectional conflict" hypothesis, while not wrong, is at least incomplete. First, it is somewhat difficult to make sense of Jackson's years of efforts to purchase Texas from Mexico if his primary concern was sparking a sectional conflict over slavery. As late as 1834, Jackson was still actively seeking to acquire Texas through his chargé d'affaires in Mexico via negotiation and purchase, and, in January 1837, in a meeting with the former Mexican president Santa Anna, Jackson, again, offered to buy the state for $3.5 million.[142] It seems, to an important extent, that Jackson was more concerned with the *way* Texas was acquired than with the simple fact of its acquisition. Second, the victory of Vice President Van Buren in the November 1836 election, of which the administration was assured by the beginning of December, should have allayed at least some of these domestic political concerns, but it seemed not to.[143] The administration still had three months of annexation opportunities until the end of its term in March 1837, which it elected not to avail itself of. In meetings with Texas commissioners from December through February, Jackson and other members of the administration exhibited the same reluctance toward annexation that they had all along.[144]

The third and most important reason the sectional conflict hypothesis appears to be incomplete is that there is a lot of evidence that the Jackson administration had other concerns; namely, the geopolitical risk associated with annexing Texas.[145] This concern over the possibility of war can be seen clearly in two episodes that occurred during the crisis over Texas. First, in January 1836, as the revolution was heating up, Major General Gaines was dispatched by Secretary of War Cass to establish a defensive position near the Louisiana border with Texas. Gaines was explicitly reminded, in line with administration policy, that it was "the duty of the United States to remain entirely neutral."[146] In late March and early April, Gaines reported back to Washington that he had intelligence that several tribes of Native Americans were preparing to attack the American frontier from within Texas and requested permission to cross the border if necessary.[147] Secretary Cass replied on April 25, clarifying that it was "not the wish of the president to take advantage of present circumstances, and thereby obtain possession of any portion of the Mexican territory," but that Gaines was, indeed, "authorized to take such position on either side of the imaginary boundary line as may be best for your defensive operations."[148] Perhaps out of concern that he had given the major general too much discretion, Cass followed up with dispatches on May 4 and 12, reminding Gaines to "act cautiously," to not cross the border "unless circumstances distinctly show this step is necessary," and, if so, to "return as soon as the safety of the frontier will permit."[149]

In June 1836, Gaines crossed the Sabine River into Texas and occupied the town of Nacogdoches, some 80 km from the border.[150] The major general then called up militia forces from Tennessee, Kentucky, Mississippi, and Louisiana to provide additional personnel, which their governors were only-too-eager to provide.[151] When President Jackson learned of the occupation and the militia requisition in early August, he was "much astonished."[152] Within a few days, he had contacted the state governors in question and had countermanded Gaines's requisition, ordering the militia forces to be discharged.[153] In an August 12 letter to Amos Kendall, Jackson's postmaster general and a key member of his Kitchen Cabinet, Jackson explained his reasoning, arguing that Gaines's action "was a violation of that nutrality which we had assumed, and *was in fact*, and which Mexico might have viewed as[,] *an act of war upon her if it had been carried into effect*." Thankfully, Jackson continued, he had "stopped it in the bud."[154] In a letter to Gaines himself, on September 4, Jackson reminded the major general that "ours is a state of strict neutrality" and that Gaines, "as the commander of our forces on that frontier[,] must religiously observe and maintain it."[155] Thus, it is clear that Jackson's reversal of what was a golden opportunity to gain territory in Texas was motivated, in important part, by the desire to avoid war with Mexico.

There was a second episode that makes clear the administration's concerns over geopolitical risk. In June 1836, President Jackson dispatched an agent to Texas, by the name of Henry R. Morfit, to gather "detailed information of the civil, military and political conditions" there.[156] The contents of Morfit's reports would play an important role in shaping the thinking of the Jackson administration. As Secretary of State Forsyth told the Texan commissioners in July 1836, the president "would not act definitely upon the subject of Texas until the report of a Confidential Agent sent to that country should be received."[157] In his first detailed report, September 9, Morfit cast doubt on Texas's prospects, and his primary reason for doing so was that "the Mexicans it is said are preparing to invade Texas during this winter."[158] In his second report, the following day, Morfit emphasized the vast imbalance of power that Texas faced vis-à-vis Mexico, noting that the Mexican population was "about 8 million" and that of Texas "between 40 and 50 thousand." In his view, it could not "be supposed that under ordinary circumstances the issue of this war would remain long undecided." In closing this second report, Morfit argued that Texas's "future security must depend more upon the weakness and imbecility of her enemy than upon her own strength."[159]

President Jackson seemed to take these findings to heart. Annexation would be definitively off the table, and he even decided to refer the matter of diplomatic recognition to Congress. Jackson's reasoning for doing so is also telling. As he wrote to Amos Kendall on December 8, 1836, with "the Constitutional power of declaring war being vested in Congress, and [as] the *acknowledgment of the Inde-*

pendence of Texas might lead to war with Mexico," the subject should be referred to that body.[160] In a special message to Congress on December 21, Jackson noted that a "premature recognition under these circumstances, *if not looked upon as justifiable cause of war,* is always liable to be regarded as proof of an unfriendly spirit." Jackson added that there was, "in appearance at least, an immense disparity of physical force on the side of Mexico." Thus, Jackson argued, the United States "should still stand aloof and maintain our present attitude."[161] For the time being, Texas was on its own.

After contemplating the matter for two months, Congress would pass a series of resolutions appropriating the funds necessary for the diplomatic recognition of Texas in late February 1837. In his very last day in office, on March 3, Jackson formally recognized the independence of Texas by nominating a chargé d'affaires to the republic.[162] Texas would continue to unsuccessfully press for annexation after the inauguration of President Martin Van Buren. A Texas diplomatic official explained the United States' continued reticence to consider annexation in January 1838 by, among other things, pointing to a fear "of involving this country in a war, in which they are now doubtful whether they would ever be supported by a majority of their own citizens, and which would be at once branded by their enemies at home and abroad as an unjust war, instigated for the very purpose of gaining possession of Texas."[163] Texas would remain a ramshackle independent republic until March 1845, when it would be formally annexed to the United States during the transition period between Presidents John Tyler and James K. Polk. This annexation of Texas would, of course, spark the war with Mexico that Jackson had so feared.

In closing, it is worth reflecting on the sea change observed in the perceptions and behaviors of Andrew Jackson across the two cases. Jackson, as a field commander in the case of Florida, argued that "the whole of East Florida [should be] seized" and that he would happily do it himself. In the course of carrying out the conquest, Jackson also rashly put to death two British subjects for little more than being in the wrong place at the wrong time, and whose execution, he hoped, would "prove an awful example to the world." Yet, his behavior as president was strikingly different. In the case of Texas, Jackson characterized the revolution as a "rash and premature act," decided that his government would maintain "strict neutrality" in the conflict, and urged the US Congress to "stand aloof." And when he heard that the Texans had captured the Mexican president Santa Anna and were considering putting him to death, he argued vehemently against it. In a letter to Sam Houston on September 4, 1836, Jackson argued that "nothing *now* could tarnish the character of Texas more than such an act at this late period," and he urged his friend to "preserve [Santa Anna's] life and the character you have won . . . this is what I think, true wisdom and humanity dictates."[164] And this was Santa Anna, who had, just a few months earlier, ordered the slaughter of hundreds of Texan (and American) revolutionaries at the Alamo and Goliad. It is difficult to imagine a more fitting illustration of the difference between the "view from the capital" and the "view from the frontier" discussed in chapter 1.

This chapter has presented comparative case studies of successful and failed inadvertent expansion by the United States in Florida and Texas. Both cases strongly support the theory of inadvertent expansion presented in chapter 1. First, the case of Florida showed how unauthorized peripheral expansion is enabled by a lack of adequate control by the capital over its agents on the periphery—that it is a manifestation of a principal-agent problem. Second, both cases support the argument that unauthorized peripheral expansion places constraints on leaders in the capital that make a simple withdrawal significantly more difficult. In both Florida and Texas, peripheral expansion sunk the costs of acquisition for leaders in the capital and generated domestic political pressure in favor of acquisition. And third, in both cases the decision of whether to accept or reject the territorial fait accompli was crucially determined by expectations of the geopolitical risk associated with doing so. In the case of Florida, the Monroe administration deftly retained partial control of the Spanish province, without fear that this would lead to war with Spain. In the case of Texas, President Jackson feared that accepting the Texan fait accompli would mean war with Mexico, which led to its rejection. Across the two cases, what I referred to in chapter 1 as the "view from the capital" and the "view from the frontier" was powerfully illustrated—showing Andrew Jackson to be the hot-blooded frontier agent in the case of Florida but the cool-headed leader in Washington in the case of Texas.

INADVERTENT EXPANSION ON THE EURASIAN STEPPE

Russia

> Such has been the fate of every country which has found itself in a similar position. The United States of America, France in Algeria, Holland in her Colonies, England in India—all have been irresistibly forced, less by ambition than by imperious necessity, into this onward march, where the greatest difficulty is to know when to stop.
>
> —Prince Alexander M. Gorchakov, 1864

This chapter examines inadvertent expansion in two cases from the Russian Empire in Central Asia. The first case focuses on the Russian acquisition of territory in the Khanate of Kokand in 1864–66. The second case examines the Russian Empire's nonacquisition of the Ili region of western Qing Dynasty China in 1871–81. The purpose of this chapter is to present the book's second pair of comparative theory-testing cases, showing how variation in geopolitical risk across the two cases helped produce the divergent outcomes observed. The comparison of the Russian Empire in the Khanate of Kokand and in the Ili region is useful in that the two cases hold many factors fixed—the same great power, operating in the same region, with most of the same leaders in the capital, and separated by only five years—while the outcomes vary for reasons of geopolitical risk.

Russia in the Khanate of Kokand, 1864–66

The Russian Empire acquired the Khanate of Kokand's cities of Chimkent (now Shymkent, Kazakhstan) and Tashkent (now Tashkent, Uzbekistan) between July 1864 and August 1866. The conquest of these cities was independently planned and executed by a local officer of the Imperial Russian Army, both exceeding (in Chimkent) and disregarding (in Tashkent) the orders of his civilian and military superiors in the capital, Saint Petersburg. The theory of inadvertent expansion makes three central arguments that are borne out in this case. First, that peripheral expansion is the result of a principal-agent problem: that a combination of a divergence of preferences between leaders in the capital and their agents on the periphery and information asymmetries favoring the agents lead to a loss of control over the agents' actions. In the case of Russia in Kokand, there was a significant divergence of preferences between leaders in the capital and members of the Imperial Russian Army on the Central Asian frontier, and the vast distances separating the two led to dramatic information asymmetries in favor of the army. Second, that once a territory is partly or wholly acquired, a number of constraints emerge that make it difficult for leaders in the capital to simply withdraw. In the case at hand, the frontier army's striking successes in acquiring these cities sunk the costs of their acquisition, and broader concerns for Russian national honor meant backing down seemed out of the question. And third, that a lack of perceived geopolitical risk associated with acquisition will encourage leaders in the capital to accept the fait accompli, resulting in territorial expansion. In the case of Russia in Kokand, the Central Asian khanates were relatively weak, and concerns over a potentially adverse reaction by the British were quickly alleviated by their muted response. These facts strengthened the case for central authorization, which would occur when Tashkent was formally annexed to the Russian Empire in August 1866.

Historical Background

The Russian Empire began to advance deep into the Kazakh Steppe of Central Asia in the 1840s. From its base in Orenburg, at the southern tip of the Ural Mountains, a string of forts was established through the late 1840s and early 1850s, culminating in the conquest of Ak Mechet and the founding of Fort Perovsk there in 1853. Further to the east, from Omsk in Western Siberia, a similar southward advance ensued, which itself would culminate in the founding of the town of Vernyi in 1854. These two lines each penetrated over 1,000 km southward into the Kazakh Steppe, fully enveloping it. Yet they themselves were separated by over 1,000 km of uncharted territory.[1] To the south of the Russian lines were the three Uzbek khanates of Bukhara, Khiva, and Kokand.[2] Established at the turn of the previous century, these Islamic kingdoms were militarily weak, prone to warfare among themselves, and often internally divided in ways that made them vulnerable to outside influence and attack.[3] The Khanate of Kokand—with a population of approximately 1.5 million—sat further north than the other two, and its affluent urban centers of Chimkent and Tashkent made it an enticing target for the expanding Russian Empire.[4]

By the early 1860s, the central question of Russian imperial policy in Central Asia was when—and, more importantly, where—to connect Russia's two strings of forts and establish a defensible southern border for the empire.[5] The foreign minister at the time was the esteemed diplomat, Alexander Gorchakov, who was unusually cautious and averse to the use of military force for interests he deemed peripheral.[6] The war minister was Dmitry Miliutin, a brilliant military strategist who tended to be more forward leaning in his advocacy for the use of force.[7] Their principal role in imperial policy was to inform and advise the Russian czar, Alexander II. These three individuals—Gorchakov, Miliutin, and Alexander II—were the leaders in the capital who were primarily responsible for Russian imperial policy. It is they who would be dragged unwittingly into more territorial acquisitions than they had bargained for in Central Asia.

In February 1863, a special committee on Central Asian policy was held in the capital, Saint Petersburg, and it was agreed that reconnaissance between Russia's two lines was a necessary first step.[8] The individual tasked with this reconnaissance would be a lieutenant colonel in the Imperial Russian Army, Mikhail Grigorevich Cherniaev. A career military officer and decorated veteran of the Crimean War, Cherniaev had a strong independent streak and was often impatient and quarrelsome with his superiors.[9] Lieutenant Colonel Cherniaev was the key actor on the Russian imperial periphery who would independently launch the conquests in the Khanate of Kokand.

Cherniaev began his reconnaissance of the territory separating Fort Perovsk and the town of Vernyi in the spring of 1863. The instructions given to him by the governor-general of Orenburg were to "display the greatest peaceableness, and use arms only in case of extreme necessity."[10] However, Cherniaev's actions on this exploratory mission would be a strong indication of what was to come. On May 30, he came upon the town of Suzaq, some 400 km down the Syr-Darya River from Fort Perovsk. Cherniaev was then fired on, and he ordered a retaliatory bombardment of the town, leading to its prompt surrender. News of the acquisition of Suzaq shocked the governor-general of Orenburg but was met with praise in Saint Petersburg. Even the usually cautious Foreign Minister Gorchakov noted in July 1863 that the "successful actions of Colonel Cherniaev, without special expenditures and sacrifices have brought us closer to the goal [of connecting the lines] which we had in view originally."[11] The following month, Gorchakov and War Minister Miliutin agreed that the lines should be joined expeditiously, and this was officially ordered by Czar Alexander II on December 20, 1863.[12] The key question was where they would be connected.

It was agreed in early 1864 that an initial line would be drawn north of the Syr-Darya and Arys Rivers, and it would be connected from Suzaq through the town of Aulie-Ata. The line could then, according to Miliutin, be moved further south and connected through Chimkent "when the time is favorable."[13] On February 9, 1864, Cherniaev was appointed commander of the Western Siberian detachment based in Omsk and was given orders to occupy and fortify Aulie-

Ata.[14] While Cherniaev's orders do mention that there were longer-term plans to incorporate Chimkent into the empire, his specific orders were to capture and garrison of Aulie-Ata and then to connect with another Russian force to the west, thereby establishing the empire's Central Asian frontier.[15] In late April, Cherniaev departed Vernyi with twenty-five hundred personnel, and he succeeded in taking Aulie-Ata by early June.[16] By the end of the month, the lines between Perovsk and Vernyi were connected, and Cherniaev was promoted to major general.[17] His orders had been fulfilled with striking success, and Cherniaev clearly understood this. As he wrote to his parents in a letter on June 6, 1864, the capture of Aulie-Ata was "the final goal proposed for the force's activities this year."[18]

Saint Petersburg and Russian Central Asia

Saint Petersburg suffered severe principal-agent problems with respect to Cherniaev and its other agents on the Central Asian frontier. First, the vast distance between Saint Petersburg and Russian Central Asia, and the rudimentary state of transportation and communications technology, meant that there were important information asymmetries favoring the periphery. While Orenburg had been connected to Saint Petersburg by telegraph since the 1850s, Russian territory deep in Central Asia would not see a telegraph station until 1873, and the region would not be fully accessible by rail until 1898.[19] It took a full month's difficult journey to travel the approximately 1,500 km from Orenburg to the front lines in Russian Central Asia, and, therefore, communications sent from Saint Petersburg would take at least two months to receive a reply.[20] According to historian David MacKenzie, this distance "stimulated initiative and independent judgment but encouraged ambitious commanders seeking decorations and promotion to commit their government to a course contradicting its general policy."[21] It also meant that frontier agents such as Cherniaev were often the only source of information on happenings in the region, and they could (and did) distort events in their favor, exaggerating the severity of local threats and glossing over their own mistakes and misdeeds.[22]

Second, there was a divergence of preferences between the leaders in Saint Petersburg and the actors on the Central Asian frontier when it came to Russian imperial policy there. In general, leaders in Saint Petersburg were not in favor of significant expansion in the region.[23] Perhaps, in the relatively near future, Chimkent could be added to Russian holdings, but Tashkent, further to the south, was seen as off limits by most. While there had been regular calls from within the Russian government for Tashkent's acquisition since the late 1850s, those whose opinions mattered most—Alexander II, Gorchakov, and, to a lesser extent, Miliutin—were opposed.[24] They preferred to consolidate existing Russian gains in the region rather than add to them, were concerned about the potential for sparking conflict with Britain, and thought it better to influence these territories as independent entities from the outside rather than directly controlling them from within.[25] In sum, leaders in the capital embodied what I referred to in chapter 1 as the "view from the capital"—the responsibilities of rule were weighty, the dangers were distant, and the incentive to act quickly was weak.

In contrast, many actors near and on the Central Asian frontier advocated for a more expansionist policy for Russia there. As MacKenzie notes, in Central Asia, the Russians "close to the scene of action were usually the most militant and impatient."[26] Cherniaev, in particular, had long argued for a more forceful policy in the region and had come to see Chimkent and Tashkent as particularly enticing possibilities. As he wrote, while posted on the Central Asian frontier in the late 1850s, advocating for an advance beyond Fort Perovsk, "We have the resources for this, but they are being kept under wraps . . . We need this region to extend our influence over Central Asia."[27] Hardened frontier agents such as Cherniaev exemplified what I referred to as "the view from the frontier"—their responsibilities were narrow, the dangers were near, and, therefore, their temptation to act was high. Thus, as a result of a divergence of preferences and information asymmetries, leaders in Saint Petersburg had a very difficult time controlling the actions of agents on the periphery, and this opened the door to a great deal of independent action.

Chimkent

Within just days of taking Aulie-Ata and connecting the Russian lines, Cherniaev began eyeing Chimkent, a Kokandian city roughly 160 km to the southwest. In the first week of July 1864, Cherniaev resolved to advance on the city, writing to the governor-general of Western Siberia that because "Kokanese concentrations grow daily . . . I have decided to protect Aulie-Ata and nearby nomads by advancing toward Chimkent and operating there according to circumstances."[28] Cherniaev then set out from Aulie-Ata with a force of fourteen hundred toward Chimkent, arriving at the city walls on July 19. After a battle with Kokandian forces that resulted in a resounding Russian victory, Cherniaev realized his own force was insufficient to capture the city outright and so returned to Aulie-Ata.[29]

This initial, abortive attempt did not dissuade Cherniaev from his goal of acquiring the city. In an August 1864 letter to the Imperial Russian Army's general staff, Cherniaev wrote that by "taking Chimkent we shall deliver a decisive blow to Kokand," and he argued that the city's "seizure before winter is not only beneficial but essential for the region's peace."[30] Cherniaev then pointedly asked, with characteristic threat inflation, "Should we wait until, with the help of Europeans, military science in Kokand compares with our own, or should we now remove their power to resist?"[31] The major general summed up his message by declaring: "I have decided to conquer Chimkent on my own responsibility," and this is precisely what he would do.[32]

On September 12, 1864, Cherniaev once again set out from Aulie-Ata, this time with a force of seventeen hundred.[33] The number of Kokandian forces at Chimkent had declined in the preceding weeks, and the prospects for a successful attack looked much improved. Cherniaev's forces arrived at Chimkent on September 19, and after a two-day siege, they stormed the city. The invasion itself reportedly took place through a sixty-foot water pipe extending through the city wall, with Cherniaev audaciously plunging into the pipe before any of his subordinates.[34] Within a few hours, Chimkent had fallen and Cherniaev was in control of the city. He had pulled off his fait accompli and the Russian Empire had gained a new territory.

When news of Cherniaev's attacks on Chimkent began to filter back to Saint Petersburg, reactions were mixed. When he heard of Cherniaev's first, abortive attack on the city, War Minister Miliutin grumbled that such "an extension of our frontiers never entered into our plans; it lengthens our lines unduly and requires considerable increases of forces." The problem they faced, the War Minister added, was that "communications are so slow that any instructions arrive too late."[35] However, this would not stop him from engaging in the largely futile exercise of telegraphing the governor-general of Western Siberia the following day, ordering him to instruct Cherniaev "in no case . . . to go further than was proposed."[36] A few weeks later, when he learned of Chimkent's successful acquisition, an exasperated Miliutin asked, "Who will guarantee that after Chimkent Cherniaev won't consider it necessary to take Tashkent, then Kokand, and there will be no end to it."[37] Foreign Minister Gorchakov felt similarly and was ultimately in favor of withdrawal.[38]

However, the very fact of Cherniaev's successful acquisition of Chimkent placed constraints on leaders in Saint Petersburg, making the territory very difficult to readily relinquish for two reasons. The first was the simple fact that the territory had already been acquired: the costs of acquisition had been sunk. While leaders may not have wanted it to be taken just then and there, longer-term plans to add Chimkent to the empire existed, and so Cherniaev was largely insubordinate with respect to the timing of the conquest rather than the conquest itself.[39] And once it was in Russian hands, some in Saint Petersburg, such as many in the War Ministry, saw it as too strategically valuable to give up.[40] The second were the concerns over Russian national honor, particularly those of Czar Alexander II. He was far more enthusiastic than his advisers regarding the whole venture, awarding Cherniaev with the Saint George's Cross, Third Class, and referring to the conquest as "a glorious affair."[41] Alexander II was prone to fall prey to concerns over Russian national prestige, and given that it was his opinion that mattered most, his enthusiasm meant that reversal was not an option.[42] Chimkent was to be part of the Russian Empire. Cherniaev would get his way.

Tashkent

After the fall of Chimkent, history would repeat itself with the next major Kokandian urban center, Tashkent. Sitting just 120 km south of the walls of Chimkent and being the largest and most prosperous city in Central Asia, it would prove to be an even more enticing target for Cherniaev and his forces. Again, just days after the successful conquest of Chimkent, Cherniaev decided to move on Tashkent. Citing rumors of a threat from the neighboring Khanate of Bukhara, Cherniaev informed the governor-general of Western Siberia on September 25, 1864, that he was advancing on Tashkent, "not to occupy it, but if circumstances prove favorable, to forestall the plans of the emir of Bukhara."[43] Two days later, he departed Chimkent, heading south toward Tashkent with fifteen hundred personnel.[44] Cherniaev and his forces arrived at the Tashkent city walls on October 2 and initiated a preparatory barrage. Thinking the walls had been breached, Cherniaev's force advanced, only to find the wall intact and themselves in a highly vulnerable position. Cherniaev ultimately ordered a retreat, but only after suffering sixteen dead and sixty-two wounded, including the deaths of two of his top commanders.[45] While not an enormous loss in an absolute sense, with no gains to show for it and in terms of Russia's wars of empire in Central Asia, this was seen as an unmitigated disaster.

When news of Cherniaev's advance on Tashkent reached Saint Petersburg, leaders there were infuriated. In a memo to the emperor on October 31, Foreign Minister Gorchakov argued that such a move was "extremely dangerous and not only would place no limits on our advance into the heart of Central Asia but would . . . involve us directly in all the wars and disorders there."[46] That same day, Gorchakov memorialized that "we have firmly resolved not to occupy additional lands" and recommended that Tashkent be promptly evacuated if it were occupied.[47] A few weeks later, Gorchakov and War Minister Miliutin penned a joint memorandum, arguing that every "new conquest, by lengthening our frontiers, requires a considerable increase in military resources and expenditures . . . and weakens Russia," and recommended drawing the line at Chimkent.[48] While Cherniaev would deliberately drag his feet in filing the report on the disastrous results of his attack, details of his failure and the associated casualties reached the capital in late November, and this only made matters worse.[49] When the czar finally heard of Cherniaev's failed attack on December 2, he wrote: "I greatly regret that he decided upon a useless assault costing us so many men."[50]

Foreign Minister Gorchakov was particularly worried about the reactions of the other great powers and, especially, that of the United Kingdom. In an effort to allay any concerns, he wrote a memorandum on November 21, 1864, to be circulated among Russia's European embassies and presented to local counterparts.[51] In what has become known, simply, as "The Gorchakov Memorandum," the foreign minister justified recent Russian expansion by pointing to the challenges posed by the Russian Central Asian frontier. In order to ensure the security and prosperity of its frontier regions, the foreign minister argued, Russia is forced to choose between two unwelcome alternatives: to "abandon its frontier to perpetual disturbance" or to "plunge deeper and deeper into barbarous countries, where the difficulties and expenses increase with every step in advance." However, with the connection of Russian lines through Chimkent, Gorchakov assured his counterparts that this advance would come to an end. Going forward, they would make every effort "to prove to our neighboring states . . . that Russia is not their enemy, [and] that she entertains towards them no ideas of conquest."[52] While some scholars have dismissed the memorandum as merely a "smoke screen" for further expansion, the evidence suggests that Gorchakov's message was sincere.[53] The plan in Central Asia, as far as Saint Petersburg was concerned, was for Russia to expand no further.

But Cherniaev, predictably, had other ideas. Cooling his heels for the winter at Chimkent, he itched for another shot at Tashkent. As he complained in a letter to a friend on the Russian general staff on January 22, 1865, "The attack on Tashkent was not as pointless as my friends in St. Petersburg claimed. Had it not been for my instructions, by now I would have driven the Kokanese from that little town." But "in St. Petersburg," he continued sarcastically, "of course, they know better."[54] But his orders were clear. On February 2, War Minister Miliutin dispatched a message to Orenburg, reminding them that Cherniaev should "undertake nothing" without specific orders and reinforcements, and, in a separate dispatch on February 23, Foreign Minister Gorchakov noted that "we have decided not to include [Tashkent] within the empire, because we consider it incomparably more beneficial to limit ourselves to indirect influence over it."[55]

However, even these most direct of instructions would not deter the major general. Once again citing a Bukharan threat to Tashkent, Cherniaev set out from Chimkent in late April 1865 with a force of thirteen hundred personnel and twelve cannons.[56] He sent a message to the governor-general of Orenburg on May 2, arguing that he "could not remain indifferent to the [Bukharan] Emir's machinations and was compelled, without awaiting the arrival of reinforcements on the line, to advance now along the road to Tashkent."[57] Cherniaev's force first cut off Tashkent's water supply from a nearby fortress then laid siege to the city itself on May 7.[58] Cherniaev's sieging army was attacked, by the Kokandian warlord Alimqul with a force of six thousand, but made easy work of them, inflicting three hundred deaths on the Kokandians, including Alimqul himself, and losing only twenty wounded of their own.[59]

By early June, the effects of the siege were beginning to bite. Hunger and drought were affecting the populace, and a Bukharan army had surreptitiously slipped into the city one night to take over its defenses. Cherniaev saw his window of opportunity closing, and, at this point, he did not see backing down as an option. As he wrote to the governor-general of Orenburg on June 11, to "withdraw from the city would give the [Bukharan] Emir vast prestige in Central Asia and strengthen him with all the sinews of war concentrated in Tashkent. Consequently, I decided to seize the city by open force."[60]

With a reinforced army of 1,950 personnel, Cherniaev launched the assault on Tashkent in the early morning of June 15.[61] Despite being surrounded by a moat, 26 km of twelve-to-fifteen-foot walls, twelve fortified gates, and sixty-three cannons, Cherniaev's forces were able to penetrate the city with the aid of internal collaborators.[62] Tashkent's much larger Kokandian and Bukharan force of 30,000, it would turn out, was no match for the Russian army, and on June 17 the city surrendered.[63] Tashkent, a city of 150,000 and the largest in Central Asia, had been acquired at a cost of twenty-eight Russians killed and eighty-eight wounded.[64] He triumphantly reported to Orenburg that, with Tashkent's occupation, "we have acquired in Central Asia a status consonant with the interests of the Empire and the might of the Russian people."[65] The fait accompli was complete. (See figure 4.1.)

The reaction from Saint Petersburg was, again, mixed. On the one hand, official policy was still guided by the Gorchakov Memorandum: Russia's Central Asian border was to run through Chimkent, and Tashkent was to remain firmly outside the bounds of the empire. Gorchakov and Miliutin agreed that Cherniaev should, ultimately, withdraw and that Tashkent should be independent, in line with this policy.[66] On the other hand, many leaders in the capital found it difficult to not get swept up in the excitement of the moment. Czar Alexander II, employing the same language he did after the acquisition of Chimkent, referred to Cherniaev's actions as "glorious" and ordered the presentation of "rewards to those who distinguished themselves."[67] The Russian interior minister captured the mood of many in Saint Petersburg when he summed up the situation on July 20, 1865: "General Cherniaev took Tashkent. No one knows why or to what end. . . . There is something erotic about our goings on at the distant periphery of the empire."[68]

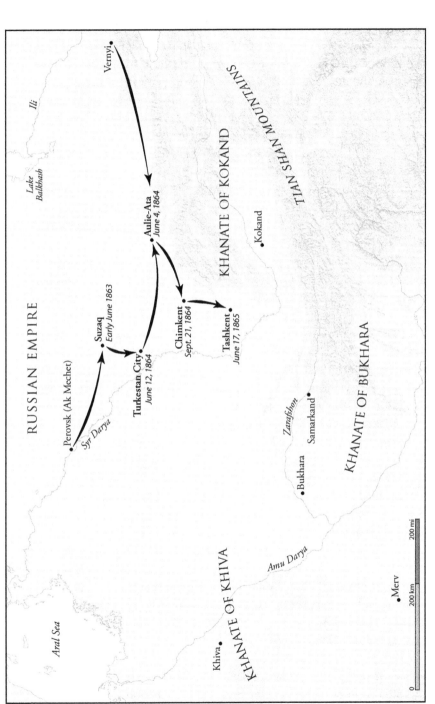

FIGURE 4.1. Mikhail Cherniaev Kokand campaign, June 1863–June 1865. Created by Beehive Mapping.

Cherniaev's successful acquisition of Tashkent, as with Chimkent, placed constraints on leaders in the capital that made withdrawal appear very difficult. The most important of these was the engagement of Russian national honor and prestige, and the Bukharan emir's demand that the Russians withdraw only strengthened these pressures. On July 29, in a memo to the governor-general of Orenburg, Miliutin argued that "the dignity of the Empire and the interests of Russia do not allow us even to consider the possibility of retreat or concession to the Emir of Bukhara's arrogant demands. Our whole future in Central Asia depends on [it]."[69] Even the usually cautious Gorchakov raised such concerns. In a memo to Miliutin on July 23, he complained about Cherniaev's insubordination but affirmed, "We cannot retreat now. It is unthinkable to bow before the emir."[70] The need to defend Russian honor, and to not appear weak before Central Asian rivals, was a powerful motivating force in this instance.[71]

And, besides, there were few geopolitical risks associated with retaining Chimkent and Tashkent. The Kokandian armies had shown themselves to be no match for the Russian forces, and the armies of Bukhara and Khiva, too, were poorly equipped, trained, and disciplined and tended to fight among themselves.[72] The khanates were highly unlikely to be able to mount an effective collective defense. There were also few rival great power interests at stake. Chimkent and Tashkent were at least 350 km from the Afghan border and nearly 600 km from British India. During Russia's conquests, the Kokandian leaders sent envoys to Calcutta, requesting aid and protection against the expanding Russian Empire, but the British were unwilling to get involved.[73] The United Kingdom, in this period, embraced a policy in Central Asia known as "masterly inactivity," a strong commitment to avoid potentially entangling alliances and interventions in the region.[74] Once Tashkent fell, London, for its part, was willing to accept Russian assurances and largely acquiesced to the conquest.[75] The lack of adverse reaction by Britain weakened arguments made within the czarist cabinet for withdrawal from Tashkent, and strengthened arguments for its retention.[76] It would take two more decades of steady Russian gains for the British to push back, as they did with the Russian annexation of Panjdeh in 1885, nearly sparking a war between the two great powers.[77] This is where Russian expansion in the region would come to an end. As MacKenzie notes, "What eventually set limits to Russian expansion in Central Asia were . . . mountain barriers and British power."[78] Both were conspicuously absent in this case.

Cherniaev, it would turn out, was a better warrior than administrator. He not only continued to routinely defy the orders of his superiors in Orenburg and Saint Petersburg but badly mismanaged the finances of the occupation as well.[79] By November 1865, Saint Petersburg had had enough, and the emperor ordered

Cherniaev recalled. As Miliutin later explained the decision, Cherniaev's "willfulness, disobedience, and petty tyranny amounted to clear violations of the basic rules of the military service."[80] However, it turned out that removing so popular an officer was not totally straightforward, and it would take until the end of April 1866 for Cherniaev to finally arrive back in the capital, where he was received at the Winter Palace. After a frosty reception by both Gorchakov and Miliutin, Cherniaev was brought in for an audience with Czar Alexander II. While Cherniaev was initially apprehensive, the czar's warm welcome and affectionate embrace moved the major general to tears.[81] It also is noteworthy that official War Ministry accounts written soon after Cherniaev's dismissal largely exonerated the major general and placed the blame squarely on the shoulders of Bukhara.[82] Saint Petersburg, it seemed, was eager to quickly and quietly put the past behind it.

Tashkent was formally annexed to the Russian Empire by the governor-general of Orenburg in August 1866. Renewed conflict with Bukhara that had bubbled up since Cherniaev's conquest put an end to any idea of its independence.[83] In July 1867, after much discussion, the area was organized as the governate-general (*krai*) of Turkestan, with Tashkent as its political and administrative center.[84] Chimkent, Tashkent, and their surrounding areas would not see true independence until the collapse of the Soviet Union over 120 years later.

The individual who would be given the difficult task of administering this new Russian territory was a lieutenant general in the Imperial Russian Army, Konstantin Petrovich von Kaufman. Unlike Cherniaev, Kaufman was not expected to engage in insubordination. As he personally told Czar Alexander II before departing for Tashkent, "I do not fear supervision over me and my activities . . . , nor do I seek to escape it."[85] However, things would be different once he was on the ground in Russian Central Asia. And Kaufman would prove to be just the latest peripheral agent to nearly drag his superiors in Saint Petersburg into an unplanned territorial acquisition.

Russia and the Ili Region, 1871–81

The Russian Empire refrained from acquiring the Ili region of western China (now Ili Kazakh Autonomous Prefecture, Xinjiang, China) between June 1871 and February 1881. The conquest of this area was planned and ordered by the governor-general of Russian Turkestan, acting without orders from his superiors in Saint Petersburg. The theory of inadvertent expansion makes three central arguments that are supported in this case. First, that unauthorized peripheral expansion is the result of a principal-agent problem, combining a divergence of preferences between the capital and the periphery and information asymmetries favoring the latter. In the case of Russia in the Ili region, the absence of rapid communications greatly hampered central control, and there was a divergence of preferences between those in Saint Petersburg and those on the Chinese frontier. Second, that once territory is acquired, a number of constraints arise that make it difficult to readily relinquish it. In the Ili region case, concerns over domestic political pressure and Russian national honor gave leaders in Saint Petersburg pause before they decided to withdraw. And third, that significant geopolitical risk associated with acquisition of a given territory will discourage leaders from subsequently authorizing their peripheral agents' faits accomplis, leading to relinquishment. In the case of Russia in Ili, China's clear willingness to fight over the territory, and a locally adverse balance of power in China's favor, pressed Russian leaders to return the territory, which they did with the Treaty of Saint Petersburg in February 1881.

Historical Background

On the eve of the Russian invasion in 1871, the Ili region was an area of roughly 3,200 km^2 in the northwest of Qing Dynasty China's protectorate of Xinjiang, right on the Russian border.[86] The Ili region was lush and fertile compared to its more arid surroundings, consisting of the Ili River and its valley, which flowed from its source in the Tian Shan Mountains westward to the border with Russian Turkestan.[87] It was also remote, sitting nearly 3,000 km from Beijing and over 3,800 km from Saint Petersburg. Qing China's presence in the Ili region—and Xinjiang more broadly—was thin, and its hold over the region, precarious, and the region experienced regular unrest and rebellion.[88] One such rebellion would eventually serve as a precipitating cause of the Russian invasion.

A major Muslim rebellion broke out in 1862 in the northern Xinjiang region of Dzungaria.[89] By 1864, it had reached the Ili River valley, and it began to cause problems all along the Russo-Chinese frontier, including the interruption of trade, cross-border raids, destruction of Russian property, and massive refugee flows.[90] Observing events from across the Russian border in Turkestan was its governor-general, Konstantin Petrovich von Kaufman. Kaufman had an esteemed military career and was a veteran of the Russian conquest of the Caucasus and the Crimean War. He had also been a personal aide to War Minister Dmitry Miliutin, which won him the minister's friendship and confidence—and, eventually, his recommendation for the governor-generalship in 1867.[91] This would be a challenging assignment for Kaufman: the territory had just recently been conquered, he had no regional experience, and he needed to establish an administrative structure from scratch, all while being overseen by superiors some 3,500 km away in Saint Petersburg.[92] But Kaufman had their every confidence, being granted broad economic, political, and military powers to enable him to organize the new governate-general as he saw fit.[93] And, contrary to his earlier-mentioned assurances of obedience, Kaufman would show an independent streak once he was on the ground in Tashkent, effecting the conquest of the Khanate of Bukhara in June 1868 without authorization from Saint Petersburg.[94] Kaufman was the frontier agent who would nearly drag the leaders in the Russian capital into acquiring the Ili region.

The cast of characters in Saint Petersburg had changed little from the conquests of Chimkent and Tashkent just a few years earlier. Alexander II was still czar and Dmitry Miliutin, war minister. Alexander Gorchakov was technically still the foreign minister, however, the director of the ministry's Asiatic Department, Nikolay K. Giers, was increasingly acting in that role, partly due to Gorchakov's health and, later, partly due to his political sidelining after Russia's embarrassing political defeat at the Congress of Berlin in 1878.[95] These were the leaders in the capital who would be dragged unwittingly into nearly acquiring the Ili River valley from China.

Saint Petersburg and Turkestan

Saint Petersburg faced serious principal-agent problems with respect to its agents on the Chinese frontier in Russian Turkestan. First, there were stark information asymmetries in favor of the frontier agents such as Kaufman. The region would not see a telegraph connection with Saint Petersburg until 1873, when Tashkent and Vernyi extended connections.[96] The closest existing telegraph station to the Ili River frontier with China was in Omsk, nearly 1,400 km away. Under these circumstances, it was incredibly difficult to communicate with, and thereby potentially control, wayward peripheral agents. According to a contemporary member of the Russian Finance Ministry, due to "the remoteness of the region and the lack of telegraph, [Kaufman] was compelled by force of circumstances . . . to take measures for which under normal conditions he would have needed to ask permission."[97] Even after the installation of a number of telegraph stations in the region, it was still widely known that the government in Saint Petersburg was "very badly informed as to what actually goes on" in Russian Central Asia.[98]

Beyond the information asymmetries, there was also a divergence of preferences between the leaders in Saint Petersburg and their frontier agents, with leaders in the capital tending to be more defensively oriented and the frontier agents more expansionist. This was put in stark relief with Kaufman's unauthorized conquest of the Khanate of Bukhara in 1868, where, when ordered by the capital to return the territory, Kaufman flatly refused to "commit such sacrilege against the prestige, honor and rights of Russia."[99] With respect to China in particular, leaders in the capital, and the Foreign Ministry in particular, did not want to disturb Russia's good relations with the Qing Empire and, therefore, were opposed to any territorial acquisitions there.[100] When Kaufman suggested in 1870 that Russian forces should occupy the Ili River valley, the idea was summarily rejected by the government in Saint Petersburg.[101] Thus, information asymmetries favoring the periphery, and a preference divergence with the capital, made unauthorized peripheral expansion a distinct possibility in this case.

The Ili Region

By April 1871, the turbulence along the Sino-Russian border had only gotten worse and the Russian government in Saint Petersburg decided it was time to develop a plan to work with the Chinese government to put down the uprisings.[102] However, Kaufman was a few steps ahead of his metropolitan superiors. While he understood, as he wrote to Miliutin in February 1871, that he was prohibited from conquering Qing territory "by categorical order from the Highest Authority," he had been working on a plan to occupy the Ili River valley on his own accord since August 1870.[103] And when he received intelligence that Yaqub Beg's armies were moving on the Ili region, Kaufman decided he could wait no longer.[104] In May 1871, he ordered the military governor of Semirechye, Major General G. A. Kolpakovskii, to conquer the Ili region. On June 24, 1871, with a force of 1,850, Kolpakovskii crossed the Chinese border and began to move rapidly up the Ili River, eventually creating a Russian occupation area that extended roughly 400 km up the valley.[105] While there were armed clashes with local rebel forces, they were, ultimately, no match for the Russian army, and, on July 4, 1871, Kolpakovskii declared the Ili region annexed to the Russian Empire "in perpetuity."[106] This had all been accomplished without the knowledge or authorization of leaders in Saint Petersburg.[107] Kaufman's fait accompli had been successfully executed.

Saint Petersburg Reacts ... and Delays

It took about three weeks for news of the conquest to begin to filter back to Saint Petersburg and even longer to reach Beijing.[108] In his report back to the capital, Kaufman justified his action based on the danger associated with rebel forces looking to consolidate power in the Ili River valley.[109] Once most of the facts had become clear, the Russian minister in Beijing was instructed to inform the Chinese government of the conquest, which he did on September 1, 1871. China's control over, and communications with, its western territories was so weak that this was when its government first became aware that the Ili River valley had come under foreign occupation.[110] However, to their relief, from the get-go Russian officials were interested in discussing when and how they would retrocede the territory back to China. The Russian position was that the occupation was a necessary, but temporary, expedient to protect their border from Muslim rebels. Once China had suppressed the rebellion and retaken control over Xinjiang, the Russians argued, they would be prepared to return the territory.[111] According to a report from the Russian Foreign Ministry, the return of the Ili region "can only take place in the event that the Chinese Government presents us with adequate guarantees of an enduring reestablishment of its authority there."[112] This policy was made official in December 1872, when Czar Alexander II issued orders requiring the return of the Ili region once China had reestablished control in Xinjiang and the Russian border was secure.[113] And, having lost control of most of its western territories, China was hardly in a position to resist.

The Chinese took these conditions seriously; perhaps more seriously than the Russian leaders had expected.[114] The government entrusted the recovery of Xinjiang to the famed Chinese general Zuo Zongtang.[115] General Zuo had spent decades suppressing the Taiping Rebellion, and then various Muslim rebellions in the west, and so he was the perfect person for the job.[116] General Zuo began his campaign in March 1876 and, in less than two years, had successfully pacified the rebellion and was in control of all of Xinjiang except the Russian-occupied Ili River valley.[117] Chinese leaders felt they had accomplished what the Russians had required of them and were ready to negotiate Russia's withdrawal.

In March 1878, Czar Alexander II constituted a committee under War Minister Miliutin to discuss the Ili problem. The committee, again, recommended the return of the Ili region to China but had moved the goalposts in the intervening years. According to Miliutin, the committee "came to the conclusion that dignity of the state demands from us the honourable fulfillment of the promise" to return Ili, "but not before we have received from the Chinese the appropriate concessions."[118] These concessions would prove to be onerous. China's newly constituted foreign office, the Zongli Yamen, sent an envoy to Saint Petersburg who would arrive in late 1878 to negotiate the return of the Ili region.[119] For reasons that remain a matter of historical debate, the envoy effectively agreed to all of Russia's terms and came to an agreement, against the explicit orders of the Zongli Yamen.[120] The result was the Treaty of Livadia of October 2, 1879, which granted to Russia the Ili region's most strategic territory, a five-million-ruble indemnity, the right to establish seven new consulates in Xinjiang, and substantial new trading privileges, among other benefits.[121] It was an overwhelming diplomatic victory for Saint Petersburg and an outright disaster for Beijing.

The Qing court was thrown into turmoil by news of the treaty's signing.[122] The territorial cessions in the Ili River valley were particularly alarming, including key strategic passes through the Tian Shan Mountain range, which would have given Russia effective military control of the entirety of Xinjiang.[123] China's leaders were furious. Upon learning of the concessions made by the envoy, Empress Dowager Cixi, China's de facto ruler, was said to have burst out in exasperation that he "must die!"[124] In February 1880, a conference established by the Qing court officially renounced the Treaty of Livadia, disavowed the actions of the envoy, and threw him in prison with a sentence of death by beheading.[125] The court then appointed another envoy to renegotiate the settlement of the Ili crisis, who would arrive in Saint Petersburg in July. The envoy carried with him a document of core principles for the negotiations and was under strict orders to follow them precisely.[126]

Saint Petersburg's Calculus

After hearing the demands of the Chinese envoy, the czar convened another grand conference on August 13, 1880, which was attended by War Minister Miliutin and the acting foreign minister Giers, among others.[127] The committee, which would meet several times over the coming months, was tasked with making a final decision on the fate of the Ili region. Despite Chinese demands for a prompt withdrawal from the territory, it was not quite so simple from the Russian leaders' perspectives. This is because the conquest itself, and the now-nine-year occupation that followed, had placed some constraints on Russia's leaders that made relinquishing the Ili River valley somewhat difficult. The first and most straightforward of these was that the costs of the conquest had been sunk. Kaufman had acquired the Ili River valley at minimal cost, in terms of lives and treasure, and the territory was effectively theirs for the keeping. Perhaps aware of these pressures, from the outset, Major General Kolpakovskii made the case for retention of the Ili region in economic terms, arguing that "millions" could be made from the local tea trade.[128] And, as the occupation continued, Russian properties and businesses would be established in the area, and abandoning these would come at a cost for Saint Petersburg.

A second reason leaders in Saint Petersburg felt bound to seriously consider retaining the Ili region was concern over domestic politics in Russia. Despite the harsh autocracy of the czarist regime, Alexander II's program of domestic reform in the 1860s had helped create a modicum of space for popular dissent, and this was recognized by leaders at the time.[129] For instance, in the run-up to the signing of the Treaty of Livadia, the acting foreign minister Giers repeatedly showed concern over what newspapers were printing about the possibility of returning the Chinese territory.[130] After China had renounced the treaty in early 1880, leaders in Saint Petersburg agreed that in view of Russian "public opinion, it was desirable that the restitution [of Ili] was not carried out purely and simply."[131] The acting foreign minister Giers was of this mind as well, writing to one of the Russian negotiators in September 1880 that Russia needed serious concessions from the Chinese in the Ili negotiations, "so as not to hurt public opinion."[132] Thus, Russian leaders were clearly concerned about the public's reaction to any return of the Ili River valley.[133]

A third reason Russian leaders had difficulty relinquishing the territory and turning it back over to the Chinese was concern over Russian national honor, prestige, and reputation.[134] Some, for instance, argued that conceding too much would only invite further demands and challenges, from the Chinese and others in the region. In September 1879, War Minister Miliutin opposed the return of China's territory on the grounds that "the Asiatics will attribute generosity, or even justice, solely and simply to incapacity to retain what had been taken."[135] A government committee held in the spring of 1880 agreed, arguing that, if Russia returned the territory outright, "we would appear to have claimed an excessive territorial extension only to renounce it following threats from the Chinese"— an unacceptable outcome.[136] And the acting foreign minister Giers shared these concerns, writing in October 1880 that "it is to be feared that [Russian] moderation only serves to encourage" the Chinese to ask for more.[137]

There is also a striking number of references to Russian "prestige" and "dignity" in correspondence between leaders in these months. For instance, the spring 1880 committee cited Russian "prestige" as a reason to avoid promptly returning the territory.[138] In September of that year, an exasperated Giers wrote, "We want to emerge with dignity from this detestable affair."[139] Giers reiterated these concerns the following month, writing in mid-October that Russia would "not be able, without compromising our dignity, to submit to Chinese demands and give in on all points."[140] In some cases, Russian leaders seemed to take these honor concerns personally. For instance, Giers wrote on October 14 that "we will have to show them our teeth, because it is impossible to allow us be scoffed at by these wretches."[141] A few days later Giers claimed that the Chinese envoy's attitude "revolts me" and argued that "the more we show ourselves to be conciliatory and polite towards him—the more arrogant he will become."[142] Thus, for reasons of sunk costs, domestic political pressure, and concerns over national (and personal) honor, it appeared difficult for Russian leaders to simply and straightforwardly return the Ili region to China.

However, as the crisis unfolded, it became increasingly clear that there were serious geopolitical risks associated with standing firm and refusing to withdraw from Ili. China appeared to be willing to wage war over the territory, and as Russian leaders would learn over the course of the crisis, they themselves were not.[143] After China's rejection of the Treaty of Livadia in February 1880, many in and around the Qing court began to call for a campaign to retake the territory by force.[144] In March, the Chinese government put General Zuo in charge of defense of the northwest, with orders to raise new forces, reenlist veterans of the pacification campaigns, and develop a plan to invade Ili.[145] In May, Zuo moved his headquarters to Hami, in eastern Xinjiang, and dramatically carried a coffin with him in order to show his willingness to die for his country.[146] Beijing also began to acquire a large number of guns and other munitions from the United States and other European countries.[147] Russia, too, would begin preparing for war in April 1880, with Kaufman shifting his headquarters from Tashkent to Vernyi, near the Chinese border, and Saint Petersburg sending a powerful naval fleet of twenty-six ships to the Chinese coast.[148] In late October and into November 1880, the negotiations became tense, involving open talk of the possibility of war.[149] As the Chinese negotiator said to his Russian counterpart on November 5: "China does not want there to be war. Should this misfortune come to pass, the . . . Chinese can endure difficulties imposed by others and work long hours. Even if China were not to win the first battle, as China is the largest country in the world, were it to go on for a decade or more, they could still endure it. I think that your honorable country definitely would not be able to avoid losses."[150]

However, despite their preparations, Russian leaders had little real interest in fighting over the Ili River valley. This was so for three key reasons. First, the local balance of power strongly favored China.[151] While Russia had a relatively large and powerful military, the Ili region was a long way from Saint Petersburg, and transport and supply were slow and incredibly costly. Russia had only approximately 5,000 military personnel in the area and would be hard pressed to produce many more. The Chinese, by contrast, had been waging pacification campaigns in the west for years under General Zuo and were believed to have as many as 180,000 troops in the area.[152] These numbers, and China's preparations more broadly, were sobering for Russian leaders.[153] As a Russian negotiator wrote to the acting foreign minister Giers in October 1880, "Of course, [the Chinese] don't want war and they dread it. But they have convinced themselves that we want it even less and that we are hardly in a state to wage it."[154]

Second, the balance of resolve also appeared to favor China in Ili. From the perspective of Saint Petersburg, the territory was small, distant, incredibly difficult to administer and defend, and without much intrinsic value. For Beijing, in contrast, it was highly strategically valuable. As noted earlier, the Ili River valley contained key mountain passes in the Tian Shan range and was critical to the military control of Xinjiang as a whole. And Xinjiang itself was viewed as an important strategic buffer with which to defend Beijing and the Chinese heartland from the west.[155] This, too, was recognized by Russian leaders at the time.

As the Russian negotiator wrote to the acting foreign minister Giers in August 1880, referring to Ili, "this territorial concession, so precious to the Chinese . . . so worthless to us."[156] This sentiment was reiterated by this same negotiator six weeks later, who pointed out to Giers that the "final possession of [Ili] . . . would hardly compensate for our expenses" in any war over it.[157]

Third, Russia had only recently finished waging a major war in the Balkans, the Russo-Turkish War (1877–78), having mobilized 934,000 personnel and suffering 118,000 deaths in its victory.[158] This had two effects on the Ili crisis. First, many of Russia's best and most experienced military personnel were still tied up in the Balkans, with few left to spare for a distant Far Eastern contingency.[159] And second, the Ottoman War had been very hard on Russian finances, and Russia was simply in no position to wage another costly war.[160] And its leaders were keenly aware of this. As the Russian negotiator wrote to the acting foreign minister Giers in October 1880, "Only a good beating can bring [the Chinese] to their senses. But I admit that while this is a necessity, it would be very hard on our poor finances!"[161] Chinese leaders were also aware of the dire state of the Russian treasury, and this increased their confidence that their coercive diplomacy would soon bear fruit.[162]

All of this meant that time was clearly on China's side.[163] As the negotiations dragged on, the perception among leaders in Saint Petersburg was that it only redounded to China's advantage, giving them more time to increase their troop numbers, import arms from Russia's European rivals, and put further strain on the Russian treasury. From early on in the negotiations, Russian officials showed concern that the Chinese might be "dragging us along so they can complete their armaments."[164] Russian negotiators also saw great importance in "putting an end to current expenses as quickly as possible."[165] Similar views were present among key Russian leaders in Saint Petersburg, such as the acting foreign minister Giers. As he wrote on September 23, 1880, *what matters most to us is to carry out the negotiations as quickly as possible* so that we can recall the fleet and put our troops back along the Chinese border on a footing of peace."[166] An important reason for this haste was a concern that the conflict with Turkey might reignite—a far less peripheral concern—and that the Russian navy would be tied up thousands of kilometers away in the East China Sea.[167] As Giers wrote on September 25, they needed "a good solution as soon as possible—because all our attention must be directed towards Turkey where one can foresee great complications."[168]

This clash of incentives put Russian leaders in a bind. On the one hand, they had incentives to retain the Ili River valley, based on sunk acquisition costs, domestic political pressure, and concerns over Russian national honor and prestige. On the other hand, there were severe geopolitical risks associated with retaining the territory—namely, the risk of war with China over a concern that was, at best, peripheral to Russia's interests. A key Russian negotiator described the position as an "inextricable dilemma," lamenting that he did "not forgive those who got us stuck here by protesting last year against the outright restitution of the territories which we had temporarily occupied with the promise to return them!"[169] The problem, he wrote a few days later to the acting foreign minister Giers, is that the Russian government was rapidly approaching a point at which it would have "no choice but between a risky war, costly and dangerous, or an evil and precarious peace."[170] It was an unenviable position, to be sure.

Saint Petersburg Decides

The determination to avoid war with China would ultimately be Saint Petersburg's primary political aim, necessitating the relinquishment of the Ili region. The central importance of avoiding war had been present in the writing of Russian leaders over the months of the negotiations. The key Russian negotiator, for instance, wrote on October 1 that "war would be a deplorable end. It would be ruinous, endless, and of no benefit to us."[171] This sentiment was echoed by the acting foreign minister Giers, who wrote that same month that "it is to avoid war that we enter into negotiations" with the Chinese.[172] Even War Minister Miliutin—who had strongly opposed returning Ili a year earlier—would agree. By mid-October, he reportedly saw a potential war with China as "a misfortune without any possible compensation" and argued that it was "necessary to absolutely avoid it."[173] For nearly a decade, the Chinese and the Russians had stood toe-to-toe over the Ili region. In the end, Russia would blink.

Czar Alexander II called a final conference in December 1880 to settle the Ili crisis, attended by Giers, Miliutin, and other key Russian leaders.[174] All present agreed that, to avoid war with China, the return of the Ili region was necessary.[175] After a few days of discussion, the Russian negotiators approached the Chinese with a compromise, the core of which would result in the Treaty of Saint Petersburg of February 12, 1881.[176] Under the terms of this treaty, the Ili region would be returned to China, Russia would receive minimal trade and political concessions, and their shared border would remain almost entirely unchanged.[177] While Russia was awarded a rather large nine-million-ruble indemnity, and a small strip of territory west of Ili was ceded to Russia to settle refugees of the rebellion, this was a clear diplomatic victory for China and a complete reversal of fortunes from the Treaty of Livadia less than two years earlier.[178] After the treaty was ratified in the respective capitals, the Ili River valley was returned to

China in February 1882, nearly eleven years after Lieutenant General Kaufman had independently ordered its occupation.[179]

One month after the Treaty of Saint Petersburg had been signed, an assassin's bomb detonated and killed Czar Alexander II on March 13, 1881.[180] The news of the czar's death badly shook Kaufman, who himself would suffer a massive stroke only three weeks later, leaving him paralyzed and without the ability to speak.[181] He would technically remain governor-general of Turkestan for the following thirteen months as his health deteriorated, until he died on May 16, 1882.[182] Kaufman's dying wish, as a true Russian nationalist and imperialist, was to be buried in Tashkent, "so that everyone will know that here is true Russian ground where it is no dishonor for a Russian to lie."[183] And, in a final twist of irony, Kaufman's replacement as Turkestan's governor-general would be none other than Mikhail Grigorevich Cherniaev.[184]

This chapter has presented the comparative case studies of inadvertent expansion and nonexpansion by Russia in the Khanate of Kokand and the Ili region of western China. Both cases strongly support the theory of inadvertent expansion presented in chapter 1. First, both cases showed how inadvertent expansion is a manifestation of a principal-agent problem, based on divergent preferences and information asymmetries. Divergent preferences for expansion between Saint Petersburg and Central Asia, as well as the lack of a telegraph connection in Kokand or the China border region, hampered central control and enabled unauthorized peripheral expansion to take place. Second, both cases showed how unauthorized peripheral expansion can create constraints on leaders in the capital that make it difficult for them to easily withdraw. In Kokand and the Ili region, unauthorized peripheral expansion sunk the costs of acquisition and generated concerns over prestige and national honor in Saint Petersburg. In the Ili region case, there were also some domestic political concerns weighing on the minds of Russian leaders as they navigated the crisis. And third, in both cases the decision of whether to accept the territorial fait accompli was importantly conditioned by the geopolitical risk associated with acquisition. The absence of such risks cleared the way for acceptance of Cherniaev's fait accompli in Kokand, whereas the risk of war with China led to the rejection of Kaufman's fait accompli in Ili.

INADVERTENT EXPANSION IN SOUTHEAST ASIA

France

> In this Indo-Chinese enterprise . . . events have more often shaped
> our policy than our policy has directed the course of events.
>
> —Jules Ferry, 1884

This chapter examines inadvertent expansion through two examples from the French Empire in Southeast Asia. The first case study focuses on the French Empire's nonacquisition of the northern Vietnamese region of Tonkin in 1873–74. The second case examines France's eventual acquisition of that territory in 1882–83. The primary purpose of this chapter is to present the book's third pair of comparative theory-testing cases, illustrating how variation in geopolitical risk produced the divergent outcomes observed.

The two Tonkin cases provide a unique inferential opportunity for comparison, in that they are strikingly similar in nearly all respects. History, in these two cases, seems to repeat itself in a way it very rarely does. As the historian of the French Empire Raymond Betts puts it, referring to the two key peripheral actors from the Tonkin cases: "One can find, in the annals of French colonial history, no better examples of this sort of individualized behavior than those afforded by François Garnier and Henri Rivière. As if in tandem, these two men performed similar military actions in the same setting, with the same disregard for orders, with the same disastrous personal results and in the same geographic situation—almost exactly a decade apart."[1] What Betts does not add here is that while Garnier fails to have his fait accompli accepted by the French government in Paris in 1874, Rivière succeeds in his venture just ten years later. This chapter traces the processes of these two cases, showing the crucial role played by varying geopolitical risk.

L'Affaire Garnier: France and Tonkin, 1873–74

France refrained from acquiring the northern Vietnamese region of Tonkin (now northern Vietnam) between October 1873 and March 1874. The ultimately failed conquest of Tonkin was independently planned and executed by a young French naval officer, with the support of the governor of the French colony of Cochinchina. This case supports two of the central arguments of the theory of inadvertent expansion. First, that inadvertent expansion is a manifestation of a principal-agent problem, combining a divergence of preferences between leaders in the capital and their agents on the periphery and information asymmetries favoring the agents. In the case at hand, peripheral actors in Saigon and Tonkin were far more open to conquest than leaders in the capital, and the vast distances separating the two, and the lack of telegraphic communications to Tonkin itself, meant that their behavior was very difficult to monitor and control. And second, that expectations of significant geopolitical risk associated with acquisition will discourage leaders in the capital from retaining the territory, leading to a rejection of the fait accompli. In this first case of France in Tonkin, French military weakness in the wake of its catastrophic loss in the Franco-Prussian War (1870–71), as well as its fear of sparking a crisis with Germany or Britain in Europe, led leaders in the capital to precipitously withdraw from the newly conquered territory.

Historical Background

On the eve of the French invasion in 1873, Tonkin comprised the northern region of the Vietnamese Empire, ruled by the Nguyen Dynasty emperor Tu Duc, out of Hue, in the central region of Annam. Southern Vietnam, known to the French as "Cochinchina," had been colonized between 1862 and 1867 after the invasion of the French emperor Napoleon III.[2] At over 116,000 km^2 and containing a few million people, Tonkin bordered the Chinese provinces of Yunnan and Guangxi to the north, the Thai vassal state of Louangphrabang to the west, and the Gulf of Tonkin to the east.[3] With the French annexation of Cambodia in 1863, Annamese leaders in Hue began to feel the French noose tightening around them.[4]

In 1871, a French arms dealer based in Hankou, China, Jean Dupuis, began transporting trade cargo up and down the Red River through Tonkin with the knowledge (though not the official backing) of the French Ministry of the Navy and Colonies.[5] After having completed several successful missions, in June 1873, Dupuis was detained by authorities in Hanoi, the capital of Tonkin, being told that his trade activities were in violation of a Franco-Annamese treaty. Dupuis had an official arms commission from Chinese authorities in Yunnan and a crew of approximately three hundred and was incensed at being detained. Being at an increasingly tense impasse, both Dupuis and local Vietnamese officials reached out to the governor of French Cochinchina to resolve the conflict.[6]

The governor of Cochinchina at this time was Admiral Marie Jules Dupré, a naval officer and veteran of the Crimean War (1853–56). To help him deal with the Hanoi conflict, Dupré would call upon fellow French naval officer, Captain Marie Joseph François Garnier. Garnier was young (just thirty-four on the eve of the French conquest), ambitious, and a hot-headed advocate of a more aggressive French colonial policy.[7] When Garnier received a note from the admiral, in early August 1873, saying "I have to talk to you about important matters, so please come as soon as you can," he wasted little time.[8] Admiral Dupré and Captain Garnier were the key peripheral actors who would aim to drag their superiors in Paris into the acquisition of Tonkin.

Paris and Tonkin

Leaders in Paris faced severe principal-agent problems with respect to their subordinates in the Southeast Asian periphery. First, there were stark information asymmetries in favor of the peripheral agents. While, by this time, telegraph technology was becoming established globally, and there was a telegraph connection between Paris and Saigon, communication with Tonkin itself remained slow, being carried by boat along the Vietnamese coast and up the Red River. The fastest a letter from Saigon could be delivered to Hanoi was eleven days, and, therefore, it would take, at the very least, three weeks to get a response to a message sent from Paris to Hanoi.[9] Under these conditions, monitoring—and thereby controlling—the behavior of any potentially wayward agents was incredibly difficult.

Second, there was a sharp divergence of preferences between the leaders in Paris and their agents in Saigon and Tonkin. Dupré had long pushed for a more aggressive colonial policy in the region.[10] Since taking up his position as governor in Saigon in 1871, he had been aiming to get Hue to recognize France's annexation of Cochinchina, and he thought this could be facilitated by a more coercive approach.[11] As he wrote to the naval and colonial minister in Paris in December 1872, "The time for talks and reasoning has passed"—it was time for "the occupation of Kécho [Hanoi], the capital of Tonkin, and the mouth of the Song Koi [Red River]."[12] Dupré followed these letters with similar appeals to Paris in both March and May 1873, arguing that France's "establishment in Tonkin is a matter of life and death for the future of our domination in Cochinchina."[13] Dupré's views are a clear manifestation of what I have referred to as the "view from the frontier"—his responsibilities were narrow, the dangers and opportunities were near, and the felt need to act urgently was great.

However, winning over the cabinet in Paris would be no small feat. In the wake of France's loss in the Franco-Prussian War, and the civil war with the Paris Commune (1871), there was little appetite in the capital for imperial adventures. The naval and colonial minister at the time, Louis Pothuau, responded to Dupré's appeal of December 1872 by pointing out that the foreign minister "does not think (and I share this view) that the present circumstances allow us to resort to violent means against Emperor Tu Duc."[14] Upon reading another of Dupré's letters of March 1873, a cabinet minister penciled in the margin: "He absolutely insists on waging war and we will have great difficulty in preventing him from moving forward. However, it is important to do so and in the most formal way."[15] These views were shared by the French prime minister Jacques-Victor Albert, the fourth duke of Broglie. As he plainly put it in a dispatch to Dupré in July 1873, "Under no circumstances, for any reason whatsoever, should you engage France in Tonkin."[16] Most leaders in Paris embodied what I have referred to as the "view from the capital"—their responsibilities were weighty, the dangers of the frontier were distant, and the perceived urgency to act was very low.

Despite this resounding message coming out of Paris, the conflict between the French arms trader Dupuis and the local officials in Hanoi seemed too good an opportunity for Governor Dupré to pass up. A few days after he had summoned Captain Garnier to Saigon, Dupré sent yet another appeal to the new naval and colonial minister, Admiral Charles de Dompierre d'Hornoy on July 28, 1873. Dupré reported that the Tonkin "question has just taken a new and decisive step" and argued that, under the circumstances, he deemed "it necessary to occupy the citadel of Kécho or Hanoi (the capital of Tonkin) and points along the coast."[17] The governor added that he was ready "to assume all the responsibility of the consequences of the expedition," which he knew would expose him "to disavowal, recall, or the loss of rank." Dupré added that he was not "asking for approval or reinforcements"; he was simply asking Paris to be allowed to proceed.[18]

On September 8, 1873, Dupré received a brief telegraphic reply, stating only that he should "do nothing that could expose France to dangerous complications"—not a flat veto, but certainly not a ringing endorsement either.[19] However, a few days later, Naval and Colonial Minister d'Hornoy followed up with a longer response to the governor's plea. He began by pointing out that he was put "on guard" by the "bold" and "adventurous" nature of Dupré's proposal. He further noted that "at any other time than the sad time we are in, I would have admired and perhaps even pushed for these grand ideas of conquest."[20] However, these were not normal times, d'Hornoy pointed out, and the circumstances "prevent the government from agreeing to any aggressive measures" in Tonkin. "It is necessary to wait," the minister continued, "prepare for more prosperous times, leave France to regain its strength, [and to] reconstitute itself militarily, fundamentally and politically."[21] Thus, while Governor Dupré would receive authorization to negotiate with Hue in October, any sort of armed conquest was definitively off the table.[22]

But mere orders would not suffice to deter the governor. Captain Garnier arrived in Saigon in late August 1873, and Dupré and Garnier immediately set about planning the expedition. What was discussed between Dupré and Garnier in these weeks is not entirely known, and the evidence is somewhat contradictory.[23] On the one hand, the official instructions Dupré gave to Garnier on October 10 were surprisingly cautious in tone.[24] Garnier was ordered not only to investigate the conflict between Dupuis and local authorities, to insist on the merchant's prompt departure, and to negotiate the opening of the Red River to trade but also to "abstain from any intervention."[25] On the other hand, Garnier may have received private verbal instructions, for he later claimed to have complete freedom of action, writing to his brother: "As for instructions, *carte blanche*! The Admiral is relying on me! Forward then for our beloved France!"[26] And Dupré also wrote, just nine days after issuing his instructions for Garnier, that the "occupation of a military position in the heart of Tonkin will very probably be a necessary step toward the conclusion of the treaty, which must be equivalent to the protectorate of France over the entire kingdom."[27] Thus, principal-agent problems between Paris and the French Indochinese frontier helped set the stage for the unauthorized conquest that followed.

Tonkin

Garnier set off from Saigon on the evening of October 11, 1873, with a force of about eighty personnel and two small gunboats. A second, slightly larger, reinforcement force, which would meet them in Hanoi, was set to depart two weeks later. Garnier ominously signaled his intentions when he wrote to a friend en route, on October 20, that things "must be in a very bad state in Tonkin for the Annamese to so kindly welcome the wolf into the sheepfold."[28]

He arrived in Hanoi on November 5. It was evident from the beginning that Garnier had little interest in fairly adjudicating the dispute between the arms trader Dupuis and the authorities in Tonkin.[29] Garnier quickly established friendly relations with Dupuis and his associates while throwing his weight around in his dealings with Hanoi officials. Within just five days of arrival, Garnier wrote to his brother he had made up his mind: "On November 15, I will attack the citadel with my eighty men: I will arrest the Marshal and send him to Saigon," and "I will officially declare . . . the country open to trade."[30]

By this point, Garnier's reinforcement force of 88 troops had arrived with two more gunboats from Saigon.[31] Combined with Dupuis's accompanying guard, with whom Garnier was now openly collaborating, their total force was approximately 450 personnel.[32] On November 16, Garnier decided to try to force the issue, putting forth a decree that declared the Red River open to trade and referring to himself as the "Great Mandarin Garnier."[33] A few days later, on November 19, Garnier sent Marshal Nguyen an ultimatum: disarm the citadel and comply with his decree or face attack. The marshal had until 6:00 p.m. to decide.[34] At 10:00 p.m., having heard nothing from the marshal, Garnier again wrote to his brother: "'The die is cast' . . . I attack tomorrow, at dawn."[35]

The attack on the Hanoi Citadel—a Vauban-style fortress complex and the center of Annam's military power in the area—opened at 6:00 a.m. on November 20, 1873. The citadel was shelled by French gunboats from the Red River while Garnier's forces streamed to a number of the complex's weakly fortified gates, managing to shell and batter them open with relative ease. The Vietnamese forces were soon in disarray, for while the garrison was numerous, they were abysmally armed—carrying only swords, spears, even stones—and the attack caught them largely by surprise. One by one, each of the citadel's five fortified gates was taken by Garnier's forces in rapid succession. By 8:00 a.m., the French tricolor was flying over the complex.[36] Two thousand Vietnamese forces were taken prisoner and thousands of others fled. Marshal Nguyen was gravely wounded by the shelling and would later succumb to his injuries. The French had no wounded and only a single soldier killed, likely the result of friendly fire.[37] The capture of the heart of Hanoi's military power had been executed in less than two hours.

The very next day, on November 21, Garnier and his small army began the systematic conquest of the entire Tonkin region. They took Hung Yen and Phu Ly on November 23 and 26, respectively.[38] Then Hai Duong and Nam Dinh on December 4 and 11, respectively.[39] Finally, Nin Binh was seized on December 17 by a force of fewer than a dozen personnel.[40] With each acquisition, Garnier's forces installed pro-French authorities and a small French garrison and then moved onto the next. On December 13, when the conquest was nearly complete, Garnier wrote to Governor Dupré from Nam Dinh, putting forth his view "that a General Protectorate of the entire Empire of Annam would be the best result to draw from the current situation."[41]

On December 18, 1873, however, Garnier was forced to rush back to Hanoi. Chinese river pirates known as the "Black Flags," who operated and controlled territory in the upper reaches of the Red River, were massing alongside Vietnamese provincial forces at the town of Son Tay, some 40 km upriver of Hanoi.[42] Annamese authorities in Hue had simultaneously sent envoys to the Hanoi Citadel to negotiate an end to the conflict with Garnier.[43] On December 21, the day peace negotiations were set to commence, approximately six hundred Black Flags and two thousand Vietnamese provincial forces began to move toward the citadel. After a very brief attack by the Black Flags, they withdrew upon contact with French artillery.[44] Garnier then decided to give chase, leading a small column of just eighteen personnel up the road in the direction the Black Flags had withdrawn. Just over a kilometer from the citadel, Garnier was ambushed and overwhelmed by Black Flags forces, who hacked and stabbed him to death. In a grisly denouement, Garnier's head was taken as a trophy by the Black Flags.[45] The following day, on December 22, Jean Dupuis, the French arms merchant whose expedition had initiated the whole conflict, went in to view Garnier's body after it had been recovered and returned to the citadel. "Nothing is quite as horrible as these headless corpses," Dupuis noted, "Garnier's clothing is in tatters, his body is covered in wounds made by sabers and spears, he is savagely mutilated. . . . I strongly squeeze his cold right hand for the last time."[46]

Paris Reacts

News of Garnier's initial conquest of the Hanoi Citadel on November 20 did not reach Saigon until the end of that month. Initially, Governor Dupré tried to use the conquest to bend Hue to his will, writing to the court on December 1 that "if you do not hurry to make the treaty, our stay in Tonkin will be extended; we will be forced to complete the occupation to directly administer the country."[47] However, as more news filtered back to the governor, he became increasingly uneasy about what was transpiring in Tonkin. Then, on January 3, 1874, the news of Garnier's death reached the governor, and he cabled Paris the very next day, reporting "the most painful news. On December 21, Mr. Garnier, who had attacked the citadel of Hanoi, was struck dead." Dupré tried to distance himself from the operation, referring to the "excess of confidence" and "imprudence" with which Garnier had acted and emphasizing that the situation in Tonkin was "imperfectly known" to him.[48] But the ball was now in the Paris cabinet's court—what was to be done with their newly conquered territory?

The truth was that there were very few incentives to retain Tonkin from Paris's perspective. While Garnier's successful conquest had sunk the costs of acquiring Tonkin, there was very little domestic political support for its retention, and news of the death of Garnier did little to ignite concerns over French honor and prestige.[49] France had lost the war with Prussia and put down the revolt of the Paris Commune only two-and-a-half years earlier and had just finished paying reparations to its newly unified German neighbor.[50] A bitter political contest between republican and monarchical factions would consume much of France's energy for the first decade of the Third Republic, leaving little room to consider imperial activity abroad.[51]

However, a more specific reason for Paris's reticence was the perceived geopolitical risk associated with retaining Tonkin. While some scholars have pointed to French concerns over conflict with China or Vietnam to explain this reticence, the evidence suggests that French concerns lay much closer to home.[52] The risk of igniting geopolitical competition with Britain and Germany in this time of vulnerability is what seems to have primarily stayed the hands of French leaders.[53] The preeminence of the European threat in French leaders' minds can be seen in many of the communications within and between both Saigon and Paris in the run-up to the conquest of Tonkin. For instance, in his September 11, 1873, reply to Paris, Governor Dupré assured Naval and Colonial Minister d'Hornoy that he would "not lose sight of all the precautions imposed on us by the present situation in Europe."[54] On September 22, in a letter to a colleague in the navy, the French prime minister Broglie pointed out that "what concerns me in particular with the occupation of the capital of Tonkin and the taking possession of the mouth of the river . . . [is that it] would excite the discontent of foreign powers, notably, England. There is no doubt that the London cabinet . . . would not care to see us become masters of Tonkin."[55] The prime minister similarly wrote to d'Hornoy on November 6 that "prudence advised us not to resort to arms" in Tonkin, since the "strengthening of our influence" would be "against the desires of the other powers."[56] Even Garnier himself seems to have known of this potential source of opposition. In his letter of November 10 to his brother Léon, announcing his plans for conquest, he wrote that he hoped "that soon after, despite the fear we have of England, it will be recognized that I have rendered service to my country!"[57]

However, the most detailed piece of evidence supporting the idea that France's concerns were geopolitical and lay in Europe is Naval and Colonial Minister d'Hornoy's September 12 letter to Dupré, forbidding him from engaging in conquest in Tonkin. In it, d'Hornoy points out to the governor that, in terms of foreign policy, "this is where we are. Not a single ally! Our immediate neighbor, from whom we are no longer separated except by a frontier which no longer offers us any means of defense, is a powerful enemy."[58] d'Hornoy worried aloud that Bismarck was seeking some motive to, again, declare war on France and that France's relatively rapid recovery alone was making the Iron Chancellor wary. He pointed out that the conquest would be costly in terms of money and personnel. But "the most serious obstacle, in my opinion," the minister emphasized, the "most dangerous would be the jealousy of England and Germany to see our power extend thus in the East, and I fear that the difficulties that would emerge would be the repercussions felt in Europe."[59] Given their relatively weak position in Europe, it was the reactions of the European great powers that French leaders most feared.

Paris Decides

Given these perceptions of geopolitical risk, and the lack of constraints placed on French leaders by the conquest, the decision for the leaders in Paris was relatively easy. The cabinet quickly ordered the immediate withdrawal from Tonkin and the return of conquered territories to local authorities.[60] In an almost-lecturing tone, Naval and Colonial Minister d'Hornoy replied to Dupré's report on the death of Garnier on January 7, noting that the "sad event you are announcing justifies the thoughts I expressed to you about the mission to Tonkin and whose departure I couldn't prevent." The minister ordered Dupré to hasten the evacuation of Tonkin, for, as he put it, "the government demands in the most absolute way that there is no question of a prolonged, let alone a permanent, occupation of any part of Tonkin."[61]

This time Dupré did as he was told. He ordered the immediate evacuation of French forces from Tonkin, and, by February 1874, they had been withdrawn.[62] On March 15, 1874, France and Annam signed the Treaty of Saigon, settling the conflict in Tonkin.[63] Hue's most important concession was the recognition of French Cochinchina whereas France's was the recognition of the independence of Annam and its authority over Tonkin. Hue additionally pledged to protect the rights of Catholics; to open ports in Hue, Hai Phong, and Qui Nhon for commerce; to open the Red River for trade; and to not allow any other power, including China, to intervene in its territory. But none of these would be adhered to in practice.[64] Ultimately, little changed as a result of the French intervention in Tonkin. However, Garnier's unauthorized conquest and the resulting 1874 treaty would itself set the stage for yet another French naval officer to follow in his footsteps just a few years later.

L'Affaire Rivière: France in Tonkin, 1882–83

France acquired the northern Vietnamese region of Tonkin between April 1882 and August 1883. The conquest of this region was independently carried out by a French naval officer, exceeding the limits of his orders and defying his superiors in Paris and French-held Saigon. The theory of inadvertent expansion makes three key arguments that are supported by this case. First, that unauthorized peripheral expansion is the result of a principal-agent problem, combining diverse preferences between capital and frontier and information asymmetries favoring the latter. In the case of France in Tonkin in 1882–83, a lack of telegraphic communication with Tonkin itself hampered control over actors operating there, and leaders in Paris were far less aggressive than their peripheral agents would ultimately prove to be. Second, that the acquisition of territory often places constraints on leaders that make it difficult to simply withdraw and return the territory to local governing authorities. In the case at hand, the territorial acquisitions ignited concerns of French national honor and prestige that made backing down seem unthinkable to many, if not most, in the capital. Third, that a lack of geopolitical risk associated with acquisition will encourage leaders in the capital to accept the fait accompli, resulting in territorial expansion. In this Tonkin case, while there were no rival great power interests at stake, there was the risk of conflict with a regional power, China, which had a tributary relationship with Tonkin. However, French officials from Tonkin to Paris did not see it that way, consistently ignoring and downplaying the risks of impinging upon China's interests, and it is their estimations, perceptions, and risk tolerances that guided their behavior. French leaders would be proven wrong in this regard, as the French conquest would ultimately spark the Sino-French War in December 1883. But not before leaders in Paris authorized the acquisition of Tonkin, which was successfully carried out in August of that year.

Historical Background

With France's withdrawal from Tonkin in February 1874, French expansion in the region was put on hold. The domestic political battle between monarchists and republicans raged on, and the economic effects of France's war indemnity to Germany, though by this point fully paid off, continued to be felt.[65] Furthermore, in their relatively weakened state, French leaders remained wary of antagonizing the other great powers of Europe.[66] Under these conditions, the state of play in Vietnam returned to much as it was before the abortive French conquest of 1873. French missionaries, traders, and consuls were harassed and hindered in their duties.[67] Hue continued its subordinate relationship with the Qing Empire, sending tribute missions and requesting their assistance in putting down a domestic rebellion.[68] And the Black Flags continued to operate in the upper reaches of the Red River, collecting customs and hindering the free passage of French exploration and trade.[69] However, despite all of these challenges, France took little action. As the French foreign minister Louis Decazes said of Tonkin, in September 1877, "We have renounced openly establishing a protectorate. . . . [We are] not in a position to undertake aggrandizement."[70] It was almost as if Garnier's intervention had never happened, and the treaty of 1874 had never been signed.

The new French governor in Cochinchina was Charles-Marie Le Myre de Vilers, the first civilian to hold that position. The new commander of Saigon's naval station was Henri Laurent Rivière. Despite being a veteran of the Crimean War, the Mexican Expedition (1861–67), and the Franco-Prussian War, Rivière had a rather undistinguished naval career, which, at age fifty-four, he seemed unlikely to improve on.[71] Personally, Rivière had little interest in colonialism or empire and was instead an esteemed writer of novels and plays who frequented Paris's most exclusive salons.[72] Henri Rivière was the key actor on France's Southeast Asian frontier who would drag his superiors into the conquest of Tonkin.

The key leaders in Paris who were responsible for French imperial policy were the prime minister, the foreign minister, and the naval and colonial minister. There was a great deal of turmoil in French domestic politics in these years, and, over the course of the Tonkin expedition, the French prime ministership was held by five individuals (Léon Gambetta, Charles de Freycinet, Charles Duclerc, Armand Fallières, and Jules Ferry), the position of foreign minister was occupied by six (Gambetta, Freycinet, Duclerc, Fallières, Paul-Armand Challemel-Lacour, and Ferry), and the naval and colonial ministry changed hands four times (Bernard Jauréguiberry, François de Mahy, Charles Brun, and Alexandre Peyron). While some had much greater influence on the process than others, the individuals in these positions were the leaders in the capital who Henri Rivière would drag unwittingly into conquering Tonkin.

Paris and Tonkin

Leaders in Paris would face significant principal-agent problems in dealing with Rivière and other agents on the ground in Tonkin. First, there were important information asymmetries favoring their peripheral agents. While, as noted earlier, there was a telegraph connection between Paris and Saigon, Tonkin itself still lacked a telegraph station, with communications from Saigon continuing to be carried upriver by boat. The fastest a message from Saigon could be delivered to Hanoi in these years was approximately six days, and, therefore, it would take, at the very least, twelve days to get a response to a message sent from Paris to Hanoi.[73] These communication delays made monitoring—and thereby potentially controlling—the behavior of peripheral agents like Henri Rivière incredibly difficult for leaders in Paris.

Second, there was a divergence of preferences between many leaders in the capital and their agents in Saigon and Tonkin. While there were advocates in Paris of a more aggressive approach to Tonkin—most notably, Naval and Colonial Minister Jean Bernard Jauréguiberry—the general posture of most leaders in the capital was one of aversion to intervention.[74] And while there was one French prime minister that hoped, and even planned, to possibly acquire Tonkin by force—Charles de Freycinet—his cabinet did not last long enough to put its plans into action.[75] In general, leaders in Paris wanted to avoid an entangling engagement in Tonkin, embodying the "view from the capital."

Those on the periphery, by contrast, often took the "view from the frontier" and were typically more aggressive in their orientation. The Cochinchina governor Le Myre de Vilers, for instance, was a proponent of an aggressive regional posture. In the summer of 1881, he personally advocated for a small armed expedition to the region, to clear the Red River of the Black Flags and to strengthen the existing French garrisons there. The governor's plan was agreed to by the cabinet and approved by the Chamber of Deputies in July 1881, yet the government in Paris made the limitations on this mission unmistakably clear. In the cabinet's instructions for Le Myre de Vilers in September, he was told to "raise the prestige of French authority" in the region and to "protect the interests and rights of Europeans in these parts," but, "above all, [to] refrain from embarking on adventures of military conquest." This was to be, in their words, "a material demonstration which in no way has the character of a military operation."[76]

By late December, Governor Le Myre de Vilers saw the opportune moment approaching.[77] On January 16, 1882, he notified Paris that, while he planned to double the garrison in Hanoi, he was quick to emphasize that there "will be no military operation; I will only take preventive measures."[78] The following day, the governor issued his orders for Commander Rivière, instructing him to double the Hanoi garrison, from one hundred to two hundred personnel, and to clear the Red River of the Black Flags.[79] And the very same constraints that Paris had placed upon Le Myre de Vilers were, in turn, placed upon Rivière. As the governor put it:

> You know the views of the government of the Republic. It does not want at any cost to wage, four thousand leagues from France, a war of conquest that would drag the country into serious complications. It is POLITICALLY, PEACEFULLY, ADMINISTRATIVELY that we must extend and strengthen our influence in Tonkin and Annam . . . the measures we take today are essentially preventive. So, you will use force only in case of absolute necessity and I am counting on your caution to avoid this eventuality.[80]

To hammer the point home, Le Myre de Vilers closed his orders by pointing out to Commander Rivière that the government's wishes could "be summed up in this sentence: Avoid gunfire; it would serve no other purpose than to embarrass us."[81] The governor seems to have had confidence that his subordinate had gotten the message. In a note to the commerce and colonial minister in Paris the following day, he pointed out that Rivière had promised to strictly comply with his instructions and that they could "count on his prudence and moderation."[82]

However, there were obvious limits to Le Myre de Vilers's ability to control Rivière once he had left Saigon, and the governor was sensitive to this. As he wrote in his January 17 orders for Rivière: "I don't think I can give you more detailed instructions . . . most likely, things will happen and necessities will arise that I cannot foresee; but I count on your patriotism and your wisdom not to lead the government of the Republic in a way that it does not want to follow."[83] And while Rivière was not known to have an aggressive streak, things often appeared different once one was on the frontier. And without telegraphic communications as a means of monitoring him, there was no telling what might unfold.

Before Rivière had a chance to depart, the ruling ministry of Léon Gambetta fell on January 30, delaying the expedition's departure by a few weeks.[84] On March 4, the returning naval and colonial minister Admiral Jauréguiberry approved Rivière's instructions, telling Le Myre de Vilers that by ordering the commander "not to use force except in the case of absolute necessity, you have followed exactly the intentions of my Department."[85] On March 16, the returning prime minister Charles Freycinet also approved of the instructions, similarly reiterating that the mission "cannot include . . . the occupation of any neighboring territory."[86] With his orders approved in Paris, Rivière was ready to depart.

Tonkin

Henri Rivière left Saigon for Hanoi with a force of 233 personnel aboard two naval vessels on March 26, 1882.[87] After a brief stop at Hai Phong, on the Tonkin coast, the expedition made its way up Tonkin's river system, arriving at Hanoi in the late afternoon of April 2.[88] For the commander's first few days in Hanoi, everything seemed to be going relatively smoothly. He met with local officials, exchanged gifts, was transparent about his plans and intentions, and, in contrast with François Garnier a decade earlier, was sensitive to, and accommodating of, their concerns regarding the expedition's sudden appearance.[89] However, during the second week of their stay, concerns among the Tonkinese began to creep in. Knowing from experience that the sudden appearance of a French expedition often spelled trouble, local Tonkin officials continued to reinforce their forces at the Hanoi Citadel, which Rivière watched with increasing alarm.[90] As the commander wrote to Governor Le Myre de Vilers on April 18, "The citadel continues to fill with soldiers and to strengthen itself " and that this "state of affairs can only continue at the expense of our influence" in the region.[91] When Rivière received a force of 250 reinforcements from Saigon on April 24, bringing his total to just shy of 600, he decided that it was time to take action.

At 5:00 a.m. on April 25, Commander Rivière—like Garnier before him—sent the governor of Hanoi an ultimatum.[92] He gave the governor until 8:00 a.m. to hand over the citadel or face attack.[93] At 7:30 a.m., the governor asked for a twenty-four-hour delay, but Rivière simply ignored it, taking the request as a sign of hostility.[94] At 8:15 a.m., Rivière's gunboats on the Red River initiated a two-and-a-half-hour preparatory bombardment on the citadel's north face.[95] Meanwhile, the assault force divided into two columns and got in position to move on the fortress. When the guns went silent at 10:45 a.m., one force feigned an attack on the citadel's east gate, while the main assault force attacked where the barrage had taken place, the north gate. By 11:15 a.m., both forces were inside the citadel, finding that most of its defenders had fled. Before noon, the citadel was secured, and the French tricolor was flying at its highest point. The conquest cost the French just four wounded, while at least forty Annamese defenders were killed, and an unknown but significant number of Annam's soldiers were wounded. The citadel's governor perished as well, having hung himself during the attack.[96]

Rivière wrote to Le Myre de Vilers that very day, informing him of the conquest. However, without a telegraph connection in Hanoi, it would take nearly a week for his letter to arrive on the governor's desk. "I had to take the Hanoi citadel," Rivière wrote, "It couldn't go on." He promised his superior that the new acquisition would be "all profit for us and no pain" and begged the governor "to believe that I had to act as I did. The citadel openly fortified near us; it was a danger which we had to cut short."[97] On April 27, Commander Rivière sent a similar letter of notification to Naval and Colonial Minister Jauréguiberry in Paris, pointing out that, given the "preparations of defense" he observed at the citadel, he simply "had to prepare to act."[98] The day after the conquest of the citadel, Commander Rivière issued a proclamation to the people of Hanoi, claiming that his intention was not to take over the country and blaming the conquest on the "reprehensible conduct" of the citadel's governor.[99] In an attempt to signal his good faith, the commander lowered the French tricolor on April 27 and replaced it with the Annamese flag. In the days that followed, he also returned much of the citadel to local authorities, only retaining the Royal Pavilion, the military heart of the fortress.[100] Even Rivière himself was stunned by the sudden turn of events and his place in them. "It is quite astonishing," he wrote to a friend on May 2, "I have thus become a man of war."[101]

Saigon and Paris React

It took until May 1 for news of the citadel's seizure to reach Saigon. It clearly came as a surprise to Governor Le Myre de Vilers, for just days earlier he had been assuring Naval and Colonial Minister Jauréguiberry that Commander Rivière was "too careful and too sensible a man to engage lightly on a path contrary to the spirit of your instructions."[102] The governor was clearly irritated with his subordinate and even considered recalling him.[103] In his reply to Rivière on May 2, the governor pointedly asked, "Was this measure essential?" noting that "fortresses that are taken without firing a shot are rarely to be feared." However, from Le Myre de

Vilers's perspective, what was done was done, and he was willing to accept his share of the responsibility, though he reiterated his orders "not to use force against the regular authorities except when absolutely necessary."[104] In a series of cables and letters sent back to Paris, Governor Le Myre de Vilers stood behind Rivière, pointing to the "threatening attitude" of the Hanoi authorities, noting that there was "nothing to fear" in response, and assuring his metropolitan bosses that they were "not on a war footing."[105] In the meantime, the governor continued to urge Rivière to expand no further and to await instructions from Paris.[106]

For their part, leaders in Paris took the news in relative stride. On June 20, Naval and Colonial Minister Jauréguiberry gave his approval for the steps taken thus far, though he agreed that there was a "need to make our success effective by limiting our occupation."[107] France, in these months, was swept up in a crisis over Egypt that would precipitate a British invasion, in July 1882, and had little time or attention to devote to Southeast Asia.[108] In fact, the decision in Paris, for the time being, was to not make a decision. Rivière was to maintain his position, expand no further, and do nothing that would cause complications for France in the region. In Le Myre de Vilers's view, they could reopen diplomatic negotiations with Hue over the future of Tonkin from this new position of relative strength, possibly gaining a protectorate once they had come to an agreement.[109] As he saw it, time was on their side.[110] For the time being, he wrote to Rivière on July 27, they had to "be patient" and "await the auspicious hour."[111] Rivière, for his part, was unsure what the future held but seemed to have few regrets. As he wrote to a friend that same month, "I do not know whether it will be approved or not; but it does not matter; I did what I had to."[112]

Back in Tonkin

After many months of inactivity, Rivière received a reinforcement force of seven hundred that had been organized by Naval and Colonial Minister Jauréguiberry in late February 1883.[113] Their timing was impeccable, as the commander would soon receive intelligence from a reliable source that a Chinese company was in the process of gaining mining concessions near the port of Hon Gai on the Tonkin coast; alarmingly, with the apparent backing of mining interests in the United Kingdom. Rivière was also disturbed by a proposal recently put forward by the French minister to China, Frédéric Bourée, to cede the port area to China in a broader division of spheres of influence in Tonkin.[114] Thus, on March 12, Rivière decided once again to take matters into his own hands, ordering the occupation of the port, which was carried out by one of his field commanders two days later.

Rivière then set his sights on the citadel of Nam Dinh, about 100 km down-river from Hanoi. According to Rivière, the citadel's governor and his army were displaying "the most hostile attitude" toward the French and were apparently preparing to create barriers along their stretch of the Red River, potentially cutting off French access to the sea.[115] This posed, according to Rivière, an intolerable risk. On March 19, he wrote to Le Myre de Vilers's replacement as governor of Cochinchina, Charles Thomson, announcing that the "situation is serious enough in Nam-Dinh for me to decide to attack the Citadel."[116]

On March 26, Rivière arrived at Nam Dinh at the head of a force of eight hundred and sent the governor an ultimatum: hand over the citadel or be removed by force. When no surrender was forthcoming, the French forces initiated their attack at 7:00 a.m. the following morning. While the Annamese defenders put up a spirited resistance, they were, ultimately, no match for French firepower and tactics, and, by nightfall, the French tricolor was flying over the citadel. The attack cost the French just one dead and two wounded, while they inflicted as many as one thousand casualties on their Annamese opponents.[117] The following day, on March 27, Rivière wrote to Governor Thomson, proudly informing him that he had taken the Nam Dinh citadel and that, between Hanoi and Nam Dinh, France was now in control of the Red River Delta.[118] It is clear that Rivière had broader motivations for these conquests, beyond the case-specific factors he cited for each. Reflecting on events a few weeks later, Rivière wrote to a friend, "I decided myself to do what [the Government] couldn't make up their minds to make me do." With these acquisitions, he continued, the government "will be forced to move on the Tonkin question. . . . I do not yet know if they will be happy in France with what I did. [But] I have done what had to be done."[119] Rivière was clearly frustrated by his government's inaction and was aiming to force its hand.

While Rivière was carrying out the conquest of Nam Dinh, Black Flags and Vietnamese armed forces carried out a large-scale counterattack on the Hanoi Citadel.[120] They were repelled by the French garrison defending the fortress, but news of the attack alarmed Rivière, leading him to rush back upriver to Hanoi where he arrived on April 2.[121] In the weeks that followed, Commander Rivière became increasingly concerned about reports of large concentrations of Black Flags and Vietnamese troops gathered in the villages of Bac Ninh and Son Tay, each within 35 km of Hanoi. Contributing to the tension, a series of provocative placards were posted at the gates of the Hanoi Citadel, purportedly by the Black Flags, taunting and threatening the French occupiers.[122] In what, it turned out, would be his final letter to Governor Thomson, on May 16, Rivière pointed out that the "situation is not without a certain gravity" and argued that it was "necessary[,] to get out of the difficulties we are in, to capture Bac-Ninh and Son-Tay."[123]

At 4:00 a.m. on May 19, 1883, Rivière and a force of approximately five hundred headed out from Hanoi toward Son Tay.[124] Little did they know but a staff member of a local Hanoi hostel where some of the French soldiers were staying had caught wind of the planned attack and informed the Black Flags in advance.[125] Just 4 km from Hanoi, the French force was ambushed and surrounded on three sides by a Black Flags army, forcing them into a disorganized fighting retreat.[126] In the course of the retreat, the commander was shot in the shoulder, where he collapsed—not far from where François Garnier himself was killed nearly ten years earlier. He was then dragged off alive by the Black Flags to a military base nearby, where he soon thereafter perished. And, like Garnier before him, Rivière too had his head removed after his death.[127] (See figure 5.1.)

Back in Paris

While Rivière had been engaging in the conquests of Hon Gai and Bac Ninh, political winds were shifting back in the capital. After the three-week tenure of a brief caretaker ministry in early February 1883, Jules Ferry formed his second

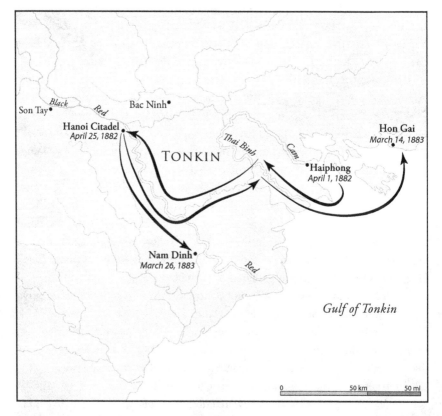

FIGURE 5.1. Henri Rivière Tonkin campaign, April 1882–May 1883. Created by Beehive Mapping.

ministry on February 22, approximately three months before Rivière was killed in Tonkin. He named Paul-Armand Challemel-Lacour as his foreign minister and Charles Brun as his naval and colonial minister. From the second day of his appointment, Challemel-Lacour got to work on the Tonkin crisis, finding it both more serious and more urgent than he had supposed from the outside.[128] Challemel-Lacour conferred with Naval and Colonial Minister Brun and Prime Minister Ferry, and they decided to hold a cabinet meeting on March 5 to decide the fate of the Tonkin question.[129]

Effecting a prompt withdrawal would have been no small feat. It turned out that Rivière's actions had placed constraints on French leaders that made pulling out of Tonkin and relinquishing the captured territory exceedingly difficult. For one, Rivière had independently conquered much of the Tonkin Delta and, in doing so, had substantially sunk the costs of acquiring this territory. However, a second and more important reason it would have been difficult to retrench was the engagement of French national honor and prestige.[130] French leaders both in Saigon and in Paris clearly saw France's honor as being at stake once Tonkin had been partially acquired. For instance, on June 11, 1882, just six weeks after Rivière's seizure of the Hanoi Citadel, Governor Le Myre de Vilers wrote in a letter to Naval and Colonial Minister Jauréguiberry that, if France did not take further action in the region, "we will lose our influence, because our abstention will be considered an act of weakness and cowardice."[131] In another report from the governor, sent a week later, Naval and Colonial Minister Jauréguiberry penciled on the margin: "We cannot go back now!"[132] The naval and colonial minister had made similar arguments when he requested additional troops to establish a protectorate in the fall and winter of 1882. In his letter of October 15 to Prime Minister Duclerc, he wrote that France in Tonkin was in "a state of affairs which, if continued, could compromise our honor." He claimed it was "too late to abandon a country where our flag has been flying for eight years" and added that "what was possible without dishonor to the Republic at the beginning of 1880 is no longer [possible]."[133] The interim naval and colonial minister François de Mahy agreed, writing in February 1883 to incoming Prime Minister Jules Ferry that the abandonment of Tonkin "may have, for our influence in the Far East . . . consequences such as I cannot call enough to your utmost attention."[134] In short, concerns about French national honor and prestige made backing down in Tonkin appear very difficult to leaders in Paris.[135]

Furthermore, the geopolitical risk associated with retaining the territories, and even pushing further into Tonkin, appeared to be manageable to most leaders in Paris. There were few great power interests at stake in Tonkin, and the threat of China—which had tributary interests in Tonkin—forcibly resisting a French advance was consistently downplayed or ignored.[136] In the view of many

French leaders, China had acquiesced to the annexations of Cochinchina in the 1860s without protest and similarly accepted the 1874 treaty with Hue, which stated that it was to be "independent of all foreign powers," including China.[137] As a contemporary chronicler of events in Tonkin put it, to most French leaders, "China was considered *une qualité négligeable*" (a negligible quality).[138]

These views were present in the years and months preceding Rivière's conquest of Hanoi as well. For instance, in July 1880, when Prime Minister Freycinet agreed to the plan to occupy Tonkin just before his ministry fell, he wrote to the naval and colonial minister that there "would be no complications to fear on the side of China, which perhaps would even gladly see that it is relieved of the intermittent policing that it is currently conducting" on the Red River.[139] The Cochinchina governor Le Myre de Vilers similarly argued in a letter to Paris in December 1881 that, if they occupied Tonkin, the "Chinese government will abstain; we won't provide it with a basis for intervention because we will make no declaration of war."[140] This argument was passed on almost verbatim from Naval and Colonial Minister Jauréguiberry to Prime Minister Freycinet during his second ministry in March 1882.[141]

This downplaying of the China threat persisted in the aftermath of Rivière's April 1882 conquest of the Hanoi Citadel.[142] For instance, in a letter from Governor Le Myre de Vilers to Naval and Colonial Minister Jauréguiberry on May 22, the governor wrote, referring to the possibility of Hue seeking the aid of Beijing, that it "is possible even probable; but it is not dangerous, for the moment at least."[143] In another letter on July 19, reporting on Chinese troop increases on the Tonkin border, Le Myre de Vilers wrote, "I don't think that . . . the Chinese demonstration is of serious importance,"[144] and this message was passed on to Prime Minister Duclerc in September.[145] In response, the prime minister wrote on September 26 that France had "every reason to hope that our good relations with China will not be seriously disturbed by our expedition on the Song-koi [Red River]" and added that the reported troop increase on the border was likely "a measure taken by the Government of Beijing to inspire the confidence in the Court of Hué, and to maintain in it the illusion of an intervention."[146]

This is not to say that there were no concerns in the French government. Frédéric Bourée, the French minister to China, sent a series of letters and cables to Paris through the fall and winter of 1882, reporting on Chinese troop increases and infiltration into Tonkin.[147] At one point, he even claimed he saw war as essentially "inevitable."[148] However, even Bourée had played a part in minimizing the China threat, claiming in an October 1882 letter to the prime minister that he was "almost certain that the Chinese Government will not care to expose its soldiers to compete with ours and that the imperial forces will retreat everywhere at our approach."[149] This downplaying of the geopolitical risk posed by China led to some wildly optimistic views among leaders in Paris. For instance, Naval and Colonial Minister Jauréguiberry wrote to Prime Minister Duclerc in October 1882 that the Chinese "would have nothing to lose, but everything to gain, on the contrary, from recognizing our Protectorate."[150] In sum, while there were pockets and periods of concern, the general trend among government officials in Paris and Saigon was to perceive relatively little geopolitical risk posed by China's interests in Tonkin.

Paris Decides

The cabinet of Prime Minister Jules Ferry decided in their March 5 meeting that France would establish a full protectorate over Tonkin, by military force if necessary. Minister Bourée in Beijing was recalled and Foreign Minister Challemel-Lacour was tasked with explaining the cabinet's decision to the French legislature, which he did on March 13. In his remarks, the foreign minister leaned heavily on themes of French national honor, claiming that "France had obligations that it could not shirk" and that prolonging the situation in the region would only cause "a deep attack on our authority in Annam, in Tonkin, and in Cochinchina." He further argued that a "retreat" from Tonkin would result in "the certain ruin of our influence, and the loss of our prestige throughout the Orient."[151] And the government's optimism with respect to the China threat continued apace. On March 14, Challemel-Lacour wrote to the recently recalled Minister Bourée (who would not leave Beijing until his replacement arrived a few months later) that the establishment of a French protectorate in Tonkin "can only be profitable to China itself, by ensuring order on its borders."[152]

The decision on Tonkin having been made, all that was left for the Ferry cabinet was to put forward a specific plan and to request the necessary funds from the Chamber of Deputies, which it did on April 26. Along with the request, Foreign Minister Challemel-Lacour included an explanatory statement for French legislators, where the government, again, heavily emphasized the importance of protecting French honor and prestige. France's inaction, he noted, "could be considered as marks of indecision or weakness and have not been without damaging the reputation of France in Asia." "A new abandonment of Tonkin," the foreign minister continued, "would be considered an abdication in these regions of the Far East, where our flag appears with honor among those of the main trading powers." Thus, Challemel-Lacour noted in closing, the government's policy was to "establish ourselves firmly in Tonkin, and to affirm in the eyes of all our resolution to stay there."[153]

The Chamber of Deputies voted on a request of 5.5 million francs to cover three thousand French soldiers, one thousand locals, and nine additional gunboats for Tonkin on May 15, 1883. The measure passed by the wide margin of 351–48.[154] The bill was amended in the days that followed and was returned to the chamber for a second vote on May 26—the very day that news of Rivière's killing and beheading at the hands of the Black Flags had reached Paris.[155] This time it passed unanimously, with Naval and Colonial Minister Brun writing to the Cochinchina governor Thomson that the legislature had "voted unanimously on credit for Tonkin. France will avenge its glorious children!"[156]

The French minister Bourée finally left Beijing in mid-May 1883. This put an end to any consistent warnings of the risks of war with China for good. In his instructions to Bourée's successor, Foreign Minister Challemel-Lacour casually noted that recent events had "cooled our relations with China" and asked the new minister to "facilitate a rapprochement between our two countries."[157] In a separate set of instructions, the foreign minister pointed out that China had "no valid motive to take umbrage with a project which it will naturally be called upon to take advantage [of]" and argued that China's "military preparations . . . should only be considered as attempts at intimidation."[158] The new minister in Beijing, for his part, took an entirely more laid back approach than his predecessor had. He reported on June 18 that China's military preparations "have been exaggerated," and he argued a few days later that a "powerful maritime diversion made on the coasts of the Celestial Empire would suffice" to keep it from intervening.[159] In early July, the French minister similarly argued in a letter to Foreign Minister Challemel-Lacour that the Chinese "will be careful not to declare war, because peace is too advantageous to them." And, even if it came to conflict, he continued, "China's forces on land and sea are singularly overrated . . . poorly armed, most of them undisciplined, they would certainly not hold in front of six battalions supported by a strong artillery."[160] Prime Minister Ferry had a similar impression. In a June 21 conversation with the Chinese minister in Paris, Ferry was told that "China has no thoughts of aggression; it knows that France is strong enough to do what it wants in the Kingdom of Annam" and that China "will not consider [French] actions in Tonkin as a cause of war or rupture."[161] This conversation, along with the messages he was getting from other members of his ministry, gave Prime Minister Ferry the impression that France's "firm attitude and known resolve" was working. He saw China as backing down.[162]

Conquest and War

The initial French force of three thousand, along with its native recruits, reached the Tonkin shores in early July 1883.[163] With the force having taken a few coastal territories and worked its way through the Tonkin Delta, the determination was made in Paris in late July to bring the invasion to the heart of Annamese power, in Hue.[164] On August 16, French naval forces assembled in the harbor of Danang and two days later initiated a bombardment of the Thuan-An fortresses, which protected the imperial palace at the entrance to the Hue River.[165] On August 20, an armistice was agreed to and, on August 25 1883, France and Annam signed the Treaty of Hue, establishing a French protectorate over both Annam and Tonkin.[166] The entirety of what is now Vietnam was in French hands, where it would remain until after France's catastrophic loss at the Battle of Dien Bien Phu in 1954.

France's conquest of Tonkin and Annam would, indeed, spark the war with China that French leaders had seen as so unlikely. Beijing's refusal to withdraw its forces from northern Tonkin, as well as its continued support for the Black Flags, led French forces to attack the Black Flags' stronghold at Son Tay in December 1883, sparking the Sino-French War. At its peak, France had some 35,000 forces engaged in the war, which would last until June 1885, when China recognized France's protectorate over Tonkin and Annam with the Treaty of Tientsin.[167] Between the French conquest of Tonkin and Annam and the Sino-French War that followed, France lost 4,222 killed and wounded in combat as well as an additional 5,223 French and colonial soldiers lost to disease. Chinese and Vietnamese deaths are estimated to have exceeded 10,000.[168]

This chapter has presented comparative case studies of failed and successful inadvertent expansion by France in Tonkin in 1873–74 and 1882–83. Both cases strongly support the theory of inadvertent expansion presented in chapter 1. First, both cases show how inadvertent expansion is a manifestation of a principal-agent problem—that divergent preferences and information asymmetries favoring the periphery enabled agents to engage in unauthorized conquests. Second, the 1882–83 case supports the argument that even a partial conquest of territory can place constraints—in this case, concerns over French national honor and prestige—on leaders that make withdrawal exceedingly difficult. And third, in both cases, the decision in the capital of whether to accept or reject the fait accompli was crucially determined by the geopolitical risk associated with doing so. In the 1873–74 case, French leaders were so concerned with how Britain and Germany would react to the acquisition of Tonkin that, given their weak position in Europe, they opted for an expeditious withdrawal. In contrast, in the 1882–83 case, there were no other great power interests at stake, and French leaders consistently downplayed the risk of China intervening, leading them to accept the fait accompli and establish a protectorate over Tonkin and Annam. It turned out, in this case, that they were wrong—China would indeed fight over Tonkin and the war was ultimately quite costly for France. But the expectations, perceptions, and risk tolerances that informed the decision to accept the fait accompli are in line with the theory's expectations.

Much of the power of this chapter's evidence is in the striking similarity between the two cases. Each one presents the same great power, in the same region, dealing with the very same territory, and both involve an insubordinate French naval officer, who engaged in the same process of acquisition, and in which the officer was killed by the same enemy in largely the same manner on almost the very same spot, separated by fewer than ten years. While there is no such thing as a perfect comparative case—and, in reality, all else is never held equal—the similarities across these two cases should give us confidence that the important variation observed in perceived geopolitical risk played an important role in the variation observed in the outcomes: failed inadvertent expansion in 1874 and successful inadvertent expansion in 1883.

THE DILEMMA OF INADVERTENT EXPANSION

Japan and Italy

> When the military preparations are completed we do not need to go to great lengths to find the motive or occasion. . . . (If necessary, the Kwantung Army could) create the occasion for this with a plot and force the nation to go along.
>
> —Ishiwara Kanji, 1931

This chapter examines two more "modern" cases of inadvertent expansion: Japan and Italy. The first case presents the Japanese government's acquisition of Manchuria in 1931–32. The second presents the Italian government's decision to reject the territorial fait accompli presented by its peripheral agents in the port city of Fiume in 1919–20. The primary value of this pair of cases is threefold. First, it presents the book's fourth pair of comparative theory-testing cases, showing the important role geopolitical risk plays in enabling or preventing inadvertent expansion. Second, both cases occur well into the era of modern communications, showing how inadvertent expansion can occur even with all of the benefits of near-instantaneous communication. And third, the chapter highlights the painful dilemmas that inadvertent expansion can thrust into leaders' laps, what I referred to in chapter 1 as the "dilemma of inadvertent expansion." In both cases, leaders in the capital simultaneously perceived significant geopolitical risk associated with acquiring the territories in question *and* the threat of severe domestic political punishment for backing down. And, while in both cases the leaders' decisions appear to be primarily guided by considerations of geopolitical risk, the cases highlight the delicate balance leaders must strike in these circumstances, and how they struggle to do so.

This chapter presents the book's only direct comparison of two different great powers. However, for four reasons Italy and Japan in the early twentieth century is a useful comparison to test the theory of inadvertent expansion. First, for most of their history, Japan and Italy were the "least of the great powers," existing largely in the shadows of more powerful partners and rivals in Europe and the Western

Hemisphere.[1] Second, both Japan and Italy were relatively late to modernize and, therefore, were more recent entrants to the great power club, having to catch up quickly to contend with their more established peers.[2] Third, politically, both were "mixed regimes," experimenting with electoral democracy but soon taking sharply authoritarian turns—for Italy under Benito Mussolini, in 1922, and for Japan under military dictatorship, in 1932. Fourth, in both cases, the territory in question was relatively close to the capital under conditions of rapid communications technology, ameliorating some of the more severe principal-agent problems on display in previous chapters. Therefore, while no comparison is perfect, Japan and Italy are highly comparable along many important dimensions, holding a number of factors fixed while their outcomes vary.

"Ishiwara's War": Japan in Manchuria, 1931–32

The Japanese Empire acquired Manchuria (now northeastern China) between September 1931 and March 1932. The conquest of Manchuria was independently planned and orchestrated by mid-ranking officers of the colonial Kwantung Army, defying the orders of their civilian and military superiors in Tokyo. The theory of inadvertent expansion makes three central arguments that are borne out in this case. First, that unauthorized peripheral expansion results from a principal-agent problem, combining a divergence of preferences between leaders in the capital and their agents on the periphery and information asymmetries favoring the peripheral agents. In this case, there was a strong divergence of preferences between civilian leaders in Tokyo and the Kwantung Army in Manchuria, and the Kwantung Army enjoyed considerable information asymmetries as a result of deeply pathological civil-military relations. Second, that once a territory is partly or wholly acquired, a number of constraints on leadership emerge that make it difficult to relinquish the acquisition quickly and easily. In the case of Japan in Manchuria, the Kwantung Army's early successes sunk the costs of its acquisition, and there were some truly severe domestic political costs associated with withdrawal. And third, that significant geopolitical risk associated with acquisition will discourage leaders in the capital from acquiring the territory in question, leading them to reject the territorial fait accompli. This argument is, in some ways, doubly supported in this case. In the opening weeks of the conquest, concerns over geopolitical risk led civilian leaders in Tokyo to try to rein in the Kwantung Army and to withdraw from newly acquired territories in Manchuria. However, as the crisis progressed, the manageability of these risks became clear: Chinese armies in Manchuria adopted a policy of nonresistance, the Soviets refrained from intervening, and the other great powers' reactions were largely muted. In light of these realities, resistance to the conquest by the central government progressively weakened over the course of the crisis, and the case for central authorization became progressively stronger. These pressures led to a fall of the government, its replacement with a more expansion-oriented leadership, and, ultimately, the establishment of the Japanese puppet state of Manchukuo on March 1, 1932.

Historical Background

On the eve of the invasion of Manchuria in September 1931, Japan had had a continuous presence on the Chinese mainland since its surprise victory in the Russo-Japanese War in 1905. Under the Treaty of Portsmouth, the Russian Empire ceded to Japan its lease of the Liaodong Peninsula (which would be renamed the Kwantung Leased Territory) as well as the South Manchuria Railway, the 1,129 km rail system with lines running from Port Arthur to Changchun and from Mukden to Antung.[3] Manchuria as a whole totaled roughly 985,000 km^2 in China's northeast region, bordering the Korean Peninsula to the south and the Soviet Far East to the north and east.[4] It had a population of 30 million, approximately 220,000 of which were Japanese migrants who had traveled there to work for the South Manchuria Railway or to pursue other opportunities.[5] This was shortly after the "Warlord Era" in China (1916–28), when Manchuria had been ruled by the influential warlord Zhang Zuolin. While China would be weakly unified after Chiang Kai-shek's "Northern Expedition" in 1928, Manchuria still had a great deal of autonomy from the Nationalist regime in Nanjing.[6]

Stationed in the Kwantung Leased Territory, and all along the South Manchuria Railway, was the Kwantung Army, a colonial branch of the Imperial Japanese Army, headquartered in Port Arthur.[7] Totaling just 10,400 personnel, the Kwantung Army was commanded by a series of generals on two-year rotations and staffed by a few hundred mid-ranking officers.[8] Among these was a forty-two-year-old lieutenant colonel by the name of Ishiwara Kanji.[9] A career army officer, Ishiwara was intense, idealistic, and intellectually gifted.[10] Yet, he was also strident, impulsive, and contemptuous of Japan's Taishō-era political leadership.[11] After converting to Nichiren Buddhism in his early thirties, Ishiwara developed radical, apocalyptic views of a future world-altering clash between Japan and its enemies in the West, particularly the United States.[12] Preparing Japan for such an eventuality became his life-defining mission, the first step of which was to take place in Manchuria. Ishiwara was joined on the Kwantung Army staff in June 1929 by his childhood friend and classmate, Itagaki Seishirō. Despite many personal differences, what the two shared in common were a deep conviction that Manchuria presented threats and opportunities for Japan and that outright occupation was the necessary response.[13] Ishiwara and Itagaki were the actors on Japan's imperial periphery who played a crucial role in planning and executing of the invasion of Manchuria.[14]

The prime minister of Japan at this time was Wakatsuki Reijirō. His second stint at the premiership, he and many members of his cabinet tended to take a dovish view of Japan's relations with China and Manchuria. Chief among these was the famed diplomat and foreign minister, Shidehara Kijūrō, whose very name came to be associated with the liberal views that defined Japanese foreign policy in the 1920s. Standing somewhat outside this more liberal consensus was War Minister Minami Jirō, an army general whose foreign policy views, naturally, hewed more closely to those of the Imperial Japanese Army. Finally, there was the head of state, the Shōwa Emperor Hirohito, who was only a few years into his reign but was proving to be a more politically active emperor than his recent predecessors.[15] These were the leaders in the capital Tokyo who would be dragged unwittingly, and mostly unwillingly, into further territorial acquisitions on the Chinese mainland.[16]

Manchuria, on the eve of the Japanese invasion, was ruled by Zhang Xueliang, the son and successor of the warlord Zhang Zuolin. While the father, Zuolin, had been an ally of the Japanese in Manchuria against the government in Nanjing, his unauthorized 1928 assassination by a member of the Kwantung Army would push his son, Xueliang, to cooperate more closely with Nanjing against the Japanese.[17] Zhang Xueliang was the head of what was known as the Fengtien Army, a force of approximately 250,000 personnel.[18] To the south, on the other side of the Great Wall, was the recently established Nationalist Kuomintang regime of Chiang Kai-shek, with its capital in Nanjing. And to the north of Manchuria was the Soviet Union, which had been established less than a decade earlier at the conclusion of the Russian Civil War. In any case of armed conflict involving the Kwantung Army, the key questions were what kind of resistance Zhang's forces would put up, and whether the Kuomintang or the Soviet Red Army would intervene.

Tokyo and Manchuria

Leaders in Tokyo faced severe principal-agent problems vis-à-vis the Kwantung Army in Manchuria as a result of information asymmetries favoring the army and a divergence of preferences between capital and periphery. First, there were stark information asymmetries in favor of the Kwantung Army due to its substantial institutional autonomy and unusually weak civilian oversight over the Japanese military.[19] According to articles 11 and 12 of the Meiji Constitution of 1889, the army and navy were overseen by the emperor himself, not the cabinet or the Japanese Diet (parliament). These same constitutional provisions formally institutionalized the military's traditional "right of supreme command" (*dokudan senkō*), the principle allowing staff officers of field armies autonomy from civilian control in the areas of operational planning and execution.[20] Japanese law also mandated that the military had to approve ministers of the army and navy for appointment and that the resignation of either of these officers could lead to the dissolution of the cabinet.[21] These institutional realities were not helped by the fact that the Kwantung Army itself was the primary source of information coming out of Manchuria. While there were Japanese Foreign Ministry consulates in Mukden, Antung, Dairen, and other major cities in the region, they were lightly staffed and often had to rely on army sources themselves.[22] There was also the South Manchuria Railway; however, its management was generally sympathetic to the views of the Kwantung Army and, therefore, willing to put a similar "spin" on information it sent to Tokyo.[23] These constitutional and informational conditions gave the Kwantung Army a high degree of independence, greatly hampering civilian and even central military control.

Second, there was a sharp divergence of preferences between the leaders in Tokyo and the Kwantung Army in Manchuria. Prime Minister Wakatsuki and much of his cabinet were highly cautious when it came to China policy. This was the era of "Shidehara Diplomacy," whose core tenets were international cooperation, economic diplomacy, and nonintervention in China's domestic political affairs.[24] Wakatsuki and Foreign Minister Shidehara, therefore, advocated for maintaining the territorial status quo in China and for dealing with any existing problems through negotiation. War Minister Minami's policy views on Manchuria were more hawkish than the views of his cabinet colleagues, though he did want to tread carefully, was concerned with discipline within the Kwantung Army, and was willing to restrain its more radical elements.[25] And while Emperor Hirohito's specific policy views with respect to Manchuria were not always clear or consistent, he did favor a more conciliatory approach to China and repeatedly argued for the need to maintain discipline within the army.[26] In short, leaders in Tokyo embodied what I referred to in chapter 1 as "the view from the capital." Their responsibilities were broad and weighty, being concerned not only with policy in and around Manchuria but with the well-being and defense of Japan, the interests of the empire as a whole, and relations with other regional states and global great powers. And being cloistered away in the capital Tokyo, they felt few of the daily effects of the nationalist, anti-Japanese upheaval in Manchuria and saw little urgency to act.[27]

The Kwantung Army, in contrast, was much less cautious in its China policy. They were far less concerned about the possibility of a Soviet intervention or of the reactions of the other great powers. Being away from the main islands, the Kwantung Army was largely isolated from the domestic politics of Japan.[28] With little knowledge of, or experience dealing with, international trade and finance, they were far less concerned about the risk of economic sanctions.[29] And many Kwantung Army officers were largely indifferent to the opinions of the other great powers and their publics.[30] Thus, many members of the Kwantung Army and, most particularly, officers, such as Ishiwara and Itagaki, advocated for the complete annexation of Manchuria.[31] Manchuria was a rich source of valuable natural resources, which would be necessary in the approaching war of attrition with the West.[32] And invading Manchuria would forestall what Ishiwara saw as an inevitable Soviet occupation, preventing, in his terms, the "communization of Asia."[33] Ishiwara and many of his Kwantung Army colleagues, in sum, clearly embodied the "view from the frontier." Their responsibilities were relatively narrow, being concerned with defending the roughly 3,700 km^2 that Japan possessed in Manchuria, rather than the empire as a whole.[34] And their sense of urgency to take action in Manchuria was great, as they faced Chinese nationalist upheaval daily and directly. As the historian and Ishiwara biographer Mark Peattie puts it, "Ishiwara in a very real sense was stationed on a sort of Japanese 'imperial frontier,' a semi-colonial environment in which the proximity of danger and opportunity served to reinforce the conviction that the clearest solution to national problems lay close at hand."[35]

The "Mukden Incident"

While the idea of separating Manchuria from China by force had emerged within the Kwantung Army as early as 1916, planning in earnest for an invasion began in July 1929.[36] The Kwantung Army was numerically and materially inferior to its adversaries, lacking mechanized forces and aircraft and being lightly equipped in artillery, engineering, and transport.[37] Thus, it was essential that the plans be meticulously organized, stressing the importance of intelligence, rigorous training, and the use of surprise, speed, and the concentration of force.[38] The idea was to devise a series of tightly interlinked operational plans that would trigger one another in a sequential fashion, creating a process that, once set in motion, would be very difficult to stop or reverse. Then, all that would be needed was a crisis of a sufficient magnitude to light the fuse, which would be easy to orchestrate. As Ishiwara put it in May 1931, if needed, the Kwantung Army could "create the occasion for this with a plot and force the nation to go along."[39] Operational plans were finalized by the summer of 1931.

Despite the information asymmetries favoring the army in Manchuria, it would prove difficult to keep the conspiracy a secret for long. In August and early September 1931, rumors began to circulate in the capital that trouble was brewing in Manchuria, prompting reporters to regularly press the prime minister and foreign minister for more information.[40] On August 18, a top adviser to Emperor Hirohito said to an aide, "I can't help but think the imperial army is cooking something up in Manchuria, Mongolia, and China."[41] On September 4, the Foreign Ministry received a telegram from Manchuria warning that "a plot is afoot among young officers in the Kwantung Army to thrash the Chinese army."[42] These rumors were taken so seriously that, on September 11, the emperor himself summoned War Minister Minami to question him on the state of military discipline.[43] While Minami assured him that things were under control, the emperor admonished him to "be even more cautious."[44]

On September 15, Foreign Minister Shidehara received a telegram from the consul general in Mukden, informing him that the "Kwantung Army [is] assembling troops and bringing out munitions[;] seem likely to start action in the near future."[45] That same day, the War Ministry dispatched the General Staff intelligence section chief Major General Tatekawa Yoshistugu to Manchuria to remind the Kwantung Army of the cabinet's policy of nonintervention in China and to put a stop to any impending plots. Yet, news of Tatekawa's trip was cabled from an accomplice of Itagaki's in Army Headquarters in Tokyo, warning: "Plot discovered. Tatekawa coming; strike first to avoid implicating him."[46] Ishiwara and Itagaki took this advice to heart. While the invasion of Manchuria had been planned for September 27, they moved it up to the evening of the eighteenth, the day that Tatekawa was supposed to arrive.[47] Upon his arrival, Itagaki then had Tatekawa whisked away to be wined and dined at a local restaurant, where he would ultimately pass out.[48] Just a few hours later, the invasion of Manchuria was launched.

At 10:20 p.m. on September 18, 1931, there was an explosion on the southbound track of the South Manchuria Railway at Liutiaokou, just north of Mukden. The charge had been set by a lieutenant in the Kwantung Army, with the aim of framing Zhang Xueliang's army with the sabotage. Local Kwantung Army conspirators then rushed to the scene, claimed they were fired on by Chinese soldiers and returned fire, and pursued the enemy while calling for reinforcements.[49] In accordance with Kwantung Army plans established by Ishiwara and Itagaki, a local battalion commander then ordered an attack on the Fengtien Army barracks at Mukden, which housed as many as ten thousand personnel. As Zhang had recently ordered his troops to under no circumstances resort to force in any confrontation with the Japanese, the barracks were overrun within a few hours and at minimal cost to the Kwantung Army.[50] Just four hours after the initial explosion, the Imperial Japanese Army in Korea received a request from the Kwantung Army to dispatch reinforcements, which began to mobilize immediately.[51] By 1:00 p.m. the next day, Mukden as a whole was under Kwantung Army control, and by 3:00 p.m., the South Manchuria Railway's terminal city of

Changchun, to the north, was occupied. Within less than twenty-four hours, the invasion of Manchuria was well underway.

Tokyo Reacts

The first meeting of Prime Minister Wakatsuki's cabinet to deal with what became known as the "Mukden Incident" was held in Tokyo on September 19 at 8:00 a.m., the morning after the explosion. It was agreed, in line with Wakatsuki's, Foreign Minister Shidehara's, and Emperor Hirohito's preferences, that the crisis should be localized, the spread of hostilities contained, and the dispute settled as expeditiously as possible.[52] As Wakatsuki put it that morning, the plan was to "immediately instruct the commanding officer of the Kwantung Army not to enlarge the theater of conflict nor to bombard and occupy government buildings and fortifications."[53] War Minister Minami was more sympathetic to the Kwantung Army's position but felt bound by the cabinet's, and especially the emperor's, wishes, and so he relayed these orders to the Kwantung Army at 6:00 p.m. that evening.[54] The desire to promptly settle the crisis, and to contain and even reverse the Kwantung Army's expansion to the greatest extent possible, would be the Wakatsuki cabinet's position for the remainder of its tenure.[55]

The cabinet's primary concern was the geopolitical risk associated with expanding further into Manchuria. To start, leaders in Tokyo were concerned about the hundreds of thousands of Manchurian forces led by Zhang Xueliang.[56] Then there was the Soviet Union to worry about. As noted earlier, the Soviet Union shared a lengthy border with Manchuria and had interests in northern Manchuria, operating the Chinese Eastern Railway there. While the Soviets had only approximately one hundred thousand military personnel east of the Ural Mountains, it was industrializing rapidly, being midway through its first five-year plan.[57] In 1929, just two years earlier, the Red Army had intervened and routed the Fengtien Army when it threatened the Chinese Eastern Railway.[58] Thus, the Soviet Union seemed to have both the capabilities and the will to intervene effectively when its interests in the region were threatened. While many military planners saw the risks of Soviet intervention to be relatively low, Tokyo's position was one of caution regarding this possibility.[59] This was especially the case when it came to the possible extension of hostilities north of the South Manchuria Railway.[60] To try to head off this potential, the cabinet issued a resolution on September 23, ordering the Kwantung Army to stay out of the north.[61] These concerns were enunciated repeatedly by Prime Minister Wakatsuki, Foreign Minister Shidehara, and even War Minister Minami over the course of the crisis.[62]

The cabinet was also deeply concerned with the reaction of the other great powers, the members of the Nine Power Treaty and the League of Nations at large. In the cabinet's first meeting dealing with the crisis, on the morning of September 19, Prime Minister Wakatsuki rhetorically queried War Minister Minami: if the Mukden incident turned out to be "a conspiracy of the Japanese army, what will Japan's position be in the eyes of the world?"[63] In the decade running up to the invasion of Manchuria, Japan's trade as a percentage of its gross domestic product amounted to an average of approximately 35 percent, and, thus, the threat of sanctions loomed particularly large.[64] In an October 1 cabinet meeting, Prime Minister Wakatsuki warned that "if Japan does not act with due consideration of her international position, Japan in the end will be isolated, and this will bring an unexpected misfortune upon the nation."[65] The following week, in response to the suggestion of setting up an autonomous regime in Manchuria, Wakatsuki said doing so would be "a violation of the Nine Power Treaty, and then the whole world will be our enemy. In view of the present economic situation, we are practically forced to be isolated."[66] Similar concerns of economic sanctions and diplomatic isolation were shared by Foreign Minister Shidehara, Emperor Hirohito, and central army authorities as well.[67]

Thus, the geopolitical risk associated with further acquisitions in Manchuria led the government in Tokyo to oppose the invasion of Manchuria and to try to rein in the Kwantung Army. However, the very fact of the Kwantung Army's unauthorized expansion constrained the cabinet in two important ways that would ultimately make withdrawal impossible to achieve. First, the Kwantung Army's quick successes in its operations in Manchuria firmly sunk the costs of the acquisition. By September 21, the Kwantung Army had secured all major centers along the South Manchuria Railway and had occupied Kirin, a city roughly 100 km east of Changchun. In mid-November, the army moved on Tsitsihar in north Manchuria, and, in early January 1932, it took Chinchow and Shanhaikwan, completing the occupation of the south right up to the Great Wall.[68] On February 5, Harbin was occupied, effectively completing the conquest of Manchuria.[69] These territories had been acquired at remarkably little cost. In taking the barracks at Mukden, the Kwantung Army suffered only twenty-four casualties in an assault on as many as 10,000 personnel.[70] The Kwantung Army suffered 155 casualties in its occupation of Changchun just days later.[71] Kirin was then occupied without firing a shot.[72] And Tsitsihar was taken over the course of less than two days, and the entry into the city itself was bloodless.[73] Overall, the Imperial Japanese Army suffered 2,530 killed in its conquest of Manchuria, a fairly low figure given the area of the territory acquired, the size of the forces it faced, and the kinds of casualties it had suffered in past wars.[74] (See figure 6.1.)

These successes were facilitated not only by the rigor of the Kwantung Army's training and the detail of its planning but also by the Fengtien Army's policy of nonresistance and the lack of intervention by the Soviet Union and the other

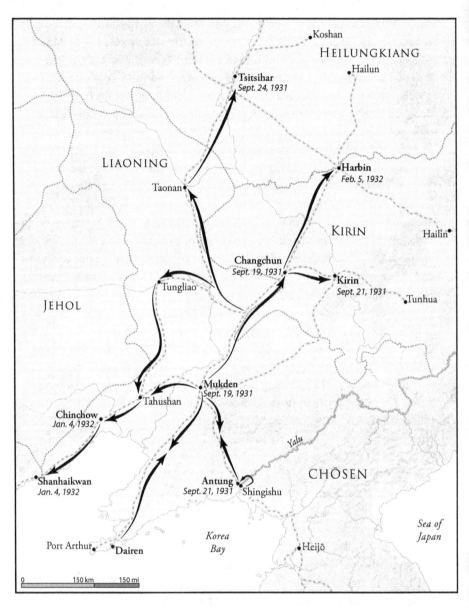

FIGURE 6.1. Kwantung Army Manchuria campaign, September 1931–February 1932. Created by Beehive Mapping.

great powers. The Soviet Union was far more concerned with domestic political issues, and with its European flank, than with events in Manchuria at this time, and Japan's leaders came to understand this.[75] In a strong signal of their defensive intentions, the Soviets proposed a nonaggression pact with Japan in December 1931 as the invasion was ongoing, an offer Tokyo ultimately passed up.[76] And the reactions of the United States and the other great powers were similarly muted.[77] This was, in part, because they were still preoccupied with the continuing fallout of the Great Depression of 1929. However, it is also clear that within a few days of the invasion, both the United States and the United Kingdom were aware that the central government had lost control of the Kwantung Army, and this, too, likely tempered their responses.[78] This absence of effective resistance severely weakened the arguments for restraint from leaders in the capital.[79] And it made the hawks, who had doubted the great powers' willingness to intervene, look prescient. Thus, the reservations of leaders in the capital would dissipate as the conquest progressed, as, one by one, their greatest fears failed to materialize.[80] And with every act of defiance committed by the Kwantung Army, the cabinet, Diet, and imperial court was rendered progressively weaker.[81]

A second important constraint that would crop up and make retrenchment difficult was the overwhelming support among the public and the press that the Kwantung Army's actions received.[82] In a severely economically depressed Japan, the idea of a resource-rich Manchuria as an "economic lifeline" came to be widely accepted among the populace, particularly in rural areas.[83] In fact, Ishiwara, Itagaki, and other conspirators had deliberately sought to shape elite and public opinion at home and in Manchuria in the months and weeks leading up to the invasion.[84] They did so by producing and distributing pamphlets, magazines, and books, and organizing speaking tours throughout Japan, with the support of some members of the General Staff in Tokyo.[85] They were greatly aided in this by the Manchurian Youth League, a nationalist organization formed with Kwantung Army backing in 1928. The league traveled widely throughout Japan in the months preceding the invasion, arguing for a stronger policy in Manchuria.[86]

Once the invasion was underway, the Kwantung Army continued to foster this support, setting up a propaganda office, holding regular briefings, distributing pamphlets, and broadcasting patriotic songs and messages over the radio.[87] All of this public support generated significant pressure on the cabinet to protect and defend Japanese nationals and soldiers in Manchuria. And the Kwantung Army would exploit this, using "false flag" operations as an excuse to occupy Manchurian cities. In Kirin, for instance, Kwantung Army agents were dispatched to foment unrest, which was then used as an excuse to invade, in September 1931, to "protect" Japanese property and nationals.[88] A similar strategy was attempted in Harbin that same month, though in this case the cabinet stood firm for the time being.[89] As time went by, the public and the press became increasingly unified behind the Kwantung Army's invasion of Manchuria. In the words of one scholar, the Japanese press had voluntarily turned itself into a "propaganda machine for the army."[90]

The overwhelming public support for the army's actions created easy avenues of attack for the cabinet's opponents in and out of government, severely raising the risk of domestic political punishment. The first attacks on the Minseitō Party cabinet of Prime Minister Wakatsuki came from the opposition Seiyūkai Party and its leaders.[91] Already prone to see the ruling cabinet's Shidehara Diplomacy in China as "weak-kneed," the opposition was quick to capitalize on the opportunity of a popular war in Manchuria to attack.[92] And these attacks ultimately paid off at the ballot box. While Wakatsuki came to office with his Minseitō Party holding a large majority in the Diet, the party would be absolutely trounced in the February 1932 elections, losing 127 seats (and their majority) to the opposition Seiyūkai.[93] This was a strong endorsement of the Kwantung Army's actions in Manchuria, and a vote against the Minseitō cabinet's cautious policy in China.[94]

Other forms of potential domestic political punishment faced by the cabinet were far more severe. For instance, the Sakurakai (Cherry Blossom Society), a secret ultranationalist organization within the Imperial Japanese Army, staged coup attempts against Minseitō cabinets in March and October 1931.[95] Since their formation in September 1930, they had advocated for a much more forceful policy in Manchuria and the establishment of a totalitarian government in Japan.[96] These plots were a grave concern for leaders in Tokyo. In late September 1931, a close adviser to the emperor pointed out that the "fact that their plot has succeeded in Manchuria will surely give a certain element of the Army the confidence that they can also do the same in Japan, and there lies the real danger."[97] While in neither case did the coup succeed, these were clear expressions of opposition to Shidehara Diplomacy in China. Coup rumors and threats continued to swirl among leaders in Tokyo through the early months of 1932 and would have a chilling effect on the cabinet, leading the foreign minister and others to soften their resistance to the Kwantung Army's insubordination.[98]

Besides coup plots, there were also assassination attempts. In November 1930, Prime Minister Hamaguchi Osachi was shot by an ultranationalist who was opposed to his signing of the London Naval Treaty, reducing Japan's naval armaments.[99] While Hamaguchi would survive the initial attempt, he would never recover his health and died from related complications less than a year later.[100] It would also come to light that the abortive October 1931 coup included planned assassinations of both Prime Minister Wakatsuki and Foreign Minister Shidehara, among others.[101] And Inukai Tsuyoshi, the Seiyūkai party leader who would succeed Wakatsuki as prime minister in December 1931, would himself be killed in office in May 1932. His residence was stormed by young officers of the Imperial Japanese Army and Navy who, despite the Inukai cabinet's more forward-leaning policy in Manchuria, were opposed to his attempts to subject the military to stricter civilian control.[102] Attempted and successful assassinations on other business and political elites in these years had profound effects on Japanese leaders and contributed to a general climate of fear among Tokyo's leadership.[103] As Shimada notes, "The spectacle of army terrorism was reducing the cabinet, and even the supreme command, to impotence."[104]

One final additional means by which the Kwantung Army manipulated the cabinet in Tokyo and enhanced their relative influence was through veiled threats of secession from Japan. In mid-October 1931, rumors began to circulate in government and military circles in Tokyo of the possibility of the Kwantung Army seceding and independently establishing itself in Manchuria.[105] While the origin of these rumors is a matter of dispute, during the invasion of Manchuria, Ishiwara Kanji is believed to have sent a telegram to Tokyo stating that "if the Japanese government constantly interferes . . . [then] we will have to break the glorious history of the Imperial army and separate ourselves from the empire."[106] The purpose of these threats was to put pressure on the government in Tokyo to support the Kwantung Army's expansionist policy in Manchuria.[107] And whatever doubts may have existed in Tokyo as to the credibility of these threats, central army authorities took them seriously enough to investigate carefully.[108] Thus, a combination of the Kwantung Army's sinking the costs of expansion and fervent support for their actions among the press and the public would effectively bind the hands of leaders in Tokyo, making restraining or withdrawing the Kwantung Army incredibly difficult.

Wakatsuki's Dilemma

Thus, the cabinet in Tokyo faced conflicting pressures in Manchuria. On the one hand, the early expected risk of Russian intervention and the potentially adverse reactions of the other great powers pushed them to tighten the reins on the Kwantung Army. On the other hand, the Kwantung Army's initial successes and the overwhelming support their exploits received from the public and the media pressed leadership to swim with the tide and accept their faits accomplis. The cross pressures created by these conflicting pressures presented the cabinet with a deeply distressing dilemma. The prime minister himself was discouraged, even despairing. As he told a secretary to the court the day following the invasion, "Under these circumstances I am quite powerless to restrain the military.

How can his majesty's military act without his sanction? What can I do? . . . I am in serious trouble."[109] Almost a month later, the prime minister was even more exasperated. As he told this same secretary on October 12:

> The present day situation is exceedingly unfavorable. I have endeav-
> ored, wholeheartedly, to better the international relations of Japan. At
> Cabinet meetings, I have frequently requested the War Minister to care-
> fully keep under control the actions of Japanese troops in Manchuria . . .
> However, Army officials act counter to this order whenever they find it
> convenient to do so. This sort of thing has its immediate repercussions
> in the League of Nations and the outcome is that the League feels it has
> been completely betrayed . . . I don't know what to do about the matter.
> Under this sort of conditions, I can't continue in my office indefinitely,
> but I can't resign right now. It is an exceedingly difficult situation.[110]

The dilemma facing the cabinet weighed heavily on Foreign Minister Shidehara as well. The Mukden consul general met with Shidehara on November 16 and described him as follows: "His demeanor seemed discouraged, disappointed, and dejected. One could recognize without words how much he was suffer-ing in this unprecedented emergency. I had unbound sympathy for him in his predicament."[111]

Tokyo Decides

These pressures were ultimately more than the leadership could bear. On Decem-ber 12, 1931, having lost the confidence of the imperial court, the Wakatsuki cabinet fell.[112] It was replaced the following day, as noted earlier, by the opposi-tion Seiyūkai cabinet of Inukai Tsuyoshi. By this point it had become clear that the geopolitical risk involved in acquiring Manchuria was far less severe than initially supposed, allowing the Inukai cabinet to adopt a more forward-leaning Manchuria policy than its predecessors. The rise of Inukai effectively ended seri-ous resistance by the central government to the Kwantung Army's conquest of Manchuria.[113]

Yet, the Inukai cabinet faced their own struggles with the Kwantung Army. Inukai, a hawk on Manchuria policy, was nonetheless concerned about the reac-tions of the great powers and was intent on restoring discipline within the army.[114] This was not just his preference; he was under orders to do so. As Emperor Hiro-hito admonished him upon his appointment as prime minister, "the Army's med-dling in domestic and foreign politics, endeavoring to have its way, is a situation which we must view with apprehension for the good of the nation. Be mindful of my anxiety."[115] The emperor again warned Inukai in late December to "maintain international trust" and to be aware of the impact the Kwantung Army's actions were having on international affairs.[116] Inukai would try, and he would worry. As he wrote to a senior army official in a February 15, 1932, letter:

> What is most worrisome is that the will of the senior officers is not thoroughly observed by their subordinates. For example, the action in Manchuria seems to have been brought about by the united power of the field-grade officers, who made their superiors acquiesce automatically. . . . It is feared that it might become customary to act single-mindedly upon the belief that should those who hold direct command over regiments unite and cause a disturbance, the superiors would finally give ex post facto approval to all matters, and that [such a trend] might create a major change in military control and discipline. . . . Therefore I wish the elders of the army to take remedial measures now, when the malady has not yet spread widely.[117]

But Inukai, too, was only minimally in control of events in Manchuria. With popular opinion surging behind the Kwantung Army, and with an incredibly hawkish cabinet advising him, in the long run Inukai had few options but to swim with the tide.[118] The invasion and occupation of Manchuria was an accomplished fact.

The Japanese puppet state of Manchukuo was proclaimed on March 1, 1932, marking the end of Japan's conquest of Manchuria. It was nominally independent but was, in fact, under the strict control of the Kwantung Army. As an internal Kwantung Army document from January 1932 put it, Manchukuo would adopt "the external form of a constitutional, republican government . . . but maintain the internal reality of a centralized dictatorship imbued with the political authority of our empire."[119] The Inukai cabinet would initially hold off on formally recognizing Manchukuo; notably, out of concern for the reactions of the other great powers.[120] Though, this, too, would occur in September 1932 with the same sense of inevitability that had characterized the entire affair. Inukai's cabinet would be the last party-led government in prewar Japan, and his May 1932 assassination was an important milestone in Japan's turn toward military dictatorship.

Despite their insubordination, Itagaki Seishirō and Ishiwara Kanji would be generously rewarded for their actions in Manchuria and would continue to rise through the ranks of the Imperial Japanese Army. Itagaki would be promoted to the rank of general and would serve as chief of staff of the Kwantung Army and the China Expeditionary Army, as well as a short stint as war minister. Ishiwara, for his part, was given the Order of the Golden Kite, third class, for the invasion of Manchuria, and was promoted to full colonel ahead of most of his Army Staff College classmates. He retired from the Imperial Japanese Army at the rank of lieutenant general in March 1941, just months before the outbreak of the Pacific War.[121] No individual had been as important to the Japanese conquest of Manchuria as Ishiwara. With the aid of Itagaki and others, he had been deeply involved in nearly all aspects of the invasion, from the Mukden Incident in September 1931 to the establishment of Manchukuo in March 1932. As Itagaki had told a friend a few weeks into the invasion, it was not Japan's war, or even the Kwantung Army's war, it was "Ishiwara's war."[122]

D'Annunzio's *Sacra Entrada*: Italy and Fiume, 1919–20

Italy refrained from acquiring the Adriatic port city of Fiume (now Rijeka, Croatia) between September 1919 and December 1920. The ultimately failed conquest of Fiume was independently planned and carried out by disgruntled members of the Italian armed forces, led by an eccentric Italian literary figure and World War I veteran. The theory of inadvertent expansion makes three arguments that are borne out in this case. First, that peripheral expansion is a manifestation of a principal-agent problem, enabled by a combination of diverse preferences between principal and agent and information asymmetries favoring the agents. In this case, the Italian government hoped to acquire Fiume by negotiation rather than by force but had only relatively weak control of the post–World War I Italian Army. Second, that once a territory is acquired, constraints emerge that make it very difficult for leaders in the capital to easily withdraw and return the territory. In the case of Italy in Fiume, early domestic political support for the venture bound the hands of the leadership in Rome. And third, that significant geopolitical risk associated with acquisition will discourage leaders in the capital from retaining the territory, leading to nonacceptance of the fait accompli. In the case at hand, Italy's World War I great power allies stood firm, absolutely refusing to accept the conquest of Fiume. These perceived risks would ultimately be decisive, leading the Italian government to sign the Treaty of Rapallo in November 1920, paving the way for the city's independence as the Free State of Fiume.

Historical Background

Fiume in the early twentieth century was a bustling small port city of approximately fifty thousand in the northeast corner of the Adriatic Sea, where the Dalmatian coast meets the Istrian Peninsula. As a port city nestled between Austrian and Hungarian territories within the Dual Monarchy's multiethnic empire and sitting just 120 km from Italy's pre–World War I border, Fiume's political and cultural identity had long been diverse and cosmopolitan. A 1910 census recorded the population as 49 percent Italian, 31 percent Slav, and 13 percent Magyar (Hungarian), with a smattering of Germans and other ethnicities.[123] Fiume was strategically and economically important as a regional economic hub with rail lines connecting Belgrade, Prague, Budapest, and Zagreb to the coast.[124]

With the collapse of the Austro-Hungarian Empire in the aftermath of World War I (1914–18), the Allies established in the city a joint occupation consisting of American, British, French, and Italian forces.[125] The Italians, for their part, were intent on ultimately annexing the city. While Fiume was not promised to Italy in the 1915 Treaty of London, which had conditioned Italy's entry into the war, many surrounding territories had been promised to it, and the city would have added to Italy's growing dominance of the Adriatic. After 462,000 dead, 954,000 wounded, and three-and-a-half years of fighting, many in Italy only hoped to receive what they saw as their due.[126] Yet, the status of Fiume would have to await the negotiations of the Paris Peace Conference, which were to begin in January 1919. And, as it would turn out, this port city of roughly 30 km² would be a major stumbling block in Italy's negotiations with its allies at Versailles.[127]

Italy's territorial ambitions in Fiume, and beyond, ran headlong into the Allies'—and particularly, the American president Woodrow Wilson's—interest in what was known as "national self-determination," the idea that nationalities should have the right to freely choose their sovereignty. Wilson flatly refused to accept the Treaty of London, arguing in the first of his Fourteen Points that only "open covenants . . . openly arrived at" should be recognized in the postwar international order. The president also claimed, for Italy specifically, that adjustment of its borders "should be effected along clearly recognizable lines of nationality," a clause that weakened many of Italy's territorial claims, Fiume included.[128] While, as noted earlier, Fiume proper had a plurality of Italians in its population, if the adjacent and deeply interconnected suburb of Suzak was added, the plurality went to the Slavs. And estimates based on political party affiliation in Fiume suggest that a narrow plurality favored annexation to the newly formed kingdom of Yugoslavia, rather than to Italy.[129] In short, Italy's territorial claims rested on shaky ground, and the American president simply would not budge.

The conflict over Fiume at Versailles would spark protest and unrest both in Italy and in Fiume itself. Italy faced severe economic hardship in the aftermath of the war. It owed the Allies the equivalent of $3.5 billion in wartime loans, saw greater inflation than anywhere in Europe with the exception of Russia, and had widespread unemployment resulting from demobilization.[130] This was the beginning of Italy's *Biennio Rosso* (Two Red Years), a period marked by mass strikes, land seizures, factory occupations, and violent conflict between socialist, anarchist, and nationalist political organizations.[131] Fiume, as well, saw roving nationalist gangs, deadly riots, and armed clashes between Italian and Allied forces in the spring and summer of 1919.[132]

Amid the political turmoil of these months, Fiume emerged in Italy as a potent symbol of Italian pride and honor; and Italy's failure to acquire it became a symbol of national humiliation. As the Italian prime minister Vittorio Orlando told his colleagues at Versailles in April 1919, "Italian public opinion is very excitable. I am doing what I can to calm it; but the consequences of disappointment of this kind would be very grave."[133] The nationalist press pushed for the annexation of Fiume, while placards were posted and walls painted throughout the country with similar demands. When Orlando eventually withdrew from the conference over disagreements regarding Fiume, he was greeted in Rome with cries of "Viva Fiume!"[134]

Prominent among those agitating for the annexation of Fiume was the Italian poet, playwright, novelist, and philosopher, Gabriele D'Annunzio. D'Annunzio was Italy's most esteemed literary figure of the time—so broad was his fame and success that most Italians simply referred to him as *Il Vate*, or "The Poet."[135] He was notoriously eccentric and famously promiscuous, carrying on dozens of affairs throughout his adult life.[136] He was also an ardent nationalist, had an immensely inflated sense of his own importance, and had a great deal of contempt for the political class in Rome.[137] Besides writing and womanizing, D'Annunzio also had a short parliamentary career and a roving commission between Italy's Army, Navy, and Air Force during World War I.[138] Back in Italy after the war, at the age of fifty-five, he became engaged in nationalist causes and organizations and was unmatched in his ability to whip crowds up into a frenzy with rousing speeches and pungent language. D'Annunzio was the actor on the periphery who would aim to drag Italian leaders in Rome into acquiring Fiume.

Fiume

Within a week of the armistice on November 11, 1918, D'Annunzio was contacted by local Italian authorities in Fiume seeking his aid in facilitating its acquisition.[139] Planning for some sort of march on the port city began in earnest between the winter of 1918 and the early spring of 1919.[140] Financing for the operation, largely through nationalist organizations and Italian industrialists, was secured in the spring of that year, as were the forces necessary to carry it out. By May 1919, D'Annunzio was enlisted to lead the march. Rumors began to circulate in Rome that summer that a conspiracy involving Fiume was being cooked up.[141] The Italian prime minister Francesco Nitti repeatedly reminded his generals in the region that the government's policy was to avoid any precipitous action in Fiume at all costs.[142] Naturally, D'Annunzio did nothing to calm nerves in Rome, asking, in a public address on May 7, "Down there, on the roads of Istria, on the roads of Dalmatia, do you not hear the footsteps of a marching army?"[143]

Prime Minister Nitti's grasp of the Italian military was not exactly firm. Civilian governments in Italy had relatively weak control of the military in these years for several reasons.[144] First, for most of its existence, the Italian military had been large and central to its political system. The final stages of Italian unification—known as the *Risorgimento*—had been accomplished through a series of wars between 1861 and 1870, which started off the unified Italy with a large military. In the years that followed, political leaders relied on the military, rather than on a large civilian police force, for domestic security and the maintenance of order, which further entrenched its position.[145] Second, as a constitutional matter, the Italian military was under the control of King Victor Emmanuel III, not the prime minister or cabinet.[146] While the Italian parliament voted on military budgets and conscription requirements, the military itself was loyal to, and was effectively run by, the monarchy.[147] And third, Italy's significant losses in World War I, perceptions that Italy had been subjected to a "mutilated peace" at Versailles, and the rapid demobilization of the Italian military that occurred in the aftermath of the war created significant resentment toward civilian leaders among military officers and the rank and file. The Italian Army went from 3.8 million personnel in December 1918 to 1.6 million just seven months later, and it would continue to be rapidly cut in the months that followed. This was accompanied by a suspension of promotions, lower pay rates, and increased requirements for pensions.[148] All of these factors—historical and constitutional—greatly hampered the cabinet's control of the military and made unauthorized peripheral expansion particularly likely in this case.

The conquest of Fiume ultimately was set for September 11, 1919.[149] D'Annunzio was to travel from Ronchi in Italy's northeast corner, across the Istrian Peninsula, arriving in Fiume in the morning, a distance of about 100 km. He began with just 186 members of the Italian military but had a Fiuman militia that was to join his forces upon arrival.[150] He and his grenadiers set off from Ronchi at midnight on the eleventh, D'Annunzio leading the column in a bright red Fiat 501.[151] Before departing, D'Annunzio sent then-nationalist journalist Benito Mussolini the first of hundreds of letters the two would exchange in the months that followed: "My dear companion, the die is cast. I depart. Tomorrow morning I will conquer Fiume. May the God of Italy help us."[152]

Along the way, D'Annunzio and his forces were met by numerous Italian soldiers who were under orders to stop, and even fire on, the Poet if he tried to pass. However, most were sympathetic to his cause and instead cheered him as he passed, with many even abandoning their posts to join his column.[153] By the time he arrived at the outskirts of Fiume on the morning of the twelfth,

D'Annunzio was at the head of between two thousand and twenty-five hundred personnel, with dozens of trucks and armored vehicles.[154] D'Annunzio was met outside of the city by the commander of Italian forces in Fiume, who implored him to turn back. When D'Annunzio refused, the general saw no other option and let D'Annunzio and his forces into the city.[155] By noon the conquest of Fiume was complete. With characteristic grandiosity, D'Annunzio would refer to his acquisition of Fiume as the *Sacra Entrada* (Sacred Entrance).[156] That evening, at 6:00 p.m., D'Annunzio appeared on the balcony of the governor's palace and addressed the crowd: "Italians of Fiume! . . . I proclaim: I, a soldier, a volunteer, a wounded veteran of the war, believe that I interpret the will of the people of Italy in proclaiming the annexation of Fiume!" a declaration that was met with an eruption of celebration.[157]

Rome Reacts and Decides

When Prime Minister Nitti learned of events in Fiume, he was visibly shocked and absolutely livid, forcefully pounding his fist on his desk.[158] He was not surprised by D'Annunzio's attempt to take Fiume; he had, after all, been receiving reports on this possibility for months. What surprised him was the Poet's *success*—and the defection of thousands of Italian soldiers that it had required. The following day, on September 13, Nitti made a statement before the Italian parliament, expressing publicly his anger and disapproval and assuring his colleagues that "the Government had taken appropriate measures."[159] A few days later, on September 18, Nitti's cabinet ordered a blockade of Fiume, with the Italian Third Army surrounding the city by land and the Italian Navy blocking the entrance to its harbor.[160] Then Nitti took the extraordinary step of requesting that Victor Emmanuel III call a meeting of his privy council, which was held a week later, on September 25. It was attended by leading Italian political figures, top military leaders, the king and his closest advisers, and the prime minister, and they were unanimous in their opposition to D'Annunzio's unauthorized conquest.[161] With this strong backing, the prime minister returned to parliament and called for snap elections to be held in November. The leadership's position was firm. D'Annunzio's fait accompli could not be accepted.

The primary reason for the government's strenuous opposition was the geopolitical risk associated with accepting the city. As noted earlier, D'Annunzio's fait accompli occurred in the context of a joint Italian occupation of Fiume alongside the United States, Britain, and France. After receiving assurances from Rome that the matter would be dealt with expeditiously, Italy's great power allies agreed to have their forces make a hasty exit, though no one was pleased with the situation.[162] Prime Minister Nitti initially thought that the situation could be used to

Italy's advantage and that D'Annunzio's escapade might help strengthen his position in negotiations over Fiume.[163] Yet, while the British and French were somewhat more sympathetic, President Wilson was absolutely firm: D'Annunzio had to go, and Fiume was to become a free city under League of Nations auspices.[164] The president made his view clear to the Italian foreign minister Tommaso Tittoni just days after D'Annunzio's march on Fiume, and Britain, France, and the United States penned a joint memorandum on December 9, pointing to the "urgent necessity" of creating an independent Fiuman state.[165] When he delivered this memorandum to the Italians, the French president Georges Clemenceau noted that "there could be no peace in Europe till this question was settled."[166] It was clear to Nitti that the Allies were in no mood to make concessions.[167]

And Italy had few other options. For one, it was militarily much weaker than any of its allies, let alone all three of them together, so it could not exactly stand and fight.[168] But more importantly, in its dire postwar economic state, it needed its great power allies, and the United States in particular, more than ever. As noted earlier, Italy had borrowed billions from its allies, and the United States was continuing to extend it credit. Rupture with the United States at this point would have meant true economic calamity for Italy, something Prime Minister Nitti, as a trained economist, understood only too well.[169]

However, the decision was complicated by the fact that D'Annunzio's conquest of Fiume itself generated constraints that made withdrawal difficult from the perspective of Rome. The first was the simple fact of his success. Fiume had been acquired by D'Annunzio at no cost in human life, sinking the costs of acquisition for leaders in the capital. But second, and more importantly, the conquest of Fiume had the backing of a significant portion of the Italian military, as well as the press and public more broadly. A perceived risk of popular backlash led Prime Minister Nitti to soften the blockade of Fiume after just a few days.[170] Its resulting leakiness meant that soldiers, sailors, and air personnel continued to desert to Fiume in droves to enlist in D'Annunzio's army and join the cause. The Fiuman forces numbered as many as nine thousand at its peak, and, at a certain point, D'Annunzio had to begin turning military defectors away for lack of accommodations.[171] The press, too, seized on the march on Fiume, painting D'Annunzio as an Italian folk hero.[172] And important sections of the public backed D'Annunzio's venture as well.

The domestic political threats that leaders in Rome faced were not merely electoral. For instance, former prime minister Vittorio Orlando claimed during the Paris peace negotiations that a secret society had pledged to assassinate him if he returned without Italy's irredentist claims.[173] Furthermore, in June 1919, a nationalist coup plot seeking to overthrow the Italian government was uncovered and broken up.[174] And there were rumors circulating about assassins sent from Fiume to kill Prime Minister Nitti and Foreign Minister Tittoni.[175] Thus, members of the Nitti cabinet were aware that rising nationalist sentiment in Italy represented a threat not only to their electoral fortunes but to Italian political institutions and even to their lives.[176]

This combination of strenuous allied opposition and public and military support created a real dilemma for the Nitti cabinet.[177] President Wilson was unwilling to give an inch on Fiume and had significant economic leverage over the prime minister. Yet, there were military and nationalist forces pressing him on, threatening not only his prime ministership but possibly his life. It was as if the ground beneath Nitti's feet, as he put it, "had been mined."[178] Under these trying circumstances, the prime minister adopted a patient and delicate strategy of assuring the Allies that Italy would clean up the Fiuman mess, while negotiating with D'Annunzio to resolve the situation.

D'Annunzian Fiume and Its End

For the fifteen months of its existence, Fiume under Gabriele D'Annunzio reflected all of the eccentricities of its leader. The outlaw city attracted curious visitors from all over Europe—gangsters and prostitutes, politicians and war heroes, famed musicians and Nobel Prize–winning scientists.[179] There were parades and political rallies by day and banquets and torchlit processions by night. And the Poet was at the center of it all, addressing throngs of admirers, glad-handing his loyal supporters, and hosting debaucherous soirees at the governor's palace. Yet, there was a much darker side to it all as well. For D'Annunzio would turn out to be not only a hopeless administrator but also a deeply authoritarian leader.[180] The Poet embraced a charismatic form of personalistic rule, in which he was entirely above the law and dissent was made a capital crime.[181] Before long, there were security forces on every corner, the prisons in Fiume began to overflow, and extrajudicial expulsions, kidnappings, and killings became commonplace.[182] In his raucous public addresses, D'Annunzio used a dialogical style that would later become associated with Italian and German fascism, employing violent and vulgar language and having crowds hurl obscenities at his political enemies in Rome. And Benito Mussolini was watching carefully, visiting the city as a journalist on a number of occasions and corresponding with D'Annunzio regularly.[183] Reflecting on this period, the famed Italian diplomat Carlo Sforza would refer to D'Annunzio as the true "inventor of fascism."[184]

It did not take long for the D'Annunzian spectacle to begin to lose its luster. In November 1919, Italians went to the polls where Nitti was confirmed in his leadership, the nationalist party won just a handful of seats, and not a single fascist candidate was elected to office.[185] In the prime minister's view, as he communicated to D'Annunzio shortly after the election, the results were a strong indication that Italians were "against any adventurous policy" in Fiume and beyond.[186] And while it would be more than a year of on-again, off-again negotiations before the Poet was finally removed, it was clear by early 1920 that his days in Fiume were numbered. Francesco Nitti would resign from office in June 1920 to be replaced by Giovanni Giolitti, a more decisive politician who soon entered into negotiations with the Kingdom of Yugoslavia over the fate of Fiume.[187] The resulting Treaty of Rapallo, signed on November 12, 1920, established the Free State of Fiume as an independent city-state between Italy and Yugoslavia. Despite the treaty passing by overwhelming majorities in the Italian parliament, D'Annunzio clung to power in Fiume and continued to call for its annexation to Italy.[188]

But enough was enough. Prime Minister Giolitti had to take action. On December 20, 1920, he sent D'Annunzio an ultimatum, demanding his exit. In response, the following day D'Annunzio declared war on Italy. On Christmas Eve, the Italian Army and Navy were ordered into action. After a few dozen casualties were taken by both sides, the Italian Navy cruiser *Andrea Doria* fired two shells on D'Annunzio's palace on December 26. This was ultimately decisive. On December 28, D'Annunzio left Fiume for good.[189]

D'Annunzio would not be punished for his open defiance of Italian authorities. Despite his reduced stature, he was still deemed too popular among important segments of the Italian public. This, and the fact that Giolitti chose December 24 for D'Annunzio's ouster to minimize press and public attention, clearly indicate the popular constraints under which Italian leaders felt they were operating.[190] D'Annunzio may have ultimately failed in his greatest ambitions, but his example would play an important role in the success of some of his fascist descendants in Italy, Portugal, Spain, and Germany.[191]

Less than two years later, Benito Mussolini seized power with his "March on Rome," establishing a fascist dictatorship in Italy and adopting many of the repertoires of rule he observed in Fiume. D'Annunzio, for his part, effectively retired to his home on Lake Garda at the government's expense. He evidently still had his hypnotic charm, and Mussolini saw him as a potential political threat in his emerging fascist movement. As Il Duce explained, "When you have a rotten tooth, you have two possibilities open to you: either you extract the tooth or you fill it with gold. With D'Annunzio I have chosen the latter treatment."[192]

This chapter has presented comparative cases of inadvertent expansion and non-expansion in Manchuria and Fiume. Both cases strongly support the theory of inadvertent expansion presented in chapter 1. First, in both cases unauthorized peripheral expansion resulted from inadequate monitoring and control over agents on the periphery—the Kwantung Army in Manchuria and D'Annunzio and important segments of the Italian Army in Fiume. Second, in both cases peripheral expansion generated constraints that made it difficult for leaders in the capital to easily withdraw—in both Japan and Italy, the most important of these were domestic political risks and costs associated with doing so. And third, in both cases the ultimate decision of whether to accept the fait accompli was crucially determined by the geopolitical risk associated with doing so. In the case of Japan in Manchuria, the perceived geopolitical risk pushed Prime Minister Wakatsuki to work strenuously to put a halt to the conquest and to rein in the Kwantung Army. Yet, once it became clear that such risks would not come to fruition, his government was replaced by the more pliant Inukai cabinet, and the invasion of Manchuria moved forward. In the case of Italy in Fiume, the strong stance of Britain, France, and, particularly, the United States in opposition to D'Annunzio's conquest gave the Italian government little alternative but to roll it back, which it ultimately did by force. In both cases, what I referred to in chapter 1 as the "dilemma of inadvertent expansion" was illustrated powerfully—the agonizing situations in which leaders simultaneously face severe domestic political costs associated with territorial withdrawal as well as significant geopolitical risk associated with territorial acquisition. Showing how leaders navigate these perilous circumstances has been an important aim of this chapter.

INADVERTENT ANNEXATION IN EAST AFRICA

Germany

> As my comrades and I sailed to Zanzibar in 1884, the German government wanted nothing to do with the founding of a colony in East Africa and she did everything in her power to prevent such a thing from happening.
>
> —Carl Peters, 1917

This chapter examines inadvertent expansion through two examples from the German Empire in East Africa. The first case focuses on the German acquisition of what would become German East Africa in 1884–85. The second examines Germany's nonacquisition of a number of territories in modern-day Kenya and Uganda in 1889–90. The purpose of this chapter is twofold. First, it presents the book's fifth and final pair of comparative theory-testing case studies, showing how variation in geopolitical risk led to divergent outcomes, with successful inadvertent expansion in the first case but failed inadvertent expansion in the second. But second, and more importantly, this chapter presents the book's only cases of inadvertent expansion via *political annexation*, as all qualitative cases to this point have focused on armed conquest. While the data presented in chapter 2 include many observations of inadvertent expansion via political annexation, this chapter allows the reader to observe how the theory works in practice in two in-depth case studies of annexation.

These two German cases are a useful comparison in that they hold many factors fixed—the same great power, operating in the same region, involving the very same individual peripheral actor, claiming directly contiguous territories, and separated by only five years—while the outcomes across the two cases vary. One important difference between the two cases is a leadership change that takes place in the German capital, Berlin. In March 1890, after twenty-eight years at the helm of Prussian and then German power, the "Iron Chancellor" Otto von Bismarck was dismissed by the new German emperor, Wilhelm II, in the midst of a process of inadvertent expansion. This presents two inferential opportunities. First, the fact that Bismarck, the famously reluctant imperialist, accepts his peripheral agent's fait accompli in 1885, whereas the more expansionist Wilhelm II ultimately rejects the territorial fait accompli in 1890, helps highlight the crucial role played by domestic political pressure and geopolitical risk in these cases. Second, the fact that the leadership transition takes place during the peripheral expansion in Kenya and Uganda also shows how different leaders with *very* different foreign policy views can be similarly influenced by expectations of geopolitical risk.

Germany in East Africa, 1884–85

The German Empire acquired what would become German East Africa (now Burundi, Rwanda, and mainland Tanzania) between November 1884 and February 1885. A series of annexations in the core of East Africa were independently planned and carried out by a private German colonial organization, despite repeated efforts at discouragement by Berlin. This case supports two of the central arguments of the theory of inadvertent expansion.[1] First, that once a territory is partly or wholly acquired, a number of constraints emerge that make it difficult for leaders in the capital to simply withdraw. In the case at hand, the successful annexation of these territories sunk the costs of acquisition and generated domestic political pressure on leaders in Berlin to accept them. Second, that the absence of geopolitical risk associated with acquisition will encourage leaders in the capital to accept the fait accompli, resulting in territorial expansion. In the case of German East Africa, Britain was simply in no position to resist the German advance and would quickly acquiesce to the annexations. These facts strengthened the case for subsequent central authorization, which would occur when Kaiser Wilhelm I signed the imperial charter on February 27, 1885, adding East Africa to the German colonial empire.

Historical Background

On the eve of the annexations in November and December 1884, what would become German East Africa was divided among dozens of small chiefdoms, many of which were under the loose control of the sultanate of Zanzibar, just across the Zanzibar Channel from central Africa's east coast. Up the coast to the north lay more of the sultanate's territory in modern-day Kenya, and to the south lay Mozambique, where the Portuguese had had a presence since the early sixteenth century. To the west, in the heart of Africa, sat what would soon become the Congo Free State, a colony that would be privately owned by King Leopold II of Belgium. These were the early days of the European "Scramble for Africa," when a great deal of territory, particularly in the interior, remained unclaimed.

There were two key leaders in the German capital, Berlin, responsible for issues of territorial expansion and empire. The first was the emperor, Kaiser Wilhelm I, the German head of state who had ultimate authority and the final word on any decisions regarding territorial acquisition. The second was Otto von Bismarck. As the chancellor of the German Empire and, effectively, its foreign minister, Bismarck's personal influence on foreign and imperial policy in this era is difficult to overstate. A leader whose very name has become synonymous with Realpolitik, Bismarck was tough, energetic, and uniquely rational in his thinking about international affairs.[2] The German Second Reich did have a state secretary for foreign affairs in Paul von Hatzfeldt, but his was much more of a supporting role, drafting memos and executing decisions made by the chancellor. The empire also had a colonial secretary in Heinrich von Kusserow, but this position was under the authority of the foreign ministry, not itself at the cabinet level.[3] Finally, until the end of World War I, Germany did not have a single national war or defense ministry, with this role being divided among several major states, such as Prussia, Bavaria, Saxony, and Württemberg. Kaiser Wilhelm I and the Chancellor Bismarck were the crucial leaders in the capital who would be inadvertently dragged into the acquisition of East Africa.

The 1880s saw the emergence of a number of German civil society organizations advocating for colonialism.[4] Among the more radical of these was the Gesellschaft für deutsche Kolonisation (GfdK; Society for German Colonization), formed in March 1884. It aimed to go beyond mere advocacy and lobbying and would actually fund and organize private expeditions and activities directly aimed at attaining colonies for the empire.[5] The GfdK was cofounded and led by a twenty-eight-year-old historian and philosopher by the name of Carl Peters. An ardent German nationalist, Peters was a firm believer in the colonial cause, could be dictatorial in his treatment of others, and was deeply and profoundly racist.[6] Peters was the key peripheral actor who would present Berlin with the East African fait accompli.

Peters made himself something of a known quantity in German Foreign Office circles. This was due not only to his leadership role in the GfdK but also to his periodically pitching various colonial schemes to foreign office personnel. By the fall of 1884, however, after a number of his proposals had been shot down by the foreign office, Peters and the GfdK were feeling pressure to get some sort of expedition underway.[7] Having raised funds from their now roughly 350 members, the organization's leadership felt it had to move forward or potentially face an open revolt among shareholders.[8]

In mid-September 1884, Peters and the GfdK came up with a plan: to acquire territory on the East African mainland across from the island of Zanzibar. On September 20, Peters once again wrote the foreign office, but this time he phrased his message as an announcement rather than a request. Then, without awaiting a reply, Peters and his colleagues hastily packed their belongings and departed.[9] The ragtag expedition consisted of Peters and three companions: Count Graf Joachim von Pfiel, a German aristocrat; Carl Jühlke, a lawyer; and August Otto, a young businessperson.[10] On October 1, they boarded a steamer at Trieste for a five-week journey that would end at Zanzibar.[11] As Peters later wrote, reflecting on this decision, he had "decided to accept the risk of retrospective rejection by the Imperial Government of the Reich."[12] Just like that, his fait accompli had been launched.

As noted earlier, Bismarck was less keen on imperial ventures than many of his European contemporaries, a sentiment well summed up by his 1881 statement that "as long as I am Reichskanzler, we shall not pursue a colonial policy."[13] This promise would not hold—of course—as Germany had recently burst upon the imperial scene, claiming South-West Africa in April 1884, Cameroon and Togoland in July, and New Britain and northeastern New Guinea in November.[14] Yet, Bismarck was often reluctant in these acquisitions and had very little interest in what Peters and his colleagues were planning in East Africa. Just two days after Peters's departure, on October 3, the German Foreign Office composed a response to the announced expedition, which was awaiting him upon arrival in Zanzibar on November 4. The cable, which had been personally approved by Bismarck, stated explicitly that the government had given them no encouragement or assistance for their venture and that they could not count on protection for any territorial claims they might stake out—they were there at their own risk and on their own responsibility.[15]

East Africa

Once in Zanzibar, Peters and his colleagues hastily prepared for their expedition to the mainland. They hired porters, servants, and interpreters and purchased food, arms, and other equipment.[16] In the early morning of November 10, they set out on a hired dhow across the Zanzibar Channel toward the mainland. They would ultimately leave behind much of the food they had purchased for the expedition to make room for gifts for local chiefs, and they lacked medicine and other essentials for tropical travel.[17] They disembarked at Saadani on the East African coast, and, after some organizing, began their expedition into the interior on November 12.[18]

Peters and his colleagues moved with speed. In a little over a month, they covered hundreds of kilometers of ground and concluded at least ten treaties with local chiefs in the regions of Usagara, Nguru, Useguha, and Ukami.[19] The process of treaty making followed a consistent pattern. They would, first, ask permission to camp on a chief's territory. They would then circulate rumors among the people of Peters's extraordinary power and influence. This was followed by offering the locals rum and gifts. Then the treaty would be signed, and the German flag hoisted. Peters followed this by giving a short speech, before the ceremony closed with a cheer for the kaiser and the firing of three volleys.[20] Then, the expedition would move onto the next chiefdom, and the process would begin anew. Peters and his colleagues ultimately claimed some 140,000 km² of territory in this manner.[21]

Yet, in almost all other respects, the expedition was an utter fiasco. Otto, the merchant, was constantly drunk, and bad blood developed between Peters and Pfiel, to the point of Pfiel apparently firing his revolver at Peters during a particularly nasty quarrel. Peters severely burnt his foot a few weeks in and thereafter had to be carried by porters in a hammock. The effects of a lack of food, medicine, and equipment quickly began to show themselves, with porters falling ill and abandoning the expedition, and the Germans suffering severe and recurrent fever. Otto would ultimately die in an Usagara goat shed, and Pfiel almost certainly would have died as well had he not been stumbled upon by a traveling French scientist after he had been abandoned by Peters. After thirty-seven days in the interior, Peters and Jühlke, starving and grievously ill, staggered into a French mission church in the coastal town of Bagamoyo on the evening of December 17.[22] Peters later recalled that, when he saw the cross and heard the resonant sound of the organ, he "broke into a cramped sobbing as all the tension of the previous weeks poured forth in a flood of tears."[23] (See figure 7.1.)

Berlin Reacts

After a few days of recovery on the coast, Peters returned to Zanzibar and telegraphed the GfdK in Berlin with news of his acquisitions. The GfdK then contacted the foreign office and a representative of the organization met with Colonial Secretary Heinrich von Kusserow on December 29, requesting government protection for Peters's claims.[24] Kusserow decided to await a more comprehensive report on the acquisitions before informing and making a recommendation to Bismarck, which would arrive in the form of a formal letter of request from Peters about a month later. In the meantime, Peters embarked on the long journey home, where he would arrive in early February 1885.[25] The GfdK followed up

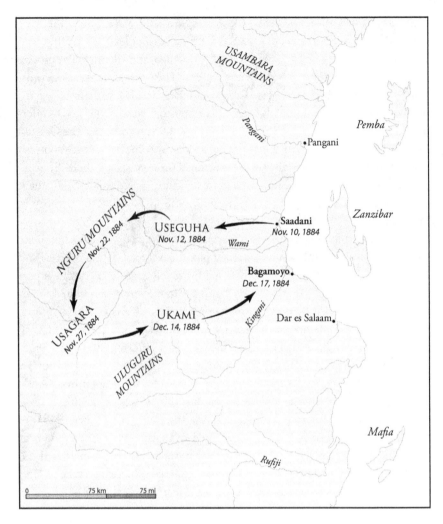

FIGURE 7.1. Carl Peters East Africa campaign, November–December 1884.
Created by Beehive Mapping.

with the foreign office a week after Peters's return, again requesting protection,
but also authorization for further annexations in the area. At this point, it had
been almost seven weeks without a definitive response from the government, and
Peters started to get anxious.[26]

By February 15, Kusserow felt that he had enough information and sent a
detailed memo to the chancellor.[27] The timing of Peters's fait accompli was complicated by the fact that the imperial powers were just wrapping up the Berlin-
hosted West Africa Conference.[28] Suddenly springing an East Africa protectorate

upon the other great powers, after having said nothing about it through months of discussion of colonial matters, would undoubtedly come as a surprise and, to some, an unwelcome one.

Despite the awkward timing, the very fact of Peters's annexations helped generate two constraints that made returning the territories difficult for leaders in Berlin. For one, the job was already half done. While Bismarck and the foreign office had tried to dissuade Peters with the strongly worded cable of October 3 referenced earlier, now the picture had changed considerably. Peters and his colleagues had laid claim, without significant resistance, to a large portion of East Africa, and they were likely to press on to the borders of King Leopold's newly constituted Congo Free State. They had also promised, in letters and memos to the government, that the colony could be operated at minimal expense, that governance and development of East Africa could be handled by the GfdK, and that the territory was suitable for the cultivation of a wide variety of valuable crops.[29] Thus, Peters's successful acquisitions presented with his persuasive arguments meant that the costs of acquisition had been definitively sunk.

The second reason Bismarck would have trouble rejecting the fait accompli was political. While the core of the colonial movement in Germany was relatively small, colonialism and empire were increasingly popular in some influential German circles.[30] A federal election had been held in late October 1884, and the Bismarck-aligned Conservative and National Liberal parties had made colonial policy an important theme of their campaigns. Their relative gains, and the losses of the Left Liberal party, were widely perceived to be due, in important part, to their divergent views on Germany's growing overseas empire.[31] By accepting German East Africa, Bismarck could strengthen his own domestic political support and that of his allies in the Reichstag (German parliament), at relatively low cost. As the chancellor had written to a colleague just three weeks before the East Africa decision landed on his desk, for "reasons of domestic policy the colonial problem is a vital question for us. . . . At present public opinion emphasizes colonial policy so strongly in Germany that the position of the Government within Germany largely depends on its success."[32]

Besides these constraints on returning the territories, there were also few geopolitical risks associated with retaining them. While clearly the British might be surprised, even alarmed, by German gains in the region, they had made very clear to Bismarck in correspondence in January and February 1885 that their interests were mainly confined to the island of Zanzibar itself, not the East African mainland.[33] London was also not in a strong position to resist any German moves in East Africa. In what would become known as Germany's "Egyptian lever" (*bâton égyptien*) the British were heavily reliant on German diplomatic support for their occupation of Egypt, and the German government used this to their advantage repeatedly.[34] As the British prime minister William Gladstone acknowledged in December 1884, the Germans "could do extraordinary mischief to us at our one really vulnerable point, Egypt."[35] And Bismarck, reflecting on this fact in January 1885, noted that "Egypt . . . is merely a means of overcoming England's objections to our colonial aspirations."[36]

The timing of Peters's fait accompli was also fortuitous with respect to the potential geopolitical risk for Berlin. British imperial forces under General Charles Gordon had been under siege at Khartoum since March 1884, and, in February 1885, Russian forces occupied the border town of Panjdeh in Afghanistan (then a British protectorate), sparking a major crisis between the two powers.[37] Under these circumstances, London could, and likely would, do little to forestall Berlin's gains in the region. As the historian Arne Perras notes, "The attractiveness of Peters's scheme [for Bismarck] lay in the fact that it made a further colonial claim possible without provoking an imperial showdown" with London.[38]

Berlin Decides

Therefore, after some brief correspondence with his consul general in Zanzibar and a few meetings with Kusserow, Bismarck decided on February 24, 1885, to establish a protectorate over Peters's acquisitions in East Africa—just nine days after becoming aware of them.[39] Two days later, Bismarck informed Kaiser Wilhelm I of the acquisitions and advised him to accept them as a protectorate. The following day, the kaiser signed an imperial charter, proclaiming East Africa as a German protectorate, and this fact was made public on March 3, 1885.[40] Without having planned on it or having played any role in its actual annexation, the German Empire had just acquired what would soon become its largest and most populous imperial holding.[41]

Bismarck would approve further annexations sought by the GfdK, informing Peters on July 11, 1885, that "the company should take what it feels confident to take. . . . We shall see later what we can back officially."[42] But Peters was already well ahead of him. He had ordered his subordinates to engage in further annexations in East Africa on February 8—nearly three weeks *before* East Africa was officially made a German protectorate—and by July they had extended the territory hundreds of kilometers in each direction.[43] The sultan of Zanzibar would raise a protest over the claims, but, in reality, there was little he could do without overt and forceful British backing. After Bismarck sent five German warships into the harbor of Zanzibar on August 7, 1885, the sultan formally recognized all German claims on the mainland.[44] East Africa was to remain German and would go on to be the Second Reich's most important colony—a status it would retain until it was invaded by a joint British-Belgian force in November 1914, in the opening months of World War I.

In November 1885, Germany and Britain agreed to set up a joint commission to determine the limits of Zanzibar's territories on the mainland and to demarcate their respective spheres of influence there.[45] The following October, the two sides came to an agreement, with Kenya, to the north, falling within the British sphere, and Tanzania, Rwanda, and Burundi, in the south, falling within the German sphere.[46] And while the sultan of Zanzibar retained control over the East African coast, Germany was able to lease the ports of Pagani and Dar es Salaam, providing it important "windows" to coastal trade.[47] However, the treaty left many areas of possible contention unsettled, the most important of these, as the following case shows, being Uganda.[48]

For his part, Peters would retain a central position in Germany's new East African empire. Far from being punished for his disregard of official orders, he was instead tapped to organize and ultimately lead the chartered company that was to run the East Africa protectorate, the Deutsch-Ostafrikanische Gesellschaft (DOAG; German East Africa Company).[49] However, titles and responsibilities were not nearly enough to put a leash on the young administrator, as Peters was far more interested in expanding the empire than running it competently.[50] And when stories began to circulate in European capitals of a certain German national under siege in southern Sudan by a large Mahdist army, Peters saw it as a golden opportunity to strike out once again.

Germany, Kenya, and Uganda, 1889–90

The German Empire refrained from acquiring a number of territories throughout Kenya and Uganda between June 1889 and July 1890. A series of annexations were independently executed over the course of a German expedition, despite efforts by the German government to discourage its launch and hinder its progress. This case provides support for the three central arguments of the theory of inadvertent expansion presented in chapter 1. First, that inadvertent expansion results from a principal-agent problem, rooted in diverse preferences between the capital and periphery and information asymmetries favoring the latter. In the case of Germany in Kenya and Uganda, a sharp divergence of preferences for expansion would develop as the expedition's launch neared, and a lack of telegraphic communications hampered central government control. Second, that once a given territory is claimed, a number of constraints emerge that make it difficult for metropolitan leaders to easily relinquish it. In the case under examination, the annexations sunk the costs of acquisition of these territories and generated some domestic political pressure on leaders in Berlin to authorize the fait accompli. And third, that expectations of unacceptable geopolitical risk associated with acquisition will discourage leaders in the capital from authorizing territorial claims, resulting in failed inadvertent expansion. In the case at hand, the importance of the Nile Valley to Britain's entire imperial strategy meant that Uganda was seen as strategically vital to London, and this was well understood in Berlin. These geopolitical risks strongly discouraged territorial acquisition among German leaders, leading to the Heligoland-Zanzibar Treaty of July 1890, in which Germany renounced all territorial claims in Kenya and Uganda.

Historical Background

Kenya and Uganda were largely independent in these years, divided up among numerous kingdoms and chiefdoms of varying size. Since 1885, Germany had had a small coastal protectorate around the mouth of the River Tana in Kenya, known as "Wituland," with the remainder of Kenya being considered as falling within the United Kingdom's sphere of influence.[51] Uganda's status had yet to be defined by the colonial powers. To the south, of course, lay the new German protectorate of East Africa, and to the east lay the Belgian king Leopold's Congo. To the north from Lake Victoria flows the Nile River, through Uganda, Sudan, and Egypt, before emptying in the eastern Mediterranean Sea, just 50 km west of the Suez Canal. Much of the interior of these territories was unknown to the imperial powers, though this was rapidly changing with all of the private-chartered companies operating in the area.

For the time being, the German chancellor Otto von Bismarck retained his position as the key leader in Berlin responsible for German imperial policy. However, with the death of Kaiser Wilhelm I in March 1888, the German throne was to be occupied by a new emperor—first in the form of Frederick III, who himself died just three months later, passing the title of kaiser to his son, Wilhelm II. Wilhelm II's accession was viewed by many with apprehension, not least by Bismarck himself. At just twenty-nine at the time of accession, Wilhelm was impulsive and confident, with only a superficial knowledge of government, military, and international affairs. Yet, he was also stridently nationalistic and expansionist in his foreign policy views, seeking to reorient the empire's foreign policy toward a more aggressive Weltpolitik.[52] It was Wilhelm II who would make the ultimate decision regarding the fate of any territory claimed in Kenya or Uganda.

The key actor on the periphery was, again, Carl Peters. Still only in his early thirties by the late 1880s, he remained very much the unconstrained peripheral agent and a thorn in Berlin's side. As the local head of the DOAG—the chartered company that administered East Africa on behalf of the German Empire—he would prove to be a hopeless administrator, with the company operating on the verge of bankruptcy until they were bailed out by the German government in 1887.[53] Peters was also a cruel administrator, having further developed the strong sadistic streak that had been evident during his earlier annexations in East Africa.[54] He and his subordinates regularly committed atrocities against the local population in and around the company's stations throughout East Africa, including arbitrary detention, torture, murder, and sexual slavery.[55] At the end of 1887, Peters was recalled to Berlin by the DOAG, though it would not be long before he returned.[56]

The occasion for Peters's return to East Africa was what became known as the "German Emin Pasha Relief Expedition." Emin Pasha (born Eduard Schnitzer) was a physician and colonial administrator of German origin who had converted to Islam and entered the service of the British Empire as a medical officer for General Charles Gordon in Sudan.[57] With the fall of Khartoum and the death of Gordon in 1885, the spread of the Mahdist Army throughout Sudan forced Emin to retreat to southern Sudan, near the Uganda border, where he put out a call for help to the British government in July 1886.[58] Word of Emin Pasha's plight reached London in late September 1886, and the news quickly spread to other European capitals.[59] His story captured the imagination of European publics and publishers, and advocacy organizations and relief committees quickly sprang into being, pushing for rescue expeditions.[60] For colonial organizations and private-chartered companies in the region, this was clearly an opportunity, and a British Emin Pasha Relief Committee was established, in November 1886, and an expedition set off in January 1887.[61]

The idea of a rival German expedition developed more slowly. The German Emin Pasha Relief Committee only formed in June 1888, with Peters—having been recently recalled from East Africa—very much at the center of it.[62] Publicly, Peters would claim that the expedition's purpose was "to furnish Emin Pacha, in his isolated position in the Equatorial Province, with ammunition and men, and to enable him to maintain his position."[63] Privately, however, he was more candid, noting that the "German Emin Pasha expedition was no pleasure trip, but a large-scale colonial, political enterprise."[64] Emin Pasha's rescue was a mere pretext. The broader aim on the part of Peters and the committee was the extension of Germany's East African empire, to encompass Uganda, southern Sudan, and the Nile basin.[65]

Like Prime Minister Salisbury, Bismarck was reluctant to get involved. When the committee made a formal request of the chancellor for German government funding in July 1888, Bismarck would decline, noting that "the rescue of Emin Bey would be primarily an Egyptian-English interest."[66] Yet, many around him were more receptive. The expedition, for instance, garnered the support of prominent figures from each of the major parties in the Reichstag.[67] And the young kaiser himself, in August 1888, had the foreign office pass on his "warmest sympathies for the success of the enterprise" to the committee.[68] Under these conditions, Bismarck felt that he had to play along, writing the committee on August 15, 1888, that, while the expedition was "alien to our colonial interests," he recognized its "high-minded purpose" and similarly wished that "the patriotic efforts of the committee may succeed in carrying out this difficult venture."[69] Peters would later write that, at this point, he and the committee felt that "His Majesty the Emperor and Prince Bismarck [were] sympathetically welcoming the carrying out of a German Emin Pasha Expedition."[70] With these endorsements, they felt they had all the backing they needed.

Berlin and East Africa

In Kenya and Uganda, leaders in Berlin faced important principal-agent problems with respect to actors such as Peters on the frontier. First, a divergence of preferences would develop between Bismarck and the expedition. While Bismarck was, at first, reluctantly supportive, events on the ground soon changed, leading the chancellor to alter his stance. In September 1888, a rebellion broke out on the coast of German East Africa.[71] The introduction of new taxes on commerce, as well as the heavy-handedness of German colonial administration, led to an armed uprising that quickly spread to the interior.[72] By the end of the year, all territory under the control of the DOAG was in open revolt. Bismarck was dismayed by this turn of events, and, in December 1888 and January 1889, he managed to convince the Reichstag to fund a military operation to suppress the rebellion.[73] As part of the pacification campaign, the chancellor announced a naval blockade of the East African coast, and Prime Minister Salisbury agreed to send British naval vessels to participate.[74] Under these conditions, an officially endorsed expedition to the interior seemed out of the question, and Bismarck began erecting barriers to its success.

On September 14, Bismarck wrote a lengthy memorandum to the kaiser, arguing against the expedition and claiming to see no advantage of "such an eccentric extension" of Germany's African territories.[75] The following day, the chancellor informed the DOAG that he would take "no further interest" in the expedition unless they got rid of Carl Peters—who Bismarck blamed for the mess in East Africa—arguing that Peters was "entirely incapable of leading such a difficult venture" due to his "lack of caution, and excessive self-confidence."[76] Bismarck then began planting stories in German newspapers, critical of Peters and the expedition, in an effort to sway public opinion. The chancellor also began meeting with members and supporters of the committee, individually lobbying them to turn against the enterprise.[77] Thus, Bismarck quickly became strongly and openly opposed to the expedition.

A second problem was that there were information asymmetries favoring the German Emin Pasha Expedition in the periphery. While Zanzibar had been connected to the global telegraph network in 1879, coastal Kenya would not see a telegraphic connection until 1890, at Mombasa.[78] This made the expedition difficult to communicate with, and potentially control, once they were on the mainland. As Peters remarked in recounting events there, once they were in the interior, the expedition would be "masters of the situation."[79] Thus, the principal-agent problems facing Berlin made unauthorized peripheral expansion more likely.

Kenya and Uganda

Peters and the committee would not be discouraged by Bismarck's opposition, completing their preparations in Berlin over the course of January 1889. On February 25, Peters left for East Africa. In contrast to his cheerful departure of five years earlier, this time he seemed to leave with a sense of foreboding, later writing that his departure "was characterized rather by seriousness and emotion than by joyful hope."[80] Peters arrived in Zanzibar on March 31, 1889, and immediately ran into trouble. For one, the Somali soldiers he had recruited in Aden for the expedition were barred from disembarking by Zanzibari authorities, forcing Peters to leave them, for the time being, on the East African coast at Bagamoyo.[81] Peters also quickly learned that the six hundred local porters he had planned on hiring had been prohibited from joining his expedition by the sultan of Zanzibar.[82] Just days before Peters's arrival in Zanzibar, Bismarck had also notified Prime Minister Salisbury that their joint blockade should apply to all armed vessels in the area, which led to the confiscation of all the weapons Peters had purchased for the expedition.[83] When Peters went and complained to the British naval officer who was holding his weapons, the captain's response was simply: *"C'est la guerre!"* (That's War!)[84] And the local German consul proved to be of no help either, refusing to mediate Peters's conflicts with the British and Zanzibari authorities.[85]

After nearly a month of frustration, Peters telegraphed the Emin Pasha committee in Berlin on April 29, asking them to contact the German Foreign Office and plead his case. When he had not heard back, he telegraphed again on May 6, and then, receiving no reply, again on May 10. On May 13, he finally received a curt telegraphic response from the committee, informing him that the "Foreign Office refuses all mediation and support."[86] Peters was livid. "If the Imperial

Government did not wish that the German Emin Pasha Expedition should be undertaken," he replied on May 17, "it should have forbidden the project" from the start. He added that "to have allowed the development of the project to the present point, and now to permit its being hindered under every imaginable pretext, . . . and even with the co-operation of the German authorities, is certainly a very peculiar method of advancing German interests and German honour." However, while Peters was outraged, he was not deterred. As he continued in the very same telegram, "in the face of the difficulties in every direction, in face of the intrigues with which we have to fight daily, all of us here, I am proud to say, are only the more firmly resolved to carry on the undertaking to the utmost verge of possibility."[87] The German Emin Pasha Relief Expedition would go on.

On June 1, Peters crossed from Zanzibar to Bagamoyo, on the mainland, in a privately chartered vessel.[88] From there he continued south to Dar es Salaam. Peters's resolve would only strengthen with time and distance, later recalling that he "considered it more consonant with our national honour and our national interest to perish, on the sea or on the land, with my whole expedition, than to retreat before this paltry mass of obstacles and intrigues."[89] From Dar es Salaam, the expedition was officially launched on June 7, heading north up the East African coast by boat, with plans to land on the Kenyan coast near Kiwayu Island, just north of the German protectorate of Wituland. Since, by this point, Bismarck had instructed local German officials to neither let the expedition through the blockade at sea nor to pass through Wituland, this seemed the most promising approach.[90] After a difficult journey up the coast, the expedition arrived at Kiwayu Bay on June 15.[91] While Peters and the committee had initially planned for an expedition of upward of seven hundred, the various hurdles put in their way by the German government had shrunk their numbers to a little over one hundred.[92] The twenty-five Somali soldiers Peters retained were armed only with hunting rifles, and the expedition had no goods whatsoever with which to buy passage through tribal territories.[93] It was not exactly an auspicious beginning.

The expedition began its march toward and then up the River Tana on July 26, 1889.[94] Their ultimate destination was Wadelai, some 1,200 km away in northern Uganda, where Emin Pasha was supposedly fending off attacks from the Mahdist Army. Once the expedition got underway, it became clear that Peters's faculties for brutality had developed considerably since his East African expedition five years earlier. Conditions were difficult early on, and, as porters began to disappear in the night, Peters had some of them flogged, others shot, and, ultimately, all of them put in chains to prevent further escape.[95] For the local population as well, the German Emin Pasha Relief Expedition would amount to a veritable campaign of terror. Peters and his followers plundered and razed villages, raided thousands of cattle, held dozens of captives, and battled anyone who resisted their advance.[96] Peters had no evident misgivings about the conduct of the expedition either, claiming to have "found that in the end only the bullets of a repeater . . . make an impression on these wild sons of the steppe."[97]

While the ultimate aim was to find Emin Pasha, and to annex territory around the Uganda-Sudanese border area, Peters would claim various territories for the German Empire as he progressed. The expedition's first protectorate treaty was made on September 12, 1889, and they claimed new territory every few weeks from then on, planting a series of German flags in their wake as they advanced.[98] Peters would discover along the way that Emin Pasha had long been rescued by the British expedition, having left from Wadelai for the East African coast in April 1889, months before Peters's expedition had even begun.[99] However, this ultimately mattered little. He resolved to press on to Uganda, where he had heard that the kabaka (king) of Buganda was in need of help against internal challenges, and Peters saw this as an opportunity to claim an even greater prize for the empire.[100] Peters would be frustrated in this final ambition—the kabaka had no interest in a treaty of protection—and he had to settle for a treaty of amity and cooperation, which was signed on February 28, 1890.[101]

Buganda would be the culmination of the expedition, and, in mid-March, Peters and his followers began their journey back to the coast, traveling south on Lake Victoria and returning through German East Africa.[102] They reached the coast at Bagamoyo on July 16, 1890, after having traveled over 3,000 km in a few weeks shy of a full year.[103] Over the course of the expedition, Peters had signed between eight and ten treaties of protection.[104] The question now was what Berlin would do with them.

Berlin Reacts

By April 1890, it was clear in Berlin that Peters had made it as far as Uganda, and by June news of his treaties began to reach European capitals.[105] While Bismarck and other German leaders had clearly tried to prevent the expedition before it was launched, now that it had seen a measure of success, Peters's actions had generated some constraints on leaders in Berlin. For one, the expedition had sunk the costs of acquiring these territories for the German Empire. Peters would be returning in mere months with a handful of admittedly dubious, though likely defensible, treaties of protection that stretched through Kenya and Uganda. If German leaders wanted these territories, they were theirs for the taking. And Peters's martial successes in dealing with local tribes, though troubling from a humanitarian standpoint, showed that resistance may not be as heavy as might have been expected.

Perhaps a more important reason it may have appeared difficult to readily relinquish Peters's claims, however, was that the expedition itself generated domestic political pressure in favor of imperial expansion. Peters had become among Germany's most famous colonial figures, and he and the expedition were glowingly presented in the press and public as the embodiment of German courage and national honor.[106] This was also the height of the "Scramble for Africa," and the German public, like most European publics, was swept up in the rising tide of colonial enthusiasm.[107] Expansionist fervor was strongest among some of Bismarck's most important supporters in the Reichstag, narrowing the chancellor's latitude in response.[108] And Britain's participation in the naval blockade only served to inflame these passions. As Herbert von Bismarck, the chancellor's son and foreign minister, wrote to their ambassador in London on July 27, 1889, news of the confiscation of Peters's weapons "had caused extreme excitement among the German public" and had "triggered a press campaign against England."[109] Peters and the committee did their own part to foster this public support. For instance, before leaving, Peters made public statements emphasizing the extent of support for the expedition in the Reichstag, in an effort to put pressure on Bismarck.[110] The committee in Berlin also helped stoke moral outrage over the confiscation of Peters's supplies by publicizing the issue, and using it to raise further funds.[111] In short, the very fact of Peters's having launched the expedition placed constraints on leaders in Berlin, hampering their ability to reject the territories he claimed.

However, there were also severe geopolitical risks associated with retaining Peters's territorial claims. The key problem, of course, was the United Kingdom. While much of Kenya was formally independent, it clearly lay within Britain's sphere of influence according to an agreement the two powers had come to in October and November 1886. This first agreement was followed up by what was known as the "hinterlands agreement" of July 1887, in which Prime Minister Salisbury and Chancellor Bismarck agreed that they should discourage territorial annexations in the hinterlands of each other's spheres.[112] Thus, Bismarck was on record, multiple times, recognizing many of these territories claimed by Peters as lying within the British sphere.

Another key factor was that Germany's position vis-à-vis the United Kingdom, while strong in 1885 when the German East Africa claims were settled, had weakened considerably. With Britain looking increasingly likely to stay in Egypt for the time being, Bismarck's support there became less crucial, and his *bâton égyptien* began to lose its bite.[113] Germany's own conflicts with both France and Russia, as well as a visible rapprochement between those two great powers, also meant that Germany increasingly needed Britain on its side.[114] Friedrich von Holstein, an influential member of the German Foreign Office, wrote in October

1888 that "our colonial crises lie upon us like a nightmare, and we need England of all places. Our relations with the English government are being most carefully cultivated."[115] This sentiment was echoed at the highest levels, with Bismarck writing in early 1889, "At present we need England if peace is to be maintained."[116] In January of that year, Bismarck went as far as to make an offer of a formal alliance to Prime Minister Salisbury.[117] While Salisbury would politely decline, it was an unmistakably clear signal of Bismarck's view of his diplomatic position at the time.

Yet, perhaps the most important reason Germany faced geopolitical risk in considering Peters's annexations was that the United Kingdom increasingly viewed the entire Nile Valley, which included large portions of Uganda and Sudan, as a core geostrategic interest.[118] When Britain invaded and occupied Egypt in 1882, it gained control of the Suez Canal, a crucial choke point in passage between Europe and British India. And the security of Egypt, in turn, was seen as depending critically on that of the Nile. Genuine, though perhaps not all that well founded, fears of a rival great power coming in and diverting or obstructing the flow of the Nile thus led the British to view the entire course of the Nile—from Lake Victoria in Uganda, through Sudan, and into Egypt—as a crucial imperial interest. Once the United Kingdom had determined it would stay in Egypt—which was publicly announced in November 1889—Uganda became utterly indispensable.[119] Even Germany's protectorate in Wituland, on the Kenyan coast, began to be looked on with increasing anxiety.[120] And the British made their feelings known. For instance, in December 1888, Prime Minister Salisbury asked Bismarck to define his attitude to the German Emin Pasha Relief Expedition, a veiled notification of Britain's special interests in the area.[121] And, during a visit to London in March 1889, Herbert von Bismarck was astonished by how quickly each of his interlocutors brought up East African affairs and potential colonial crises there.[122] As Prime Minister Salisbury put it in March 1890, his government was firmly resolved to defend the "Nile Valley against the dominion of any outside power."[123]

A Dismissal and a Decision

Given his diplomatic acumen, Chancellor Bismarck was sensitive to these risks early on. In his September 1888 memorandum to the kaiser, he argued against supporting the Emin Pasha Expedition on the grounds that it was likely to antagonize the British, which regarded Egypt as a vital interest.[124] In December 1888, Bismarck personally assured Prime Minister Salisbury that he would give the Peters expedition no official support whatsoever.[125] The following June, with the expedition just about to commence, Bismarck had his ambassador in London assure Salisbury that "Uganda, Wadelai, and other places to the east and north of Lake Victoria Nyanza are outside the sphere of German colonization."[126] And to make his views known more publicly, in August 1889, Bismarck stated in the German newspaper *Norddeutsche Allgemeine Zeitung* that his government was opposed to the expedition on the grounds that "England regards [it] as an interference in her sphere of interest." "English friendship," he added in the article, "is far more valuable for us than anything which the expedition could hope to achieve."[127] The chancellor had made up his mind before Peters's expedition even got its start.

However, a change was to come that would shake the Wilhelmstrasse to its core. As noted earlier, with the death of Wilhelm I in March 1888, the German throne was soon occupied by his grandson, Wilhelm II.[128] The young nationalistic kaiser had dramatically different foreign policy views from Bismarck and was less pliant than his grandfather had been on these issues. After clashing with Bismarck for twenty-one months, particularly on Russia policy, Wilhelm dismissed the chancellor in March 1890, while Carl Peters was still on the Emin Pasha Expedition, annexing territory deep in the East African interior.[129] This change was seen with alarm in many European capitals, not least in London. Salisbury had been deeply concerned with the rise of Wilhelm II and referred to Bismarck's dismissal as "an enormous calamity, of which the sinister effects will be felt in every part of Europe."[130] Wilhelm II was also more sympathetic to the Peters expedition than his grandfather or Bismarck had been, raising new questions about how he would respond to Peters's fait accompli.[131]

As it would turn out, the new government in Berlin would see the expedition much like the old one, desiring to avoid conflict with London rather than claim new East African territory.[132] In fact, leaders in Berlin wanted to move rapidly toward a settlement of their outstanding conflicts with London in the region, before, as their ambassador in London put it, "an intolerable situation" developed.[133] In early May 1890, the new foreign minister, Adolf Marschall von Bieberstein, gave his British interlocutors "the positive assurance that any action . . . taken by Dr. Peters would be considered as null and void by the German government."[134] He was echoed a few days later by another foreign office official, who, in conversation with a British interlocutor, affirmed that his government recognized that "Uganda at least as far as one degree south is in the British sphere."[135] And news that Peters had signed some sort of treaty with the kabaka of Buganda, which arrived in Europe in late May 1890, made leaders in Berlin only more eager to get an agreement with London as soon as possible.[136]

While the back-and-forth between the two governments would last a few more weeks, the ultimate result was the Anglo-German Treaty of July 1, 1890.[137] According to the terms of this agreement, the United Kingdom gained the German protectorate of Wituland, territory between Lake Victoria and Lake Tanganyika, and recognition of its sphere of influence over Uganda and its protectorate over Zanzibar. In return, Germany gained some small concessions in West Africa as well as Heligoland, an archipelago of less than 2 km² off of Germany's North Sea coast.[138] With this agreement, Germany's presence in the area was limited to German East Africa proper, which, after the failures of the DOAG, had recently been converted to a full-fledged state-run colony.[139] Thus, Britain effectively gained everything it wanted, and stopped the threat of German expansion in East Africa in its tracks.[140] Peters's fait accompli had been firmly and thoroughly rejected before he had even made it out of the interior.

When Carl Peters arrived back on the coast at Bagamoyo on July 16, 1890, and learned that his claims had been relinquished, he was so enraged that he was rendered speechless.[141] Upon his arrival in Zanzibar a few days later, he cabled Berlin, trying to get the decision reversed, but it was no use. What was done was done.[142] He shortly thereafter departed for home, arriving on German soil on August 18, 1890.[143] German leaders recognized, however, that they would have to handle Peters with caution. He still had a large popular following, was well connected with the German press, and had proven himself to be an able political agitator. To both placate his anger and indulge his narcissism, the new chancellor, Leo von Caprivi, personally telegraphed Peters, promising that he would be rewarded by the kaiser if he could remain on his best behavior. A few weeks later, Wilhelm II would bestow upon Peters the Order of the Crown, Third Class, and he received other decorations from the king of Saxony and the grand duke of Saxony-Weimar-Eisenach.[144] Peters would be back in East Africa just one year later, serving as an imperial commissioner for German East Africa in the Kilimanjaro region. However, he was soon forced to resign in disgrace after his penchant for brutality helped spark yet another popular armed uprising against German rule.[145]

This chapter presented the comparative case studies of successful and failed inadvertent expansion by Germany in East Africa in 1885 and in Kenya and Uganda in 1890. This chapter is unique in that it presented the book's only two cases of inadvertent expansion via political annexation, as opposed to armed conquest. Both cases support the theory of inadvertent expansion presented in chapter 1. First, the Kenya and Uganda case showed unauthorized peripheral expansion to be a manifestation of a principal-agent problem: a divergence of preferences between Berlin and the East African periphery and a lack of telegraphic communications hampered Berlin's ability to communicate with, and potentially control, the expedition. Second, in both cases the very act of engaging in territorial expansion generated constraints that made withdrawal appear difficult from the perspective of leaders in the capital. Peters's faits accomplis both sunk the costs of territorial acquisition and helped generate domestic political pressure on leaders in Berlin in favor of acceptance. And third, both cases showed how expectations of geopolitical risk play a crucial role in driving decisions of whether to accept or reject the territorial fait accompli. In the case of East Africa in 1885, a lack of geopolitical risk, when combined with domestic political pressure, convinced Bismarck that the potential costs of accepting the territory were sufficiently low as to merit its acquisition. In contrast, in the case of Kenya and Uganda in 1890, geopolitical risk in the form of British imperial interests convinced both Bismarck, and then Wilhelm II, that the costs of acceptance were far too great, resulting in territorial relinquishment.

At least part of what is striking about these two cases are the key leaders in the capital who ultimately accept and reject the faits accomplis. In the case of German East Africa in 1885, it was Otto von Bismarck, the reluctant imperialist and practitioner of Realpolitik—who famously said, "All this colonial business is a sham"—who made the ultimate decision to retain the territory his agents had claimed.[146] In contrast, in the case of Kenya and Uganda in 1890, it was Wilhelm II, the aggressive nationalist and proponent of Weltpolitik—who would aim to give Germany its "place in the sun"—who exercised restraint in deciding to relinquish the territorial claims.[147] The cases of Bismarck and Wilhelm II, and the theory of inadvertent expansion more broadly, illuminate the various constraints—both domestic and international—that leaders operate under, pressuring them to make decisions that are at odds with what might be expected based on their foreign policy views.

Leadership, calculation, control over events—these are merely the illusions of statesmen and scholars. The passions of men and momentum of events take over and propel societies in novel and unanticipated directions.

—Robert Gilpin, 1981

This book has examined inadvertent expansion in the modern history of great power politics. It has introduced the concept of inadvertent expansion, has put forward a theory to explain when and why it occurs, and has supported the theory with a great deal of quantitative and qualitative evidence. This brief final chapter concludes the book. It has two central purposes. The first is to recap what has been learned in the earlier pages, summarizing the concept and theory of inadvertent expansion and highlighting key findings in each of the quantitative and qualitative empirical chapters. The second is to discuss the contemporary relevance of the arguments and evidence in this book, as well as their implications for both international relations scholarship and the practice of foreign policy.

Arguments and Primary Findings

Inadvertent expansion is territorial expansion that is planned and executed by actors on the periphery of a state or empire, without the necessary authorization of leaders in the capital. In chapter 1, I argued that inadvertent expansion is a process that tends to unfold in two basic steps. The first step is what I referred to as "unauthorized peripheral expansion." This occurs when state and nonstate actors on the periphery of a state or empire plan and execute instances of territorial expansion, without the authorization or support of leaders at home in the capital. The second step is what I referred to as "subsequent central authorization." This occurs when these peripheral actors, having claimed foreign territory without the authority to do so, present leaders in the capital with their claims as a fait accompli, and these leaders are then forced to decide whether to accept or reject the territorial claim.

The theory of inadvertent expansion presented in chapter 1 made three central arguments. First, that the most important explanation for unauthorized peripheral expansion is the degree of control leaders in the capital have over the periphery. Unauthorized peripheral expansion is best understood as a principal-agent problem, where diverse preferences between the capital and the periphery, and information asymmetries favoring the latter, help create the conditions for peripheral actors to engage in unauthorized expansion. When leaders in the capital have the ability to regularly monitor the behavior of their peripheral agents—typically, though not exclusively, in the form of rapid communications technology—unauthorized peripheral expansion is much less likely to occur. In contrast, when leaders in the capital lack the ability to regularly monitor their peripheral agents, unauthorized peripheral expansion will be far more likely. Thus, the first step of inadvertent expansion is crucially about control. It should be most likely to occur where centralized control is at its weakest.

The second key argument in the theory of inadvertent expansion is that the very act of unauthorized peripheral expansion changes "the facts on the ground" and thereby alters the strategic calculus facing leaders in the capital. Peripheral expansion generates constraints on central leaders, pressuring them to consider retaining the territory when they otherwise would not, and it does so for three basic reasons. First, unauthorized peripheral expansion often sinks the costs of acquiring the territory in question. Because these peripheral agents have already irrecoverably expended the costs of expansion on behalf of the state or empire, leaders will tend to see withdrawal and relinquishment as a wasted opportunity. Second, unauthorized peripheral expansion will frequently generate domestic political pressure on the leaders to support their own agents and nationals, regardless of their insubordination or unscrupulousness. Leaders may be influenced by political, military, or imperial elites in and around the capital, or the public at large may become aware of events on the frontier and rally to the cause of their conationals, putting pressure on the leaders. Third, unauthorized peripheral expansion tends to engage the state or empire's prestige, honor, and reputation in a way it simply was not engaged before. Once a territory has been partly or wholly acquired, it often appears difficult, if not impossible, to back down and relinquish the claims without an unacceptable stain on the national honor. Thus, unauthorized peripheral expansion tends to generate constraints on leaders and encourage territorial retention.

The third central argument of the theory of inadvertent expansion is that leaders' ultimate decision to either accept or reject the territorial fait accompli is crucially conditioned by the geopolitical risk associated with doing so. When there are expectations of significant geopolitical risk associated with acquisition—in the form of crippling economic isolation, armed conflict with a regional power, or encroaching on the interests of a rival great power—leaders will be far less likely to accept the fait accompli and retain the territory. In contrast, when there is little perceived geopolitical risk associated with acquisition, these leaders will be far more likely to accept the territorial fait accompli, thereby completing the process of inadvertent expansion.

These arguments were supported with a variety of different kinds of empirical evidence. Chapter 2 focused on the broad patterns of strategic and inadvertent expansion over the past two hundred years. It presented data on great power territorial expansion from 1816 to the present and included three central findings. First, that inadvertent expansion is a surprisingly general phenomenon, occurring in nearly one-in-four cases of territorial expansion by the great powers. Second, that cases of great power territorial expansion are significantly *more* likely to be inadvertent when the territory in question lacks a connection to the global telegraph network. And third, that cases of great power territorial expansion are significantly *less* likely to be inadvertent when they involve considerable geopolitical risk. These last two findings remain strong and significant even when controlling for a number of important potentially confounding variables, including the passage of time, the distance from the capital to the territory in question, whether the expansion took place as part of a broader conflict, whether the expansion took the form of annexation rather than conquest, and the strength of the great power's institutions, its regime type, and its relative power.

Chapters 3–7 then presented a series of paired comparative case studies of successful and failed inadvertent expansion in the history of great power politics. Chapter 3 presented two cases of the United States in the American South. In the case of Florida, a lack of control by Washington over its southern frontier allowed Andrew Jackson to independently claim Spanish Florida for the United States. And a combination of domestic political pressure and expectations within the Monroe administration of only modest amounts of geopolitical risk encouraged it to retain Jackson's territorial claims in 1819. In the 1836–37 case of Texas, by contrast, the desire to avoid what was seen as a likely war with Mexico pressured the administration of then-*president* Andrew Jackson to pass up the opportunity to acquire the newly independent republic, despite domestic political pressure to the contrary.

Chapter 4 presented two cases of Russia on the Central Asian Steppe. In the case of the Khanate of Kokand, a lack of control by St. Petersburg over its peripheral agents enabled Mikhail Cherniaev to independently conquer the cities of Chimkent and Tashkent. The absence of geopolitical risk associated with this acquisition, as well as honor concerns among Russian leaders, led to the retention of these Kokandian territories in 1866. In the case of the Ili region, by contrast, a similarly unauthorized territorial claim by Konstantin Petrovich von Kaufman was turned back by St. Petersburg in 1881, after a nearly ten-year occupation. Despite the emergence of both domestic political pressure in St. Petersburg and honor concerns among Russian leaders, fear of war with China over the distant territory was enough for them to relinquish the territorial claim.

Chapter 5 presented two cases of France in the Southeast Asian region of Tonkin. In the first case, occurring in 1873–74, a lack of control by Paris over its peripheral agents allowed François Garnier to independently claim Tonkin for the French Empire. However, after his death, Paris would return the territory to local Vietnamese authorities due to concerns over the potentially adverse reactions of Germany and the United Kingdom. In the second case, occurring in 1882–83, a similar lack of central control enabled Henri Rivière to, again, claim Tonkin on behalf of the empire without authorization from Paris. In this case, however, a combination of honor concerns and few expected geopolitical risks associated with retaining the territory by French leaders resulted in Tonkin's acquisition. While French leaders consistently downplayed the risks of Chinese intervention, they were ultimately mistaken, and war with China would, indeed, result. Yet, the expectations and resultant behavior of leaders in Paris were consistent with the theory of inadvertent expansion.

Chapter 6 presented the comparative cases of Japan in Manchuria and Italy in the port city of Fiume. These two cases were noteworthy in that it was pathological civil-military relations, rather than rudimentary communications technology, that led to a lack of control by these capitals over their peripheral agents. In the Japan case, the independence of the Kwantung Army vis-à-vis Tokyo allowed it to launch the invasion of Manchuria in September 1931. Domestic political pressure in this case was particularly grave, leading to the fall of one prime minister (Wakatsuki) and the later assassination of another (Inukai). And, while concerns of geopolitical risk were initially very high among leaders in Tokyo, over time these concerns dissipated, leading to the territory's retention by March 1932. In the Italy case, Gabriele D'Annunzio's unauthorized conquest of the port city of Fiume was aided and abetted by much of the Italian military, against direct orders from leaders in Rome. Yet, despite significant domestic political support for the conquest, leaders in the capital quickly decided to reject the territorial fait accompli out of concern over the harsh reactions of France, the United Kingdom, and, most important, the United States.

Chapter 7 was the final empirical chapter of the book, presenting two cases of Germany in East Africa. These two cases were also noteworthy, in that they presented the book's only two cases of inadvertent expansion via territorial annexation, the previous cases having all consisted of armed conquest. In the first case, a German colonial organization led by Carl Peters annexed a number of territories in what would later become German East Africa. And the absence of geopolitical risk associated with these annexations, along with domestic political pressure in Berlin, led the German chancellor Otto von Bismarck to retain the territorial claims in 1885. In the second case, by contrast, Peters's unauthorized annexations through Kenya and Uganda would ultimately be rejected by Kaiser Wilhelm II in Berlin in 1890. Despite domestic political pressure to the contrary, concern among German leaders regarding a potential conflict with the United Kingdom over the territory encouraged relinquishment.

In sum, the theory of inadvertent expansion was given strong support using both comprehensive quantitative data as well as a variety of historical comparative case studies. The quantitative analysis and nearly all of the cases suggest that inadvertent expansion is well characterized as a principal-agent problem, with the delegation of authority from the capital to the periphery leading to a loss of control and unauthorized peripheral expansion. It is also clear that the very act of peripheral agents engaging in unauthorized expansion helps generate constraints on leaders, which make relinquishing the territorial claims difficult. In all cases of inadvertent expansion presented, sunk costs, domestic political pressure, or honor concerns emerged to constrain leaders' freedom of choice regarding the territory. Finally, the data analysis and all cases support the idea that geopolitical risk is a crucial factor in leader decisions about whether to accept or reject their agents' territorial claims.

Contemporary Relevance

The last documented case of inadvertent expansion by the great powers was nearly a century ago, with Japan's 1931 invasion of Manchuria. The global spread of rapid modern communications technology—from the telegraph to the telephone, to the internet—has meant that central governments are much better able to monitor and control the behavior of their agents around the world. Similarly, the past few decades have seen the steady ascendancy of civilians over militaries in governments worldwide. According to data on military participation in government, the share of active-duty military in cabinets worldwide averaged around 12 percent in 1975 but had declined to around 2 percent by 2008. Among the major powers, this figure averaged between 2 percent and 3 percent between 1965 and 2008.[1] Thus, with both technology and civilian ascendancy increasing the control that central governments have over their agents on their borders and beyond, there are far fewer opportunities for inadvertent expansion than there once were, particularly among the world's most powerful and technologically advanced states.

However, inadvertent expansion is not entirely a relic of the past. Despite its historical nature, the phenomenon is contemporarily relevant in at least three important ways. The first has to do with the role inadvertent expansion may have played in the broader decline of territorial conquest. It is a well-documented research finding in international relations scholarship that large-scale territorial conquest has declined dramatically since 1945.[2] According to the "Territorial Change Data," there were 210 instances of conquest and annexation between 1816 and 1945—a rate of 1.6 per year; yet there were only 26 such instances after 1945—a rate of just 0.4 per year.[3] Among great powers, the decline is even starker. According to the data I presented in chapter 2, there were 254 instances of territorial expansion by the great powers from 1816 to 1945 but just 4 from 1946 to the present. These figures notwithstanding, it is important not to overstate the extent of this decline. As Dan Altman points out, and as I make clear regarding my own data in chapter 2, the existing expansion data typically only include successful cases of expansion, not both successful and failed expansion *attempts*. Altman examines conquest attempts from 1918 to the present and shows that smaller-scale conquests, what he refers to as "land grabs," have continued, suggesting more evolutionary change than dramatic decline.[4] Yet, it remains the case that large-scale conquest by the great powers has become exceedingly rare. Why might this be?

There are many plausible explanations for the decline of large-scale conquest. For example, the advent of the nuclear era in 1945 meant that states could pay significantly higher costs for engaging in territorial expansion, especially onto the territory of nuclear states and their close allies.[5] Economic globalization and a shift toward knowledge-based economies has also meant that many of the benefits of conquest can be acquired through much less costly means, such as trade and investment, and that extracting economic gains through occupation has become far more difficult.[6] The emergence of a territorial integrity norm—the idea that force should not be used to alter state borders—has also likely played a role in this decline.[7] And some also argue that the emergence of international law regulating conquest and conflict has itself contributed to this decline.[8] Yet, it is also noteworthy that as global communications technology has improved, and as states have become more centralized in their foreign policy decision-making, an important historical pathway to territorial expansion—inadvertent expansion— has been largely closed off, particularly among the world's most powerful states. And, while it is difficult to determine the precise extent to which the decline in great power inadvertent expansion contributed to the broader decline of conquest, it is unlikely that it played no role whatsoever.

A second point of contemporary relevance is that inadvertent expansion has not completely disappeared, particularly among the weaker smaller states. According to data collected by Dan Altman and Melissa Lee, approximately one-in-five conquest attempts since 1950 may have involved militaries acting without orders from their civilian superiors.[9] For example, in April 1983, Nigerian forces under the command of General (and later president) Muhammadu Buhari seized several islands on Lake Chad from Chadian government control, against the orders of the civilian president Shehu Shagari.[10] About a year later, in June 1984, the commander in chief of the Thai army Arthit Kamlang-ek ordered the conquest of a handful of disputed villages along the Laotian border, apparently without authorization from Prime Minister Prem Tinsulanonda.[11] And, in January 1995, Ecuadorian forces helped ignite the Cenepa War with Peru by establishing a "defensive" perimeter in the disputed Cenepa River Valley—again, without having been authorized by Ecuador's civilian president, Sixto Durán-Ballén.[12] There are other examples, but the essential point is clear: inadvertent expansion remains a problem, particularly among small states and in developing-world contexts. Under these conditions, central government authority is often relatively weak, control over parts of the state apparatus can be fairly loose, and civil-military relations can be pathological.

A third reason the theory of inadvertent expansion remains relevant to contemporary international politics is that, while the great powers engage in far less territorial expansion than they once did, decentralized foreign policy decision-making structures still exist and increase the risk of inadvertent crises and conflict more generally. For instance, in recent years the Russian government has made extensive use of semistate private military companies such as the Wagner Group in military operations in Syria, Sudan, the Central African Republic, Mali, Mozambique, Libya, and, especially, Ukraine.[13] In one particularly high-stakes incident in February 2018, Wagner forces and their Syrian allies ended up in a firefight with about forty US Army and Marine special forces in Eastern Syria, leading to somewhere between a few dozen and a few hundred casualties among the Russian mercenaries.[14] China has also regularly employed armed civilian fishing vessels known as the Maritime Militia to collect intelligence, provide logistical support, and protect and pursue its territorial claims in the Yellow, East, and South China Seas.[15] Clashes of the Maritime Militia with the Japanese Coast Guard around the Senkaku/Diaoyu Islands in September 2010 and with the Philippine Navy around Scarborough Shoal in April 2012—two US treaty allies—also illustrate the risks and stakes involved in their use.

To be clear, in none of these instances is there clear evidence that these semistate forces were operating without the knowledge or authorization of the central government.[16] In fact, in the Wagner Group in Syria case, there is at least some evidence to suggest that the Russian government was aware of and may have even authorized its operations.[17] However, the shadowy existence of such actors, and the sometimes-murky lines of authority under which they operate, clearly creates the potential for unauthorized action on their part. And it does not take much imagination to envision how, in an interstate crisis involving these kinds of actors, domestic political pressure and concerns over national honor could effectively bind the hands of civilian leaders.[18]

Consider, for instance, the Donbas War. This is part of the broader war between Russia and Ukraine, which broke out in the Donbas region of eastern Ukraine in April 2014 and is ongoing at the time of writing. The Donbas War was set in motion when a forty-four-year-old former intelligence and military officer by the name of Igor Girkin—otherwise known as "Strelkov" or "Shooter"—crossed the border from Russia into Ukraine on April 12, 2014, with fifty-two lightly armed volunteer personnel. Once across the border, Girkin and his makeshift force linked up with some anti-Kyiv militias, captured an armory and claimed a few government buildings in the city of Slovyansk, and began to fan the flames of the insurgency. Militias quickly sprang up in towns and cities across the Donetsk and Lugansk regions of eastern Ukraine, and when the self-proclaimed "People's Republics" of these two regions declared their independence from Kyiv in May 2014, Girkin was made their defense minister.[19]

While much remains to be learned about what transpired in these early months, many believe that Girkin was acting without authorization from the Kremlin in Moscow. According to historian Mark Galeotti, Girkin "was acting not just *without* orders when he led a rag-tag collection of gunmen across the Ukrainian border in April 2014, but seemingly *against* them."[20] This interpretation is shared by journalist Anna Arutunyan, who argues that in entering the Donbas, Girkin was "*defying* orders, not carrying them out."[21] And Girkin himself even claimed to be personally responsible for the outbreak of the war, telling a Russian newspaper in November 2014 that he was "the one who pulled the trigger of this war." "If our unit hadn't crossed the border," Girkin continued, "everything would have fizzled out. . . . I take personal responsibility for what is happening there."[22] It is also noteworthy that Moscow initially seemed reluctant to get involved.[23] Its primary aim of acquiring the Crimean Peninsula had just been achieved in March and at very little cost. The Donbas seemed like a costly diversion. However, given that the spark of conflict had already been lit by Girkin, leaders in Moscow felt bound to support him. According to Arutunyan, Putin likely felt that "if he backed away entirely, he would show weakness to the Americans and to his own nationalists."[24] Therefore, the Russian government deployed approximately 6,500 forces into eastern Ukraine in August 2014.[25] Russia remained mired in this hybrid war from this point until its leaders decided to dramatically escalate with the broader invasion of Ukraine in February 2022. According to United Nations' estimates, from the beginning of the Donbas War until the end of 2021, Russia suffered 6,500 killed and 16,200 wounded.[26] And all of this for a conflict it seemingly did not choose to initiate and likely felt hard pressed to extract itself from. Thus, while the outcome of inadvertent territorial expansion by the great powers has become less likely, the basic logic of the argument remains relevant in contemporary great power politics.

Theoretical Implications

The theory of inadvertent expansion and the evidence presented in this book have three important implications for international relations theory. The first has to do with how we understand a considerable portion of territorial expansion by the great powers. As discussed in this book's introduction, most theories of territorial expansion in international relations see these decisions being made by leaders in great power capitals and based on strategic assessments of cost, risk, and relative power. And even the theories that focus on the nonstrategic drivers of territorial expansion—such as those focused on domestic political regime type, leader psychology, and status seeking—still tend to see the most important decisions being made by leaders of powerful states. As is clear from the theory presented in chapter 1 and the evidence in the chapters that followed, the theory of inadvertent expansion does not completely jettison the role of state or imperial leaders when it comes to key expansion decisions. After all, it is only leaders in state or imperial capitals who have the ability and authority to decide whether to accept the territorial faits accomplis presented by their wayward peripheral agents. However, the initial impetus and decisions for expansion come from these peripheral actors, and their actions place important constraints on leaders that often effectively force them to go along. The theory of inadvertent expansion, therefore, is an important reminder of the regular influence of relatively peripheral, mundane, "everyday" actors in the process of foreign policy making. "The international system," note Margaret Keck and Kathryn Sikkink in their classic book on transnational activism, "is made up not only of states engaged in self help . . . but of dense webs of interactions and interrelations among citizens."[27] Put even more pointedly, Eric Grynaviski notes that the "consistent focus on political elites in contemporary scholarship, at the expense of individuals who live far from nations' capitals, means focusing on the agents who react to, instead of initiate, change."[28] The repeated occurrence of inadvertent expansion in the history of great power politics puts in stark relief the surprising influence of small and seemingly insignificant actors on the decisions made at the highest levels of the world's most powerful states.

The second theoretical implication has to do with how we understand state strategy. A significant portion of international relations theory depicts leaders as forward-looking and strategic actors with the ability to proactively direct state bureaucracies to meet their security needs and achieve their national interests. As two important representatives of this approach, David Lake and Robert Powell note that the "strategic-choice approach assumes that actors make purposive choices, that they survey their environment and, to the best of their ability, choose the strategy that best meets their subjectively defined goals."[29] The theory and evidence presented in this book clearly does not question leaders' ability to make strategic decisions. After all, in cases of inadvertent expansion, state and imperial leaders often make decisions by carefully weighing the relative costs of domestic political punishment and international geopolitical risk. Yet, the evidence in this book does depict national security policy as frequently made in an ad hoc manner, as haphazard, as reactive rather than proactive, and as chasing events rather than shaping them. As Richard Betts so succinctly puts it: "Strategy is not always an illusion, but it often is."[30] Despite the evidence of strategic decisions made at the individual level, the research presented in this book has uncovered a significant number of important historical cases in which broader notions of state strategy are fairly tenuous. Given such important and abundant nonstrategic state behavior, perhaps it is worth considering that, in many instances, strategic behavior will be less deliberate and more like what Henry Mintzberg and James Waters refer to as "emergent strategy," consisting of patterns of behavior realized despite, or even in the absence of, intentions.[31]

The third implication for international relations theory has to do with the idea of state unity. Large and important bodies of international relations scholarship assume that the state is a unitary actor, approaching the world and making policy decisions as a cohesive, integrated whole. As Kenneth Waltz famously argues, states "are unitary actors who, at a minimum, seek their own preservation and, at a maximum, drive for universal domination."[32] And, while he recognizes that it is a large and potentially problematic simplification, Charles Glaser, too, "assumes that states can be envisioned as unitary actors."[33] For Waltz, Glaser, and others, the assumption of state unity is clearly a theoretically fruitful one. And it is even a decent depiction of how national security policy is sometimes made.[34] However, the arguments and evidence presented in this book show the important limits of the state unity assumption. States and empires are complex, sprawling, bureaucratic bodies made up of thousands of organizations and individuals with varying authorities, interests, risk tolerances, and capabilities. It is true that, even in the theory of inadvertent expansion, final decisions are made by key representatives of the state based on their calculations of geopolitical risk. Yet, to ignore the critical role played by actors on the periphery in initial expansion decisions—and the way their actions subsequently bind the hands of central state representatives—is to miss much of what goes on in these cases. In short, a great deal of territorial expansion by the great powers simply cannot be understood without relaxing the assumption of state unity. And, if this is true in as high stakes and as consequential a policy area as territorial expansion, then it is likely true in most others.

Policy Implication

The arguments and evidence presented in this book also have one important policy implication. This is that they should lead foreign policy practitioners to be cautious in how they interpret each and every behavior they see another state engage in. "A common misperception," Robert Jervis notes in his classic work on the subject, "is to see the behavior of others as more centralized, planned, and coordinated than it is."[35] This tendency is frequently on display in how national security leaders and the media discuss state foreign policies with an almost exclusive focus on their leaders. Note, for example, how in a February 2022 speech at the White House on Russia's invasion of Ukraine, the US president Joseph Biden argued that "Putin is the aggressor. Putin chose this war," as if the invasion had been decided on and was even being carried out by Russia's leader himself.[36] Similarly, media headlines often use a leader's name as a stand-in for the government as a whole, such as "Trump Drops Mother of All Bombs" or references to "Xi Jinping's Zero-Covid Policy."[37] Clearly, states frequently act in a coordinated, cohesive way when making foreign policy decisions—it is not all chaos, all the time. Yet, this book has uncovered, explained, and exhaustively catalogued one crucially important historical phenomenon—inadvertent territorial expansion— where such assumptions would be wholly misplaced. A clearer understanding of the nature of inadvertent foreign policies, and the conditions under which they are most likely, will reduce the tendency for misperceptions to drive foreign policy decision-making. And this, it is hoped, will help us avoid the potentially gravest and costliest misunderstandings in world politics.

Notes

ACKNOWLEDGMENTS

1. Jervis 1998, 162.

INTRODUCTION

1. Moon 1989, 564, 566–567; Huttenback 1993, 228–229; James 1997, 102.
2. Huttenback 1993, 236.
3. Huttenback 1962, 99; Moon 1989, 572.
4. The Sind armies numbered approximately eleven thousand. James 1997, 103. See also Huttenback 1962, 102–103; Moon 1989, 573.
5. Moon 1989, 573–574; James 1997, 104.
6. It turned out the clever pun was not attributable to Napier. Moon 1989, 575; James 1997, 105.
7. Moon 1989, 575.
8. "Sir Robert Peel to Sir James Graham, September 19, 1843," in Parker 1899, 11; Gash 1972, 488–489.
9. Gash 1972, 488; Ansari 2005, 41–42.
10. Moon 1989, 575.
11. Gladstone 1876, 875.
12. Huurdeman 2003, 124–128.
13. "Sir Robert Peel to Lord Ripon, December 9, 1843," in Parker 1899, 18.
14. Area and population data from Territorial Change Data (v5.0). Tir et al. 1998.
15. On gains, see Gilpin 1981, chap. 3; Liberman 1998. On anarchy, see Mearsheimer 2014, chap. 2. On technology and geography, see Van Evera 1999, chap. 6; K. Adams 2004. On commitment problems, see Fazal 2007. On state institutional capacity, see Zakaria 1998. On intentions, see Schweller 1994; Glaser 2010, 35–40.
16. Gilpin 1981, 106.
17. Mearsheimer 2014, 31, 43.
18. Fazal 2007, 38.
19. Altman 2017, 2020.
20. On regime type, see Lake 1992; Bueno de Mesquita et al. 2003, 412–414. On capitalism, see Hobson 1902, chaps. 4, 6–7; Lenin 1987. On psychology, see Taliaferro 2004. On status, see J. Barnhart 2016. On nationalist mythmaking, see J. Snyder 1991. See also Kupchan 1994. On xenophobia, see Maass 2020. On the cult of the offensive, see J. Snyder 1984, 2014. See also Van Evera 1984, 1999, chap. 7.
21. Bueno de Mesquita et al. 2003, 414.
22. Taliaferro 2004, 48.
23. Krause and Eiran 2018, 480.
24. P. MacDonald 2020, 41.

1. A THEORY OF INADVERTENT EXPANSION

1. See Goertz and Diehl 1992, chap. 4.
2. On the Alaska purchase, see Alessio and Renfro 2016.

3. On military occupation, see Edelstein 2008. On neotrusteeship, see Fearon and Laitin 2004.

4. Zakaria 1998, 5.

5. Lynn-Jones 1998, 161n10.

6. For definitions of empire, see Doyle 1986, 30–47; Nexon and Wright 2007.

7. Weisiger (2014, 359), e.g., defines "conquest" as a "decisive military victory."

8. Mearsheimer 2014, 33–34.

9. Brooks and Wohlforth 2016.

10. Elman 1996, 28–29. See also Labs 1997, 12–14.

11. Schweller 2006, 112–113.

12. Though, Schweller (2006, 113) does posit that "democracies have little or no appetite for risky, aggressive expansion."

13. Doyle 1986, 25–26.

14. Gallagher and Robinson 1953; Galbraith 1960; Fieldhouse 1973, 76–84.

15. Robinson 1972; Darwin 1997; Hyam 1999.

16. P. MacDonald 2020, 43.

17. *Oxford English Dictionary*, s.v. "Autonomous, adj.," accessed July 2023, available at https://doi.org/10.1093/OED/6139242216.

18. *New Oxford American Dictionary*, 3rd ed., ed. Angus Stephenson and Christine A. Lindberg (New York: Oxford University Press, 2010), s.v. "Inadvertent."

19. For the seminal discussion of private violence in international politics, see Thomson 1996.

20. Strachan 2004, 30–31; Greenhalgh 2014, 118–119.

21. Stewart 1982, 23–24; Turnbull 2009, 27–31.

22. Esterhuyse 1968, 38–42, 46–62.

23. This is an absolutely enormous literature. For a foundational work, see Jensen and Meckling 1976. For helpful overviews, see Arrow 1984; Eisenhardt 1989; Kiser 1999; G. Miller 2005; Shapiro 2005. For a useful critique, see Moe 1984. And, for an early application in international relations, see Downs and Rocke 1994.

24. For the classic application of principal-agent theory to empire, see J. Adams 1996.

25. In a few cases, however, these agents are nonstate actors who are entirely independent of government support. When peripheral expansion occurs in these cases, it is less a principal-agent problem than a usurpation of state authority by private citizens. See, e.g., the cases of the United States in Texas (chap. 3) and Germany in East Africa (chap. 7).

26. Evans 1999, 73–74.

27. Pollack 1978, 172.

28. "Hicks Beach to Lord Beaconsfield, November 3, 1878," quoted in Brendon 2007, 180.

29. McIntyre 1967, 381; Klein 1998, 77.

30. Morris 1975, 529–530.

31. Andrew and Kanya-Forstner 1988, 13.

32. "Ellenborough to the Queen, Allahabad, June 27, 1843," in Colchester 1874, 101.

33. For foundational works, see Holmstrom 1979; Fama and Jensen 1983.

34. J. Adams 1996, 14–15; Kiser 1999, 146; Hawkins et al. 2006, 26–31.

35. Moe 1984, 769; Shapiro 2005, 267.

36. MacKenzie 1967, 272; Porch 1984, 134–135.

37. For strategic considerations, see M. Barnhart 1987, chap. 1. For economic motives, the German acquisition of South-West Africa is a useful representative case: see Esterhuyse 1968, 38–42, 46–62.

38. Galbraith 1960.

39. See Kanya-Forstner 1969, 178; Morris 1975, 535.

40. Aldrich and Connell 1992, 38.

41. On civil-military relations as a principal-agent problem, see Avant 1996; Feaver 2003, esp. chap. 3.

42. The heading for this section is from P. MacDonald 2004.

43. On the growth of empire by fait accompli, see Landes 1961, 505–506. On faits accomplis and modern territorial expansion, see Altman 2017. See also Tarar 2016.

44. On territorial expansion and sunk costs, see Taliaferro 2004, 33–35.

45. For a foundational work in behavioral economics, see Thaler 1980, esp. 47–50. For a discussion in international relations, see C. Miller 2019.

46. According to standard economic theory, sunk costs should not factor in to rational decision-making. However, this standard argument has faced criticism, as there are many conditions under which it is rational to consider sunk costs. See McAfee, Mialon, and Mialon 2010. In international relations, see C. Miller 2019.

47. For related arguments, see Hassner 2007; Krause and Eiran 2018.

48. See, e.g., Kanya-Forstner 1969, 108; Pakenham 2003, 178; W. Weeks 2013, 106.

49. Landes 1961, 505.

50. On status as a driver of territorial expansion, see J. Barnhart 2016, 2017. On status as a driver for international aggression more generally, see Dafoe, Renshon, and Huth 2014. For a useful critique, see P. MacDonald and Parent 2021.

51. On the somewhat-excessive preoccupation with reputation among leaders in international relations, see Mercer 1996, 19–21; D. Press 2005, 158–159; Tang 2005.

52. This point is similar to Barbara Walter's (2003) "reputation-building" theory of territorial conflict. In the history of empire, see Landes 1961, 505–506; Morris 1975, 535; Andrew and Kanya-Forstner 1988, 14; Hyam 1999.

53. Corrado 2014, 77. See also Paine 1996, 38–39.

54. Wesseling 1996, 295–296.

55. The "respect" quote is from MacKenzie 1988, 220. The "watching" quote is from "Konstantin Petrovich Kaufman," in Wieczynski 1980, vol. 16, 69. The "honor" quote is from Porch 1984, 134. See also Galbraith 1963, 239, 240; Pollack 1978, 124; Quinn 2000, 115.

56. See, e.g., Howe 2007, 103.

57. In the context of the British Empire, see Pollack 1978, 176–177; Ansari 2005. In the Russian Empire, see MacKenzie 1969, 307–308n86; Paine 1996, 120–121. For a related discussion in the context of the French Empire, see Porch 1984, 181. For an example from the Japanese Empire, see Matsusaka 2001, 384. In the context of American expansion, see Howe 2007, 104.

58. "Despatch from Glenelg to D'Urban, December 26, 1835 [Extracts]," in Bell 1928, 470–473; Galbraith 1963, 129, 132.

59. Quinn 2000, 157. See also Kanya-Forstner 1969, 72–83; Power 1977, 78–80.

60. Meinig 1998, 365–366; Nugent 2008, 261.

61. See J. Snyder 1991; Kupchan 1994; Taliaferro 2004.

62. On the importance of counterfactuals to causal explanation, see Fearon 1991; Levy 2008b.

63. On the different types of case studies, see George and Bennett 2005, 74–76.

64. Geddes 1990; King, Keohane, and Verba 1994, 128–139.

65. George and Bennett 2005, chaps. 3, 8.

66. George and Bennett 2005, chap. 10; Bennett and Checkel 2014.

67. Levy 2008a, 10–11.

68. On Israel, see Gorenberg 2006; Krause and Eiran 2018.

69. On case selection, see: King, Keohane, and Verba 1994, 139–149; Gerring 2001, 163–199; Bennett and Elman 2007, 172–178; George and Bennett 2005, 83–84.

70. King, Keohane, and Verba 1994, chap. 6; Gerring 2001, 165–171, 181–183.

71. See the online appendix accompanying this book. (https://doi.org/10.7910/DVN /JBGNNH)

72. This is what McAdam, Tarrow, and Tilly (2001, 81–83) refer to as an "uncommon foundations" research strategy. See also Musgrave and Nexon 2018, 604–605.

73. Gerring 2001, 174–178; George and Bennett 2005, 83–84; Bennett and Elman 2007, 174–175; Levy 2008a, 10–11.

74. On longitudinal control techniques, see George and Bennett 2005, 166–167, chap. 9; Bennett and Elman 2007, 176.

75. George and Bennett 2005, 153–166; Bennett and Elman 2007, 174–175; Levy 2008a, 10–11.

2. PATTERNS OF INADVERTENT EXPANSION, 1816–2014

1. A data codebook accompanying this book includes the full list of observations, brief narratives for each observation, coding justification for key variables, and citations of all the sources relied on.

2. Territorial Change Data (v5.0). Tir et al. 1998.

3. This was especially difficult in Russia's expansion in Central Asia as well as British and French expansion in Africa.

4. Approximately 80 percent (205/258) of the observations in my data are identifiable in the territorial change data. To some extent, this is likely due to varying inclusion criteria as well as how processes of expansion are either split up into separate observations or combined into single observations. Beyond this, given that the territorial change data cover the entire globe, whereas I focus narrowly on the nine great powers, it perhaps is not surprising that I uncovered a few more observations.

5. Cases such as the United States' purchase of Alaska in 1867 are not included on this basis.

6. Cases such as the Russian conquest of the Caucasus in the nineteenth century are not included on this basis, as the territory had been formally ceded to Russia by Persia in 1828.

7. Claims of various uninhabited islets and reefs as well as territorial claims in Antarctica are not included on this basis.

8. Cases such as the joint Anglo-French occupation of the Saar Basin after World War I are not included on this basis.

9. Cases such as the German invasion of the Soviet Union in 1941 are not included on this basis.

10. Zakaria (1998, 54–44) includes attempted, as well as considered, expansion in his study, though he is only examining a single great power (the United States) over the course of forty-three years. Dan Altman (2020) has also impressively compiled global conquest data that include attempts, though it only begins in 1918. Given that most inadvertent expansion occurs in the nineteenth century, this is a crucial limitation for the purpose of this book.

11. Fearon 2002.

12. I note that it seems at least plausible that cases of inadvertent expansion are more likely than intentional expansion both to fail in the peripheral attempt (due to inadequate planning or resources) and to be rejected by the capital, and, therefore, bias should be against finding cases of inadvertent expansion.

13. The great powers are defined as follows (modifications are underlined): United States of America (1816–2014), United Kingdom (1816–1945), France (1816–1940), Prussia/Germany (1816–1945), Austria-Hungary (1816–1918), Italy (1860–1943), Russia/Soviet Union (1816–2014), China (1950–2014), Japan (1868–1945). Correlates of War Project. 2017. "State System Membership List, v2016," available at http://www.correlate sofwar.org/.

14. This is how Goertz and Diehl (1992, 66–67) operationalize the importance of a given piece of territory.

15. In wartime, I also include the military high command among those whose orders make an observation "intentional."

16. In all but three observations of inadvertent expansion, I rely on either a primary source or at least two secondary sources. In many cases, I draw on considerably more sources in an effort to mitigate the risk of bias in individual historical sources. See Lustick 1996.

17. G. Snyder 1996.

18. For a discussion and defense, see Wendt 2004.

19. As a result, I have coded the vast majority (251/258 or 97 percent), though not the entirety, of the great power expansion observations with respect to whether they were inadvertent or intentional.

20. Region classification is derived from Ghosn, Palmer, and Bremer 2004.

21. Territorial Change Data (v5.0), "Territorial Change Coding Manual," 3, available at https://correlatesofwar.org/data-sets/territorial-change/; Kohen 2015.

22. Much of the telegraph data are from Huurdeman 2003, chap. 8, app. A; Bill Glover, "Cable Timeline: 1850–2018," in History of the Atlantic Cable and Undersea Communications, 2022, available at https://atlantic-cable.com/.

23. On the importance of the telegraph in imperial history, see P. Kennedy 1971; Headrick 1981, chap. 11.

24. Distance refers to "Great-Circle" or orthodromic distance, measured in kilometers. It is measured using the "Measure Distance" tool in Google Maps to ensure as accurate a measure between locations as possible. See Google Maps, 2023, available at https://www.google.com/maps.

25. Elman 1996, 28–29; Schweller 2006, 112–113.

26. See Alliance Treaty Obligation and Provision data (v5.1). Leeds et al. 2002. Formal Alliances (v4.1). Gibler 2009.

27. COW War Data (v4.0). Sarkees and Wayman 2010.

28. Brambor et al. 2020.

29. Polity5 Annual Time Series Data, 1800–2018. Monty G. Marshall, Ted Robert Gurr, and Keith Jaggers, "Polity5: Political Regime Characteristics and Transitions, 1800–2018," Center for Systemic Peace, 2020, available at http://www.systemicpeace.org/polityproject .html.

30. An expanding great power is considered an autocracy when its Polity score is −6 or lower. For the Varieties of Democracy data, see Michael Coppedge et al., "VDem Country–Year Dataset v12," Varieties of Democracy (V-Dem) Project, 2022, available at https://doi .org/10.23696/vdemds22; Daniel Pemstein et al., (2022), "The V-Dem Measurement Model: Latent Variable Analysis for Cross-National and Cross-Temporal Expert-Coded Data," *V-Dem Working Paper*, no. 21. 7th ed. University of Gothenburg: Varieties of Democracy Institute.

31. National Material Capabilities (v6.0). Singer, Bremer, and Stuckey 1972.

32. See the online appendix accompanying this book for more details on the analyses that follow (https://doi.org/10.7910/DVN/JBGNNH).

33. Note, however, that Italy has a failed case of inadvertent expansion (Fiume, 1919–20), which is discussed in depth in chapter 6. China, for its part, has been a regular target of inadvertent expansion (Amur Region in 1850, Ussuri Region in 1852, Manchuria in 1932, and a failed case in the Ili region in 1871–81). The failed case by Russia in the Ili region is discussed in depth in chapter 4.

34. Note also that controlling for the Asia-Pacific region increases the statistical significance of the coefficient on *risk*.

35. These are the United Kingdom in Western Peninsular Malaya (1874), North Borneo (1888), and Togoland (1914); France in Eastern Morocco (1904), Togoland (1914), and Cameroon (1916); and Japan in the Caroline Islands (1914), the Mariana Islands (1914), the Marshall Islands (1914), and Manchuria (1932).

36. These are the United States in Florida (1818); the United Kingdom in Togoland (1914); France in Togoland (1914) and Cameroon (1916); Russia in the Amur Region (1850) and the Ussuri Region (1850); and Japan in the Caroline Islands (1914), the Mariana Islands (1914), the Marshall Islands (1914), and Manchuria (1932).

37. These are the United Kingdom in Togoland (1914); France in Togoland (1914) and Cameroon (1916); and Japan in the Caroline Islands (1914), the Mariana Islands (1914), the Marshall Islands (1914), and Manchuria (1932). Note that all but one occur during World War I and onto German territory, suggesting that the "fog of war" may play a periodic role in enabling inadvertent expansion.

3. INADVERTENT EXPANSION IN THE AMERICAN SOUTH

1. "Territorial expansion of the United States—land area, by accession: 1790–2000 (Table Cf1)," in Sutch and Carter 2020.

2. Meinig 1993, 31; Nugent 2008, 111.

3. "Population: 1790–2000 (Table Aa6–8)," in Sutch and Carter 2020.

4. Nugent 2008, 117–120; Wood 2009, 686–687.

5. Nugent 2008, 119; W. Weeks 2013, 95.

6. W. Weeks 1996, 32.

7. Dangerfield 1952, 125–126; W. Weeks 1996, 41; Howe 2007, 98.

8. "Extract of a Letter from General Gaines to Major General Andrew Jackson, Fort Scott, Georgia, November 21, 1817" (686) and "General Gaines to the Secretary of War, Head-Quarters, Fort Scott, Georgia, December 2, 1817" (687), both in Lowrie and Clarke 1832.

9. "Andrew Jackson to the Secretary of War (John C. Calhoun), Nashville, December 16, 1817," in Bassett 1927, 340.

10. This is an estimate based on the fact that news of Jackson's initial attack on the Fort of St. Marks on April 6, 1818, was first learned in Washington on May 4, 1818. "May 4th, 1818," in C. Adams 1875, 87.

11. Howe 2007, 100, 106; W. Weeks 2013, 99.

12. Emphasis added. "John C. Calhoun to General Edmund P. Gaines, Department of War, December 16, 1817," in Lowrie and Clarke 1832, 689.

13. "Andrew Jackson to President Monroe, Head Quarters Southern Division, Nashville, January 6, 1818," in Bassett 1927, 346.

14. Dangerfield 1952, 138–139; Ammon 1971, 416; Cunningham 1996, 67.

15. "John C. Calhoun to Major General Andrew Jackson, Department of War, December 26, 1817," in Lowrie and Clarke 1832, 690. On Jackson's receipt, see "Andrew Jackson to Secretary Calhoun, Nashville, January 12, 1818," in Bassett 1927, 347.

16. "James Monroe to John C. Calhoun, Washington, D.C., Jany 30, 1818," in Hemphill 1963, 104; Ammon 1971, 417.

17. "John C. Calhoun to James Monroe, [Albermarle County, Va], War Dept., 12th September, 1818," in Hemphill 1967, 120.

18. "James Monroe to the Senate and House of Representatives of the United States, Washington, March 25, 1818," in Lowrie and Franklin 1834, 183.

19. "Andrew Jackson to John C. Calhoun, Head-Quarters, Division of the South, Nashville, January 20, 1818," in Lowrie and Clarke 1832, 697.

20. "Andrew Jackson to John C. Calhoun, Head-Quarters, Division of the South, Fort Early, February 26, 1818," in Lowrie and Clarke 1832, 698.

21. "Andrew Jackson to the John C. Calhoun, Head-Quarters, Division of the South, Fort Gadsden, March 25, 1818," in Lowrie and Clarke 1832, 698.

22. Remini 1977, 353; Howe 2007, 100.

23. Remini 1977, 354.

24. "Andrew Jackson to John C. Calhoun, Head-Quarters, Division of the South, Camp, Near St. Marks, April 8, 1818," in Lowrie and Clarke 1832, 700.

25. "General Jackson to F. C. Luengo, Head-Quarters, Division of the South, before St. Mark's, April 6, 1818," in Lowrie and Franklin 1834, 575.

26. "Andrew Jackson to John C. Calhoun, Head-Quarters, Division of the South, Bowleg's Town, Suwaney River, April 20, 1818," in Lowrie and Clarke 1832, 700; Remini 1977, 356.

27. "Andrew Jackson to Mrs. Jackson, St. Marks, April 8, 1818," in Bassett 1927, 358; "Jackson to Calhoun, April 8, 1818," in Lowrie and Clarke 1832, 700; Owsley Jr. 1985.

28. "General Orders, Division of the South, Adjutant General's Office, Camp Four Miles North of St. Mark's, April 29, 1818," in Lowrie and Franklin 1834, 595; Remini 1977, 358.

29. "Andrew Jackson to John C. Calhoun, Head-Quarters, Division of the South, Fort Gadsden, May 5, 1818," in Lowrie and Clarke 1832, 702.

30. "Andrew Jackson to William Davenport, Ft. Gadsden, Appelachecola, May 4, 1818," in Bassett 1927, 364–365; "Jackson to Calhoun, May 5, 1818," in Lowrie and Clarke 1832, 702.

31. "Andrew Jackson to John C. Calhoun, Head-Quarters, Division of the South, Fort Montgomery, June 2, 1818," in Lowrie and Clarke 1832, 708.

32. "General Jackson to Governor Mazot, Head-Quarters, Division of the South, On the Line of March, May 23, 1818," in Lowrie and Franklin 1834, 568.

33. "Jackson's Proclamation on Taking Possession of Pensacola, Pensacola, May 29, 1818," in Bassett 1927, 374–375.

34. "Jackson to Calhoun, June 2, 1818," in Lowrie and Clarke 1832, 708.

35. "Andrew Jackson to President Monroe, Headquarters of the South, Frt Montgomery, June 2, 1818," in Bassett 1927, 377.

36. "Jackson to Monroe, June 2, 1818," in Bassett 1927, 377.

37. Three lost in battle, one by sickness, two drowning, and one to friendly fire. See "Andrew Jackson to Rachel Jackson, Ft Montgomery, June 2nd 1818," in Moser, Hoth, and Hoemann 1994, 213.

38. Dangerfield 1952, 139; Niven 1988, 68; Howe 2007, 103.

39. "May 4th, 1818," in C. Adams 1875, 87.

40. "Don Luis de Onis to the Secretary of State, Bristol, June 17, 1818," in Lowrie and Franklin 1834, 495.

41. Ammon 1971, 421; Cunningham 1996, 60.

42. "June 18th, 1818," in C. Adams 1875, 102.

43. "July 7th, 1818," in C. Adams 1875, 108.

44. "Don Luis de Onis to the Secretary of State, Washington, July 8, 1818," in Lowrie and Franklin 1834, 496.

45. "James Monroe to James Madison, Little River, Loudoun County, Near Aldie, July 10, 1818," in Hamilton 1902, 54.

46. "July 13th, 1818," in C. Adams 1875, 107.

47. Dangerfield 1952, 137–138; W. Weeks 1992, 116; 1996, 44; Howe 2007, 103.

48. "July 10th, 1818," in C. Adams 1875, 106.

49. "July 11th, 1818," in C. Adams 1875, 106.

50. Dangerfield 1952, 143.

51. "Monroe to Jackson, July 19th, 1818," in Hamilton 1902, 58.

52. Ammon 1971, 423; W. Weeks 1996, 45; Howe 2007, 103.

53. Ammon 1971, 415; Remini 1977, 7–8, 342–343; W. Weeks 1996, 32; Brands 2005, 17, 297.

54. "July 16th, 1818," in C. Adams 1875, 109–110.

55. "July 18th, 1818," in C. Adams 1875, 113.

56. "July 18th, 1818," in C. Adams 1875, 113. See also W. Weeks 1992, 115.

57. Niven 1988, 70; W. Weeks 1992, 138.

58. "John C. Calhoun to Charles Tait, Cook's Law Office, Elbert County, Ga., War Dept., 5th September, 1818," in Hemphill 1967, 106.

59. Cunningham 1996, 64.

60. "James Monroe to James Madison, Washington, February 7th, 1819," in Hamilton 1902, 88.

61. "July 15th, 1818," in C. Adams 1875, 108; "James Monroe to James Madison, Washington, July 20, 1818," in Hamilton 1902, 61; "John C. Calhoun to Charles Tait, War Dept 20th July 1818," in Hemphill 1963, 408; Ammon 1971, 422; Niven 1988, 69, 70.

62. "July 13th, 1818," in C. Adams 1875, 107.

63. "James Monroe to General Jackson, Washington, July 19th, 1818," in Hamilton 1902, 57–58.

64. "July 20th, 1818," in C. Adams 1875, 113–114. See also Niven 1988, 69.

65. Niven 1988, 70; W. Weeks 1992, 116; Brands 2005, 340.

66. "July 21st, 1818," in C. Adams 1875, 113. See also W. Weeks 1992, 115.

67. Ammon 1971, 423; Remini 1977, 367; Niven 1988, 70–71; Howe 2007, 103.

68. "July 18th, 1818" and "July 21st, 1818," both in C. Adams 1875, 112, 114–115; Cunningham 1996, 61.

69. *Daily National Intelligencer* 1818, 2.

70. "Monroe to Jackson, July 19th, 1818" and "James Monroe to General Jackson, Washington, October 20, 1818," both in Hamilton 1902, 55, 74; "President's Message at the Commencement of the Session, Communicated to Congress, November 17, 1818," in Lowrie and Franklin 1834, 215; "The Secretary of State to Don Luis de Onis, Department of State, Washington, July 23, 1818" and "Secretary of State to Erving, November 28, 1818," both in Lowrie and Franklin 1834, 539, 541.

71. "Excerpt of a letter from J. C. Calhoun, Secretary of War, to Major General Andrew Jackson, dated, September 8, 1818," in Lowrie and Clarke 1832, 745; Ammon 1971, 426; Niven 1988, 70–71; Howe 2007, 106.

72. "James Monroe to Thomas Jefferson, Washington, July 22, 1818," in Hamilton 1902, 62.

73. "James Monroe to General Jackson, Washington, December 21, 1818" (quoted) and "Monroe to Madison, February 7th, 1819," both in Hamilton 1902, 86, 87–88.

74. "July 16th, 1818," in C. Adams 1875, 110.

75. W. Weeks 1992, 131.

76. Howe 2007, 107; Nugent 2008, 128–129.

77. Perkins 1964, chap. 15; W. Weeks 1992, 131; Nugent 2008, 123.

78. Perkins 1964, 284; W. Weeks 1996, 48–49; Howe 2007, 106.

79. "January 7 [1819]," in Rush 1833, 399. See also Dangerfield 1952, 149; Ammon 1971, 428; W. Weeks 1992, 147.

80. Ammon 1971, 422.

81. "July 15th, 1818," "July 16th, 1818," "July 17th, 1818," and "July 20th, 1818," all in C. Adams 1875, 108, 109, 111, 113–114; "Monroe to Jefferson, July 22, 1818," in Hamilton 1902, 63; Remini 1977, 366; Niven 1988, 69–70; Cunningham 1996, 61.

82. "Monroe to Jackson, July 19th, 1818," in Hamilton 1902, 57.

83. W. Weeks 1992, 122.

84. Cunningham 1996, 64.

85. "Monroe to Jackson, July 19th, 1818," in Hamilton 1902, 58.

86. *Daily National Intelligencer* 1818, 2.

87. "Secretary of State to Erving, November 28, 1818," in Lowrie and Franklin 1834, 542.

88. Remini 1977, 371.

89. Cunningham 1996, 66; Howe 2007, 104–106.

90. "'Speech on the Seminole War,' January 20, 1819," in Hopkins 1961, 659.

91. W. Weeks 1992, 160.

92. Remini 1977, 374–375; Howe 2007, 106–107.

93. Nugent 2008, 127.

94. "February 22nd, 1818," in C. Adams 1875, 275.

95. W. Weeks 1996, 52; Howe 2007, 109.

96. "James Monroe to Thomas Jefferson, Washington, May 1820," in Hamilton 1902, 123. See also W. Weeks 2013, 110.

97. The case of Texas is different from other cases in this book. While in most cases the peripheral agents who engage in conquest and present leaders in the capital with a fait accompli are members of the state apparatus, or at least are the state's own nationals, in this case they are recent émigrés to a foreign territory. Thus, the idea that unauthorized peripheral expansion is a principal-agent problem does not apply to this case, since there is no real delegation of authority. However, the recency of their emigration, as well as the fact that they were led by American political elites, make this case comparable with the others. And, despite these differences, the case shows that the dynamics of failed inadvertent expansion are broadly similar to other cases.

98. "Territorial Expansion of the United States," in Sutch and Carter 2020.

99. Meinig 1993, 129; Nugent 2008, 136.

100. Howe 2007, 660; Nugent 2008, 131, 152–153.

101. Pletcher 1973, 67; W. Weeks 1996, 86–87.

102. Pletcher 1973, 68; W. Weeks 1996, 87; Nugent 2008, 150–151.

103. Howe 2007, 661.

104. Haley 2002, 12–15.

105. Haley 2002, 87 (quote), 50–61, 64–82, 87–91.

106. Cole 1993, 134; Herring 2008, 164.

107. Remini 1984, 352; Meacham 2008, 315.

108. Remini 1981, 218.

109. Remini 1981, 202.

110. Remini 1984, 353; Cole 1993, 131; Brands 2005, 514; Meacham 2008, 316; Maass 2020, 124.

111. Brands 2005, 514.

112. Brands 2005, 516; "Andrew Jackson to President Van Buren, Hermitage, January 23, 1838," in Bassett 1931, 529.

113. "Andrew Jackson to Colonel Anthony Butler, Washington, February 15, 1841," in Bassett 1929, 245.

114. There is a broad historical consensus that the United States played no direct role in the outbreak of the Texas Revolution. See Pletcher 1973, 69; Remini 1984, 360; Cole 1993, 131; Meinig 1993, 141; Howe 2007, 669; Herring 2008, 174; Nugent 2008, 153–154.

115. Howe 2007, 661.

116. Nugent 2008, 152.

117. "Appeal by Stephen F. Austin, New York, April 15, 1836," in Bassett 1931, 398.

118. Howe 2007, 666, 669; Nugent 2008, 153.

119. W. Weeks 1996, 87; Howe 2007, 662.

120. Pletcher 1973, 70.

121. Cole 1993, 133.

122. Duckett 1962, 198–200; Pletcher 1973, 72; Remini 1984, 358, 360.

123. Nugent 2008, 153.

124. Pletcher 1973, 74.

125. W. Weeks 2013, 167.

126. W. Weeks 1996, 89–92.

127. Doc. 3342: "Powhatan Ellis, United States Chargé d'Affaires at Mexico City, to John Forsyth, Secretary of State of the United States, Mexico, May 19, 1836," in Manning 1937, 326, 327.

128. Doc. 3345: "Powhatan Ellis to John Forsyth, [Extract], Mexico, June 25, 1836," in Manning 1937, 330.

129. Doc. 3358: "Powhatan Ellis to John Forsyth, Mexico, August 26, 1836" (344), and Doc. 3374: "Powhatan Ellis to John Forsyth, Mexico, October 11, 1836" (369), both in Manning 1937.

130. Doc. 3346: "Powhatan Ellis to John Forsyth, [Extract], Mexico, June 25, 1836," in Manning 1937, 331.

131. Doc. 3353: "Powhatan Ellis to John Forsyth, Mexico, August 3, 1836," in Manning 1937, 338.

132. Doc. 3178: "Asbury Dickens, Acting Secretary of State of the United States, to Powhatan Ellis, Washington, August 19, 1836," in Manning 1937, 56.

133. Doc. 3379: "Powhatan Ellis to John Forsyth, Mexico, October 26, 1836," in Manning 1937, 377.

134. Remini 1984, 357, 362; Cole 1993, 133; Brands 2005, 520; Meacham 2008, 324.

135. "Jackson's Seventh Annual Message, December 7, 1835," in Muller 1917, 1154–1155.

136. "Appeal by Stephen F. Austin," in Bassett 1931, 398.

137. "Andrew Jackson to Governor Newton Cannon, Hermitage, August 6, 1836" (417), "Andrew Jackson to Postmaster General Kendall, Hermitage, August 12, 1836" (420), and "Andrew Jackson to Asbury Dickins, Hermitage, August 17, 1836" (422), all in Bassett 1931; Doc. 3180: "John Forsyth to Manuel Eduardo de Gorostiza, Mexican Minister to the United States, Washington, August 31, 1836," in Manning 1937, 57.

138. Duckett 1962, 199; Pletcher 1973, 73; Remini 1984, 364, 367; Cole 1993, 266; Klunder 1996, 91; W. Weeks 1996, 88; 2013, 168; Maass 2020, 127–129.

139. Remini 1984, 360; Klunder 1996, 91; W. Weeks 1996, 88; Howe 2007, 670; Herring 2008, 175; Nugent 2008, 153–154.

140. "Jackson's Eighth Annual Message, Washington, December 5, 1836," in Muller 1917, 1191.

141. "Wharton to Austin, Despatch No. 4, Washington City, January 6th 1837," in Garrison 1908, 169.

142. For 1834 efforts, see Cole 1993, 132. For 1837 efforts, see Remini 1984, 365; Brands 2005, 526.

143. See "Andrew Jackson to Maunsel White, Washington, December 2, 1836," in Bassett 1931, 440.

144. "Wharton to Austin, Despatch No. 1, Washington City, December 22nd 1836" (157–158), "Wharton to Austin, Despatch No. 4, Washington City, January 6th 1837" (169), "Wharton to Austin, Despatch No. 5, Washington City, January 15th 1837" (176), and "Wharton to Rusk, No. 9, Washington City" (191, 193–194), all in Garrison 1908.

145. W. Weeks 1996, 88; 2013, 168; Nugent 2008, 153–154.

146. "Lewis Cass to Major General E. P. Gaines, War Department, January 23, 1836," in Dickins and Forney 1861, 417.

147. "Edmund P. Gaines to Lewis Cass, Headquarters Western Department, Baton Rouge, March 29, 1836" (417–418) and "Edmund P. Gaines to Lewis Cass, Headquarters Western Department, Natchitoches, Louisiana, April 8, 1836" (419–420), both in Dickins and Forney 1861.

148. "Lewis Cass to Major General E. P. Gaines, War Department, April 25, 1836," in Dickins and Forney 1861, 418. See also Klunder 1996, 91.

149. "Lewis Cass to Major General Gaines, War Department, May 4, 1836" (421) and "Lewis Cass to Major General Gaines, War Department, May 12, 1836" (424, quoted), both in Dickins and Forney 1861.

150. Pletcher 1973, 71; Remini 1984, 357.

151. Remini 1984, 362.

152. "Andrew Jackson to Governor Newton Cannon, Liberty, Tenn., August 3, 1836," in Bassett 1931, 415.

153. Remini 1984, 362.

154. Emphasis added. "Andrew Jackson to Postmaster General Kendall, Hermitage, August 12, 1836," in Bassett 1931, 420.

155. "Andrew Jackson to Brigadier-General Edmund P. Gaines, Hermitage, September 4, 1836," in Bassett 1931, 424.

156. Doc. 5679: "John Forsyth, Secretary of State of the United States, to Henry M. Morfit, Special Agent of the United States to Texas, Washington, June 23, 1836," in Manning 1939, 3.

157. "Secretary Forsyth to Jackson, Private, Washington, July 15, 1836," in Bassett 1931, 413.

158. Doc. 5767: "Henry M. Morfit, Special Agent of the United States to Texas, to John Forsyth, Secretary of State of the United States, [Extract], Velasco, September 9, 1836," in Manning 1939, 113.

159. Doc. 5768: "Henry M. Morfit, Special Agent of the United States to Texas, to John Forsyth, Secretary of State of the United States, Velasco, September 10, 1836," in Manning 1939, 116.

160. Emphasis added. "Andrew Jackson to Postmaster General Kendall, Private, Washington, December 8, 1836," in Bassett 1931, 441.

161. Emphasis added. "Jackson's Special Message on Texas, Washington, December 21, 1836," in Muller 1917, 1220, 1222, 1223.

162. "Republic of Texas Recognized, Washington, March 3, 1837," in Muller 1917, 1231–1232.

163. "Hunt to Irion, Despatch No. 29, Texian Legation, Washington City, January 31st, 1838," in Garrison 1908, 285.

164. "Andrew Jackson to General Samuel Houston, Hermitage, September 4, 1836," in Bassett 1931, 425.

4. INADVERTENT EXPANSION ON THE EURASIAN STEPPE

1. Pierce 1960, 18–19, 43.

2. See Bregel 2009, 401–407.

3. MacKenzie 1988, 210; Becker 2004, 6–7, 9–10. See also MacKenzie 1969, 289.

4. MacKenzie 1988, 210.

5. MacKenzie 1969, 290–291; Becker 2004, 14.

6. MacKenzie 1988, 212.

7. Zakharova 2006, 600.

8. MacKenzie 1974a, 30; Morrison 2014b, 163.

9. MacKenzie 1974a, xvii–xviii, 1–20, 29–30, 63.

10. MacKenzie 1974a, 30.

11. MacKenzie 1969, 291. See also Becker 2004, 17; Morrison 2014a, 173.

12. Becker 2004, 17; Morrison 2014a, 168.

13. Morrison 2014a, 175. See also MacKenzie 1974a, 34; Morrison 2021, 219, 225.

14. MacKenzie 1974a, 33–34.

15. For Cherniaev's orders, see Doc. 45: A. O. Diugamel to Mikhail G. Cherniaev, March 12, 1864, in Serebrennikov 1914, 81–82. See also Morrison 2021, 222–223.

16. MacKenzie 1974a, 36–37; Morrison 2014a, 175–176; 2021, 226–227.

17. MacKenzie 1974a, 38.

18. Morrison 2021, 227. See also MacKenzie 1974a, 37.

19. Pierce 1960, 185–188; Becker 2004, 72–73, 111, 349n46.

20. MacKenzie 1969, 297; 1988, 221; Becker 2004, 27.

21. MacKenzie 1969, 290.

22. For examples, see MacKenzie 1988, 214–215; Sergeev 2013, 114; Morrison 2014b, 154.

23. d'Encausse 1994, 132–133.

24. MacKenzie 1974a, 21–22, 29; Becker 2004, 15–18; Morrison 2014b, 155, 161–162.

25. MacKenzie 1969, 289–290; 1988, 212; d'Encausse 1994, 133; Becker 2004, 20.

26. MacKenzie 1988, 212.

27. MacKenzie 1974a, 22.

28. MacKenzie 1974a, 39.

29. MacKenzie 1974a, 39–40.

30. MacKenzie 1969, 292; 1974a, 42.

31. MacKenzie 1969, 292–293.

32. MacKenzie 1969, 293; 1974a, 41–42.

33. MacKenzie 1974a, 42.

34. MacKenzie 1974a, 43; Morrison 2021, 234.

35. MacKenzie 1969, 293; Morrison 2021, 233.

36. MacKenzie 1974a, 43.

37. MacKenzie 1969, 293.

38. MacKenzie 1969, 295.

39. Morrison 2014a, 167; 2021, 219.

40. MacKenzie 1969, 295.

41. MacKenzie 1974a, 43; Morrison 2021, 234.

42. MacKenzie 1988, 212–213. On Alexander II's personal characteristics, see Seton-Watson 1967, 333; MacKenzie 1988, 212–213; Zakharova 2006, 595.

43. MacKenzie 1974a, 44.

44. Pierce 1960, 21; Morrison 2014a, 183; 2021, 236.

45. Schuyler 1876, 112; MacKenzie 1974a, 45; Morrison 2021, 236.

46. MacKenzie 1969, 295.

47. MacKenzie 1974a, 47–48.

48. MacKenzie 1969, 295.

49. Morrison 2014a, 184; 2014b, 154.

50. MacKenzie 1969, 295; 1974a, 46.

51. See this chapter's epigraph.

52. "Gortschakoff, 'Circular,' Nov. 21, 1864," in Causes of the Afghan War 1879, 223, 227.

53. For the "smokescreen" argument, see Saray 1982, 10. On Gorchakov's likely sincerity, see Becker 2004, 19–20; Morrison 2021, 217.

54. MacKenzie 1974a, 52. See also Becker 2004, 26; Morrison 2021, 241.

55. On Miliutin's message, see MacKenzie 1974a, 53. See also Morrison 2021, 241. On Gorchakov's message, see Morrison 2021, 241–242. See also MacKenzie 1969, 297.

56. d'Encausse 1994, 134; Morrison 2014a, 189.

57. MacKenzie 1969, 299.

58. Pierce 1960, 22; Morrison 2021, 243.

59. Schuyler 1876, 113; Pierce 1960, 22; d'Encausse 1994, 134.

60. MacKenzie 1969, 299; 1974a, 57.

61. Schuyler 1876, 114; MacKenzie 1988, 215.

62. Schuyler 1876, 101; Pierce 1960, 21; MacKenzie 1974a, 57–58.

63. Schuyler 1876, 115; Pierce 1960, 23; MacKenzie 1974a, xv; 1988, 215.

64. Schuyler 1876, 104, 115; Pierce 1960, 20–21, 23; MacKenzie 1974a, 59; Morrison 2021, 244, 250.

65. Morrison 2021, 247. See also MacKenzie 1974a, 51.

66. MacKenzie 1974a, 68–69; 1988, 216.

67. MacKenzie 1969, 299.

68. Van Der Oye 2006, 563–564; Morrison 2014b, 153–154.

69. Becker 2004, 29.

70. MacKenzie 1974a, 68.

71. Morrison 2014a, 185.

72. MacKenzie 1988, 214; d'Encausse 1994, 149; Bregel 2009, 407. For an interesting analysis of Kokand's poor battlefield performance, see Lyall 2021, chap. 5.

73. Saray 1982, 12; Sergeev 2013, 106–107.

74. Sergeev 2013, 120–121.

75. MacKenzie 1974a, 60.

76. Sadaheo 2007, 20–21.

77. Sergeev 2013, 203–209.

78. MacKenzie 1969, 310.

79. MacKenzie 1988, 217.

80. MacKenzie 1969, 306.

81. MacKenzie 1974a, 93–94.

82. MacKenzie 1969, 307n86; 1974a, 90.

83. Becker 2004, 34.

84. MacKenzie 1988, 218–219; Bregel 2009, 408.

85. "Konstantin Petrovich Kaufman (1818–1882)," in Wieczynski 1980, vol. 16, 68.

86. Hsü 1965, 2–4.

87. Pierce 1960, 28; Paine 1996, 112–113.

88. Lobinov-Rostovsky 1951, 183; Hsü 1965, 22.

89. Lobinov-Rostovsky 1951, 183–184; Pierce 1960, 28; Hsü 1965, 22–29; Seton-Watson 1967, 444; March 1996, 142; Paine 1996, 110, 118–119.

90. Pierce 1960, 28; Hsü 1965, 29–30; Paine 1996, 119–120.

91. MacKenzie 1967, 267; "Konstantin Petrovich Kaufman," in Wieczynski 1980, vol. 16, 68; Morris 1975, 536–537.

92. MacKenzie 1967, 268.

93. MacKenzie 1974b, 171; March 1996, 143; Paine 1996, 121.

94. Becker 2004, 39–42; Morrison 2021, 282–300 (esp. 283).

95. Hsü 1965, 53; "Treaty of Livadia," in Wieczynski 1981, vol. 20, 105.

96. Becker 2004, 72–73, 111, 349n46.

97. MacKenzie 1967, 268.

98. "Mr. Schuyler's Report on Central Asia," in *Papers Relating to the Foreign Relations of the United States* 1874.

99. "Konstantin Petrovich Kaufman," in Wieczynski 1980, vol. 16, 69.

100. Hsü 1965, 14.

101. Paine 1996, 121.

102. Lobinov-Rostovsky 1951, 184; "Konstantin Petrovich Kaufman," in Wieczynski 1980, vol. 16, 104; March 1996, 143; Paine 1996, 120–121.

103. Kaufman quote from Morrison 2021, 206. For Kaufman's plans, see Lobinov-Rostovsky 1951, 185; Hsü 1965, 30; March 1996, 143.

104. Lattimore 1950, 36; Lobinov-Rostovsky 1951, 185–186; Seton-Watson 1967, 444; "Konstantin Petrovich Kaufman," in Wieczynski 1980, vol. 16, 104.

105. Lobinov-Rostovsky 1951, 186; Pierce 1960, 28; Hsü 1965, 30; Seton-Watson 1967, 444; March 1996, 143; Paine 1996, 110, 121.

106. Hsü 1965, 14, 31; "Konstantin Petrovich Kaufman," in Wieczynski 1980, vol. 16, 104.

107. "Mr. Schuyler's Report on Central Asia," in *Papers Relating to the Foreign Relations of the United States* 1874; Lobinov-Rostovsky 1951, 187; Hsü 1965, 14, 31; "Konstantin Petrovich Kaufman," in Wieczynski 1980, vol. 16, 104; Paine 1996, 110, 167.

108. Hsü 1965, 31–32.

109. Lobinov-Rostovsky 1951, 187.

110. Hsü 1965, 32; Paine 1996, 121; Morrison 2021, 208.

111. Lattimore 1950, 36; Lobinov-Rostovsky 1951, 188; Pierce 1960, 28–29; Hsü 1965, 33; March 1996, 143.

112. Paine 1996, 121.

113. Paine 1996, 121; Morrison 2021, 209.

114. Hsü 1965, 34.

115. Readers may have heard of General Zuo from the popular North American Chinese cuisine dish, "General Tso's Chicken," which was named in his honor. See Coe 2009, 241–243.

116. Hsü 1965, 35–36; "Treaty of Livadia," in Wieczynski 1981, vol. 20, 105; March 1996, 143–144.

117. Lobinov-Rostovsky 1951, 188; Hsü 1965, 41–44; Seton-Watson 1967, 444; March 1996, 144; Paine 1996, 123–125.

118. Morrison 2021, 210. See also Paine 1996, 125.

119. Lobinov-Rostovsky 1951, 189; "Treaty of Livadia," in Wieczynski 1981, vol. 20, 105; March 1996, 144.

120. Hsü 1965, 57; Paine 1996, 137–140.

121. Lattimore 1950, 39; Lobinov-Rostovsky 1951, 189; Hsü 1965, 51–58; "Treaty of Livadia," in Wieczynski 1981, vol. 20, 103–107; March 1996, 144; Paine 1996, chap. 5.

122. Lattimore 1950, 39; Hsü 1965, 57; "Treaty of Livadia," in Wieczynski 1981, vol. 20, 106; March 1996, 144.

123. Hsü 1965, 60. See also Paine 1996, 112.

124. Hsü 1965, 1, 69.

125. Lobinov-Rostovsky 1951, 189; Hsü 1965, 76–77, 80–94; "Treaty of Livadia," in Wieczynski 1981, vol. 20, 106; Paine 1996, 140, 151.

126. Hsü 1965, 145–146, 151–152; "Treaty of Livadia," in Wieczynski 1981, vol. 20, 106; Paine 1996, 152–153.

127. Hsü 1965, 163–164; "Treaty of Livadia," in Wieczynski 1981, vol. 20, 106; Paine 1996, 153–154.

128. Morrison 2021, 209.

129. Hsü 1965, 155–156; Paine 1996, 154–155. On Alexander II's reforms, see Seton-Watson 1967, 332–369; Zakharova 2006.

130. "N. K. Giers to A. G. Jomini, September 4/16, 1879," "N. K. Giers to A. G. Jomini, 20 September 1879," and "N. K. Giers to A. G. Jomini, September 25, 1879," all in Jelavich and Jelavich 1959, 148–150.

131. Note that this and all other translations (from French) in this chapter were carried out by the author. "A. G. Jomini to N. K. Giers, September 22, 1880," in Jelavich and Jelavich 1959, 111. See also Paine 1996, 154.

132. "N. K. Giers to A. G. Jomini, September 27, 1880," in Jelavich and Jelavich 1959, 151. See also Hsü 1965, 177; Paine 1996, 159.

133. Hsü 1965, 172.

134. Hsü 1965, 163–164; Paine 1996, 153–155.

135. Hsü 1965, 51. Miliutin would still hold these views a full year later. See "N. K. Giers to A. G. Jomini, October 18, 1880," in Jelavich and Jelavich 1959, 154.

136. "Jomini to Giers, Sept. 22, 1880," in Jelavich and Jelavich 1959, 111. See also Paine 1996, 154.

137. "N. K. Giers to A. G. Jomini, October 14, 1880," in Jelavich and Jelavich 1959, 153. On this concern, see also "A. G. Jomini to N. K. Giers, October 3, 1880," in Jelavich and Jelavich 1959, 117–118.

138. "Jomini to Giers, Sept. 22, 1880," in Jelavich and Jelavich 1959, 111. See also Paine 1996, 154.

139. "N. K. Giers to A. G. Jomini, September 27, 1880," in Jelavich and Jelavich 1959, 151. See also Hsü 1965, 177; Paine 1996, 159.

140. "Giers to Jomini, Oct. 18, 1880," in Jelavich and Jelavich 1959, 154. See also "N. K. Giers to A. G. Jomini, October 25, 1880," in Jelavich and Jelavich 1959, 155.

141. "Giers to Jomini, Oct. 14, 1880," in Jelavich and Jelavich 1959, 153.

142. "Giers to Jomini, Oct. 18, 1880," in Jelavich and Jelavich 1959, 154.

143. Lattimore 1950, 39; Hsü 1965, 7, 9, 155, 171–172, 190; "Saint Petersburg Agreement of 1881," in Wieczynski 1983, vol. 33, 25; Paine 1996, 140–141, 143, 151; Morrison 2021, 211.

144. Hsü 1965, 75–76; "Treaty of Livadia," in Wieczynski 1981, vol. 20, 106; March 1996, 145.

145. Hsü 1965, 95–96; Paine 1996, 155.

146. Hsü 1965, 96–97; "Treaty of Livadia," in Wieczynski 1981, vol. 20, 106; "Saint Petersburg Agreement of 1881," in Wieczynski 1983, vol. 33, 25.

147. Hsü 1965, 98–99.

148. Lobinov-Rostovsky 1951, 190; Hsü 1965, 1–2, 97, 99, 100; "Treaty of Livadia," in Wieczynski 1981, vol. 20, 106; "Saint Petersburg Agreement of 1881," in Wieczynski 1983, vol. 33, 25; Paine 1996, 155.

149. Paine 1996, 158–159.

150. Paine 1996, 160.

151. March 1996, 145; Paine 1996, 110–111, 163.

152. Hsü 1965, 97, 99, 157; Paine 1996, 135, 143–144.

153. Hsü 1965, 180.

154. "A. G. Jomini to N. K. Giers, 12/24 October 1880," in Jelavich and Jelavich 1959, 121. See also Hsü 1965, 179; Paine 1996, 164.

155. Paine 1996, 112.

156. "A. G. Jomini to N. K. Giers, August 24, 1880," in Jelavich and Jelavich 1959, 102.

157. "Jomini to Giers, Oct. 3, 1880," in Jelavich and Jelavich 1959, 118.

158. Clodfelter 2008, 210–211.

159. Hsü 1965, 51.

160. Hsü 1965, 157; Paine 1996, 111, 135, 141–145, 151, 155.

161. "Jomini to Giers, Oct. 3, 1880," in Jelavich and Jelavich 1959, 118. See also Hsü 1965, 157.

162. Hsü 1965, 97–98.

163. Hsü 1965, 175.

164. "A. G. Jomini to N. K. Giers, September 10, 1880," in Jelavich and Jelavich 1959, 106. See also "A. G. Jomini to N. K. Giers, September 7, 1880" (105) and "A. G. Jomini to N. K. Giers, October 1, 1880" (115), both in Jelavich and Jelavich 1959.

165. "Jomini to Giers, Sept. 22, 1880," in Jelavich and Jelavich 1959, 111.

166. Emphasis in original. "N. K. Giers to A. G. Jomini, September 23, 1880," in Jelavich and Jelavich 1959, 150; Hsü 1965, 173; Paine 1996, 155–156.

167. Hsü 1965, 173–174.

168. "N. K. Giers to A. G. Jomini, September 25, 1880," in Jelavich and Jelavich 1959, 150. See also "Giers to Jomini, Sept. 23, 1880," in Jelavich and Jelavich 1959, 150.

169. "A. G. Jomini to N. K. Giers, October 3/15, 1880," in Jelavich and Jelavich 1959, 118.

170. "A. G. Jomini to N. K. Giers, October 10, 1880," in Jelavich and Jelavich 1959, 121. See also Hsü 1965, 179; Paine 1996, 159.

171. "Jomini to Giers, Oct. 1, 1880," in Jelavich and Jelavich 1959, 116.

172. "Giers to Jomini, Oct. 25, 1880," in Jelavich and Jelavich 1959, 155.

173. "A. G. Jomini to N. K. Giers, October 22, 1880," in Jelavich and Jelavich 1959, 128.

174. "Treaty of Livadia," in Wieczynski 1981, vol. 20, 106; "Saint Petersburg Agreement of 1881," in Wieczynski 1983, vol. 33, 25.

175. Hsü 1965, 185.

176. Lobinov-Rostovsky 1951, 190; Hsü 1965, 187; "Saint Petersburg Agreement of 1881," in Wieczynski 1983, vol. 33, 24–26; March 1996, 145; Paine 1996, 161–163.

177. Lobinov-Rostovsky 1951, 190–191; Hsü 1965, 187; "Treaty of Livadia," in Wieczynski 1981, vol. 20, 106; "Saint Petersburg Agreement of 1881," in Wieczynski 1983, vol. 33, 25; March 1996, 145.

178. Jelavich and Jelavich 1959, 138; "Treaty of Livadia," in Wieczynski 1981, vol. 20, 107; "Saint Petersburg Agreement of 1881," in Wieczynski 1983, vol. 33, 26.

179. Hsü 1965, 18; "Treaty of Livadia," in Wieczynski 1981, vol. 20, 107; "Saint Petersburg Agreement of 1881," in Wieczynski 1983, vol. 33, 25.

180. MacKenzie 1967, 276; March 1996, 145.

181. MacKenzie 1967, 276–277; "Konstantin Petrovich Kaufman," in Wieczynski 1980, vol. 16, 71.

182. "Konstantin Petrovich Kaufman," in Wieczynski 1980, vol. 16, 71.

183. MacKenzie 1967, 277.

184. MacKenzie 1988, 229.

5. INADVERTENT EXPANSION IN SOUTHEAST ASIA

1. Raymond Betts 1978, 25.

2. See Aldrich 1996, 76–78; Quinn 2000, 138–141.

3. Area data from *Statistical Yearbook of Viet Nam* 2019, 97. Population data are very hard to come by for this period. French imperial actors in 1873 would offhandedly claim that Tonkin contained over 2 million people, but the first official French estimates in 1886 were of 6.2 million. See Gourou 1936, 179; "Francis Garnier to Léon Garnier, Hanoi, November 21, 1873," in Taboulet 1956, 717.

4. Aldrich 1996, 78–80.

5. Cady 1954, 283; Roberts 1963, 423; McLeod 1991, 101; Osborne 1996, 194–195.

6. Cady 1954, 283–284; Laffey 1975, 41–42; Osborne 1996, 203–204; Davis 2017, 55–61.

7. Norman 1884, 98; Cady 1954, 282; Brunschwig 1966, 26; McLeod 1991, 99; Osborne 1995, 53–54, 104.

8. Norman 1884, 97.

9. This figure is inferred from the fact that it took eleven days for news of Hanoi's capture (November 20–December 1, 1873) and thirteen days for news of Garnier's death (December 21, 1873–January 3, 1874) to reach Saigon from Hanoi. See "Admiral Dupré to the Court of Hué, December 1, 1873," in Taboulet 1956, 721; "Marie Jules Dupré to Charles de Dompierre d'Hornoy, Saigon, January 4, 1874," in Dutreb 1924, 82–83.

10. Thompson 1937, 62–63; McLeod 1991, 100.

11. Cady 1954, 284.

12. "Marie-Jules Dupré to the Minister of the Navy and Colonies, December 22, 1872," in Dutreb 1924, 15.

13. "Telegram from Dupré to Paris, May 19, 1873," in Taboulet 1956, 694. See also "Marie Jules Dupré to the Minister of the Navy and Colonies, Saigon, March 17, 1873," in Dutreb 1924, 24–25.

14. "The Minister of the Navy and Colonies to Marie Jules Dupré, February 27, 1873," in Dutreb 1924, 22.

15. "Marie Jules Dupré to the Minister of the Navy and Colonies, Saigon, March 17, 1873," in Dutreb 1924, 25.

16. Norman 1884, 93.

17. "Marie Jules Dupré to Paris, July 28, 1873," in Dutreb 1924, 30, 33.

18. "Dupré to Paris, July 28, 1873," in Dutreb 1924, 33, 34.

19. Dutreb 1924, 35.

20. "Admiral d'Hornoy, Ministry of Marine and the Colonies to Admiral Dupré [Private Letter], Versailles, September 12, 1873," in Taboulet 1956, 699.

21. "d'Hornoy to Dupré, Sept. 12, 1873," in Taboulet 1956, 700.

22. "Paris to Marie Jules Dupré, Paris, October 22, 1873," in Dutreb 1924, 38–39.

23. Osborne 1996, 199.

24. McAleavy 1968, 128; Osborne 1996, 199.

25. "Marie Jules Dupré to Captain Marie Joseph François Garnier, Saigon, October 10, 1873," in Dutreb 1924, 50.

26. Emphasis in original quote from Osborne 1996, 205. See also McAleavy 1968, 128–129; McLeod 1991, 104, 107.

27. McLeod 1991, 104–105.

28. Norman 1884, 120.

29. McAleavy 1968, 128–130; McLeod 1991, 105.

30. "Garnier to Garnier, Nov. 10, 1873," in Taboulet 1956, 712.

31. Norman 1884, 128; Buttinger 1958, 371–372.

32. Laffey 1975, 42.

33. "Extract of Jean Dupuis' Journal, November 16, 1873," in Taboulet 1956, 712.

34. "Francis Garnier to Léon Garnier, Hanoi, November 19, 1873," in Taboulet 1956, 713.

35. "Garnier to Garnier, Nov. 19, 1873," in Taboulet 1956, 714.

36. For Garnier's description of the conquest, see "Francis Garnier to Admiral Dupré, Hanoi, December 1, 1873," in Taboulet 1956, 715–717. Also Norman 1884, 131–132; McAleavy 1968, 131–133.

37. McAleavy 1968, 133; Osborne 1996, 207.

38. Norman 1884, 132–134; Ennis 1936, 197; McLeod 1991, 113.

39. Norman 1884, 133–135; McLeod 1991, 113–114.

40. Ennis 1936, 197–198; McAleavy 1968, 134; McLeod 1991, 114.

41. "Francis Garnier to Admiral Dupré, Nam-Dinh, December 13, 1873," in Taboulet 1956, 726.

42. Norman 1884, 136; Osborne 1996, 207–208. On the Black Flags, see Laffey 1979.

43. McAleavy 1968, 135; Laffey 1975, 43.

44. Osborne 1996, 209.

45. "'The Engagement of December 21, 1873, According to Jean Dupuis,' December 21, 1873," in Taboulet 1956, 729; McAleavy 1968, 136; Osborne 1996, 209–210; Davis 2017, 64.

46. "'The Engagement of December 21,' Dec. 21, 1873," in Taboulet 1956, 729.

47. "Dupré to Hué, Dec. 1, 1873," in Taboulet 1956, 721.

48. "Dupré to d'Hornoy, Jan. 4, 1874," in Dutreb 1924, 82–83. See also Thompson 1937, 64; McAleavy 1968, 143; Osborne 1996, 211–212.

49. Brunschwig 1966, 43.

50. Thompson 1937, 62–63; Quinn 2000, 143; J. Barnhart 2020, 112–115.

51. Cady 1954, 289; McLeod 1991, 100.

52. On concerns over China, see Brocheux and Hémery 2009, 29; Finch 2013, 76. On concerns over Vietnam, see Buttinger 1958, 373.

53. Stern 1944, 198; Cady 1954, 284; Roberts 1963, 424.

54. "Dupré to the Minister, Sept. 11, 1873," in Dutreb 1924, 35.

55. "Duke of Broglie to a Colleague in the Navy, September 22, 1873," in Dutreb 1924, 40.

56. "Duke of Broglie, Minister of Foreign Affairs to the Minister of the Marine, Versailles, November 6, 1873," in Dutreb 1924, 119.

57. "Garnier to Garnier, Nov. 10, 1873," in Taboulet 1956, 712.

58. "d'Hornoy to Dupré, Sept. 12, 1873," in Taboulet 1956, 699.

59. "d'Hornoy to Dupré, Sept. 12, 1873," in Taboulet 1956, 700.

60. Cady 1954, 287; Roberts 1963, 424; Quinn 2000, 143; Brocheux and Hémery 2009, 29.

61. "Charles de Dompierre d'Hornoy to Marie Jules Dupré, January 7, 1874," in Dutreb 1924, 98.

62. Norman 1884, 145; McAleavy 1968, 144.

63. "The Treaty of March 15, 1874," in Taboulet 1956, 743–747.

64. Cady 1954, 288.

65. Munholland 1979, 84.

66. Finch 2013, 77.

67. Cady 1954, 288.

68. Norman 1884, 171, 180; Ennis 1936, 46; Eastman 1967, 44–45; Munholland 1979, 85–86, 91.

69. Roberts 1963, 425; Eastman 1967, 46.

70. Power 1977, 157n20.

71. Taboulet 1956, 766, 769n1; McAleavy 1968, 189–190; Raymond Betts 1978, 26.

72. Ennis 1936, 47n28; Taboulet 1956, 766, 770; Raymond Betts 1978, 26.

73. This figure is inferred from the fact that it took six days for news of Hanoi's capture (April 25–May 1, 1882) and of Rivière's death (May 20–26, 1883) to reach Saigon from Hanoi. See no. 107: "Mr. Le Myre de Vilers, Governor of Cochinchina, to Admiral Jauréguiberry, Minister of the Navy and Colonies (Telegram), Saigon, May 1, 1882," in *Documents Diplomatiques* 1883, vol. 1, 211; No. 199: "Mr. Thomson, Governor of French Cochinchina, to Mr. Charles Brun, Minister of the Navy and Colonies, (Telegram), Saigon, May 26, 1883," in *Documents Diplomatiques* 1883, vol. 2, 117.

74. Munholland 1979, 87–88.

75. Norman 1884, 174; Power 1977, 157; Munholland 1979, 91.

76. No. 93, Annex: "Admiral Cloué, Minister of the Navy and Colonies, to Mr. Le Myre de Vilers, Governor of French Cochinchina, Paris, September __, 1881," in *Documents Diplomatiques* 1883, vol. 1, 190–191.

77. "Charles-Marie Le Myre de Vilers to the Minister of Commerce and the Colonies, Maurice Rouvier, Saigon, December 21, 1881," in Taboulet 1956, 763.

78. No. 99: "Mr. Le Myre de Vilers, Governor of French Cochinchina, to Mr. Rouvier, Minister of Commerce and the Colonies (Telegram), Saigon, January 16, 1882," in *Documents Diplomatiques* 1883, vol. 1, 198.

79. Eastman 1967, 49–50; McAleavy 1968, 190.

80. "The Governor of Cochinchina, Le Myre de Vilers, to Mr. Henri Laurent Rivière, Saigon, January 17, 1882," in Taboulet 1956, 767.

81. "Le Myre de Vilers to Rivière, Jan. 17, 1882," in Taboulet 1956, 768.

82. No. 102: "Mr. Le Myre de Vilers, Governor of French Cochinchina, to Mr. Rouvier, Minister of Commerce and the Colonies, Saigon, January 18, 1882," in *Documents Diplomatiques* 1883, vol. 1, 201.

83. "Le Myre de Vilers to Rivière, Jan. 17, 1882," in Taboulet 1956, 768.

84. Taboulet 1956, 765; Munholland 1979, 94.

85. No. 104: "Admiral Jauréguiberry, Minister of the Navy, to Mr. Le Myre de Vilers, Governor of Cochinchina, Paris, March 4, 1882," in *Documents Diplomatiques* 1883, vol. 1, 206.

86. No. 105: "Mr. de Freycinet, Minister of Foreign Affairs, to Admiral Jauréguiberry, Minister of the Navy and the Colonies, Paris, March 16, 1882," in *Documents Diplomatiques* 1883, vol. 1, 208.

87. Taboulet 1956, 766; Eastman 1967, 50; McAleavy 1968, 190.

88. No. 111, Annex I: "Captain Rivière, Head of the Division, Commander of the Cochinchina Naval Station in Hanoi, to Mr. Le Myre de Vilers, Governor of French Cochinchina in Saigon, Hanoi, April 10–18, 1882," in *Documents Diplomatiques* 1883, vol. 1, 218.

89. No. 111, Annex I: "Rivière to Le Myre de Vilers, Apr. 10–18, 1882," in *Documents Diplomatiques* 1883, vol. 1, 219–221.

90. Norman 1884, 197; McAleavy 1968, 191.

91. No. 111, Annex I: "Rivière to Le Myre de Vilers, Apr. 10–18, 1882," in *Documents Diplomatiques* 1883, vol. 1, 222–223.

92. Maurceley 1884, 197; McAleavy 1968, 191.

93. "The Ultimatum from Commander Rivière to the Governor of Hanoi (April 25, 1882)," in Taboulet 1956, 770–771.

94. No. 118, Annex I: "Mr. Rivière, Division Chief, Captain of the Naval Station at Cochinchina, to Admiral Jauréguiberry, Minister of the Navy and Colonies, Hanoi, April 27 and May 13, 1882," in *Documents Diplomatiques* 1883, vol. 1, 247.

95. For detailed accounts of the assault, see no. 116, Annex I: "Mr. Rivière, Division Chief, Commander of the Naval Station, to Mr. Le Myre de Vilers, Governor of French Cochinchina, Hanoi, April 25, 1882" (241–242) and no. 118, Annex I: "Rivière to Jauréguiberry, Apr. 27 and May 13, 1882" (246–250) both in *Documents Diplomatiques* 1883, vol. 1; "Report from Commander Berthe de Villers to Brigadier General and Commander of Troops in Saigon, Hanoi, May 3, 1882," in Taboulet 1956, 774–776.

96. No. 118, Annex I: "Rivière to Jauréguiberry, Apr. 27 and May 13, 1882," in *Documents Diplomatiques* 1883, vol. 1, 250.

97. No. 116, Annex I: "Rivière to Mr. Le Myre de Vilers, Apr. 25, 1882," in *Documents Diplomatiques* 1883, vol. 1, 241, 242.

98. No. 118, Annex I: "Rivière to Jauréguiberry, Apr. 27 and May 13, 1882" in *Documents Diplomatiques* 1883, vol. 1, 246.

99. No. 7: "Commander Rivière to the Inhabitants of Hanoi—Hanoi, April 26, 1882," in Masson 1933, 74–75.

100. "Commander Rivière to the Head of Justice (Quan-An) of Hanoi, Hanoi, April 29, 1882," in Taboulet 1956, 778; McAleavy 1968, 191.

101. "Rivière, May 2, 1882," in Taboulet 1956, 779.

102. No. 111: "Mr. Le Myre de Vilers, Governor of Cochinchina, to Admiral Jauréguiberry, Minister of the Navy and Colonies, Saigon, April 27, 1882," in *Documents Diplomatiques* 1883, vol. 1, 216.

103. Taboulet 1956, 780; McAleavy 1968, 191.

104. No. 11: "Mr. Le Myre de Vilers, Governor of Cochinchina, to Commander Rivière—Saigon, May 2, 1882," in Masson 1933, 92.

105. No. 107: "Le Myre de Vilers to Jauréguiberry, May 1, 1882" (211) and no. 116: "Le Myre de Vilers, Governor of French Cochinchina, to Admiral Jauréguiberry, Minister of

the Navy and Colonies, in Paris, Saigon, May 2, 1882" (240–241), both in *Documents Diplomatiques* 1883, vol. 1.

106. No. 15: "Mr. Le Myre de Vilers, Governor of Cochinchina, to Commander Rivière—Saigon, May 23, 1882," in Masson 1933, 105–107.

107. No. 117: "Admiral Jauréguiberry, Minister of the Navy and Colonies, to Mr. Le Myre de Vilers, Governor of French Cochinchina, Paris, June 20, 1882," in *Documents Diplomatiques* 1883, vol. 1, 244. See also Maurceley 1884, 142.

108. Thompson 1937, 66; Taboulet 1956, 780; Munholland 1979, 95.

109. No. 112: "Le Myre de Vilers, Governor of French Cochinchina, to Admiral Jauréguiberry, Minister of the Navy and Colonies, in Paris, Saigon, May 5, 1882," in *Documents Diplomatiques* 1883, vol. 1, 227.

110. No. 119: "Mr. Le Myre de Vilers, Governor of Cochinchina, to Admiral Jauréguiberry, Minister of the Navy and Colonies, Saigon, May 22, 1882," in *Documents Diplomatiques* 1883, vol. 1, 257.

111. "Le Myre de Vilers to Commander Rivière, Saigon, July 27, 1882," in Taboulet 1956, 783.

112. "Commander Rivière to Madame de Caillavet, Hanoi, July 17, 1882," in Taboulet 1956, 782–783.

113. Norman 1884, 203; Taboulet 1956, 781, 786–787; Munholland 1979, 99–100.

114. No. 74: "Commandant Rivière to Mr. Rheinart, Chargé d'Affaires of France at Hué—Hanoi, March 14, 1883" (192) and no. 76: "Commander Rivière to Mr. Thomson, Governor of Cochinchina—Hanoi, March 17, 1883" (198, 199), both in Masson 1933. See also Taboulet 1956, 787.

115. No. 74: "Rivière to Rheinart, Mar. 14, 1883" (191 [quoted], 192) and no. 78: "Commander Rivière to Mr. Thomson, Governor of Cochinchina—Hanoi, March 17, 1883" (202–203), both in Masson 1933.

116. No. 80: "Commander Rivière to Mr. Thomson, Governor of Cochinchina—Hanoi, March 19, 1883," in Masson 1933, 208.

117. Norman 1884, 204–206; Taboulet 1956, 787–788; Eastman 1967, 68; McAleavy 1968, 200.

118. "Commander Rivière to Mr. Thomson, Governor of Cochinchina—Nam-Dinh, March 27, 1883," in Masson 1933, 212.

119. "Commander Rivière to Madame de Caillavet, Hanoi, May 8, 1883," in Taboulet 1956, 794.

120. No. 182: "Mr. Thomson, Governor of French Cochinchina, to Mr. Charles Brun, Minister of the Navy and Colonies, (Telegram), Saigon, April 26, 1883," in *Documents Diplomatiques* 1883, vol. 2, 93; Norman 1884, 207.

121. Norman 1884, 208–209; Taboulet 1956, 792.

122. Norman 1884, 210–212; McAleavy 1968, 203; Davis 2017, 85, 87.

123. No. 226, Annex I: "Commander Rivière to Mr. Thomson, Governor of French Cochinchina, Hanoi, May 16, 1883," in *Documents Diplomatiques* 1883, vol. 2, 156.

124. No. 199: "Thomson to Brun, May 26, 1883," in *Documents Diplomatiques* 1883, vol. 2, 117; Norman 1884, 216.

125. Taboulet 1956, 792.

126. No. 199: "Thomson to Brun, May 26, 1883," in *Documents Diplomatiques* 1883, vol. 2, 117.

127. "The Consul of France in Haiphong, Forestier, to Thomson, Governor of Cochinchina, May 20, 1883," in Taboulet 1956, 796, also 792–793; McAleavy 1968, 204.

128. Billot 1888, 34; Krakowski 1932, 298.

129. Billot 1888, 34–35.

130. See Cady 1954, 294; Power 1977, 159, 161, 193; Andrew and Kanya-Forstner 1988, 19. On status and French imperial expansion more generally, see J. Barnhart 2020, 111–122.

131. No. 125: "Mr. Le Myre de Vilers, Governor of French Cochinchina, to Admiral Jauréguiberry, Minister of the Navy and Colonies, Saigon, June 11, 1882," in *Documents Diplomatiques* 1883, vol. 1, 277–278.

132. Munholland 1979, 97.

133. No. 134: "Jauréguiberry to Duclerc, Oct. 15, 1882," in *Documents Diplomatiques* 1883, vol. 1, 304.

134. No. 163: "Mr. de Mahy, Interim Minister of the Navy and Colonies, to Mr. Jules Ferry, Interim Minister of Foreign Affairs, Paris, February 20, 1883," in *Documents Diplomatiques* 1883, vol. 2, 64.

135. Taboulet 1956, 787.

136. Power 1977, 164, 177–179.

137. Eastman 1967, 40.

138. Norman 1884, 177–178.

139. No. 70: "Mr. Freycinet, Minister of Foreign Affairs, to Admiral Jauréguiberry, Minister of the Navy and Colonies, Paris, July 26, 1880," in *Documents Diplomatiques* 1883, vol. 1, 156–157.

140. "Le Myre de Vilers to Rouvier, Dec. 21, 1881," in Taboulet 1956, 763.

141. No. 103: "Jauréguiberry to Freycinet, Mar. 4, 1882," in *Documents Diplomatiques* 1883, vol. 1, 205–206.

142. Thompson 1937, 66; Power 1977, 159.

143. No. 119: "Le Myre de Vilers to Jauréguiberry, May 22, 1882," in *Documents Diplomatiques* 1883, vol. 1, 256.

144. No. 129, Annex: "Mr. Le Myre de Vilers, Governor of Cochinchina, to Mr. Admiral Jauréguiberry, Minister of the Navy and Colonies, Saigon, July 19, 1882," in *Documents Diplomatiques* 1883, vol. 1, 296–297.

145. No. 129: "Admiral Jauréguiberry, Minister of the Navy and Colonies, to Mr. Duclerc, Minister of Foreign Affairs, Paris, September 12, 1882," in *Documents Diplomatiques* 1883, vol. 1, 296.

146. No. 131: "Mr. Duclerc, Minister of Foreign Affairs, to Admiral Jauréguiberry, Minister of the Navy and the Colonies, Paris, September 26, 1882," in *Documents Diplomatiques* 1883, vol. 1, 299, 300. See also no. 132: "Mr. Duclerc, Minister of Foreign Affairs, to Mr. Bourée, Minister of France in China, Paris, September 29, 1882," in *Documents Diplomatiques* 1883, vol. 1, 302.

147. Eastman 1967, 57–59; McAleavy 1968, 196; Munholland 1979, 100.

148. No. 140: "Mr. Bourée, Minister of France in China, to Mr. Duclerc, Minister of Foreign Affairs in Paris, (Telegram), Shanghai, December 5, 1882," in *Documents Diplomatiques* 1883, vol. 1, 318.

149. Note that this letter only arrived in Paris in late December 1882. No. 142: "Mr. Bourée, Minister of France in China, to Mr. Duclerc, Minister of Foreign Affairs, Peking, October 21, 1882," in *Documents Diplomatiques* 1883, vol. 1, 322.

150. No. 137: "Admiral Jauréguiberry, Minister of the Navy and Colonies, to Mr. Duclerc, Minister of Foreign Affairs, Paris, October 31, 1882," in *Documents Diplomatiques* 1883, vol. 1, 311.

151. *Journal officiel de la République française* 1883, 292, 293.

152. No. 168: "Mr. Challemel Lacour, Minister of Foreign Affairs, to Mr. Bourée, Minister of France to China, Paris, March 14, 1883," in *Documents Diplomatiques* 1883, vol. 2, 72.

153. No. 183, Annex: "Exposé of Reasons," in *Documents Diplomatiques* 1883, vol. 2, 96.

154. Norman 1884, 217–218; Eastman 1967, 72–73; Power 1977, 164; Munholland 1979, 104.

155. No. 199: "Thomson to Brun, May 26, 1883," in *Documents Diplomatiques* 1883, vol. 2, 117.

156. Norman 1884, 218. See also McAleavy 1968, 206; Power 1977, 164; Eastman 1967, 73.

157. No. 193: "Mr. Challemel Lacour, Minister of Foreign Affairs, to Mr. Tricou, Special Envoy of France in China, (Telegram), Paris, May 15, 1883," in *Documents Diplomatiques* 1883, vol. 2, 112, 113.

158. No. 197: "Mr. Challamel Lacour, Minister of Foreign Affairs, to Mr. Tricou, Special Envoy of France in China, Paris, May 18, 1883," in *Documents Diplomatiques* 1883, vol. 2, 115.

159. No. 215: "Mr. Tricou, Special Envoy of France in China, to Mr. Challemel Lacour, Minister of Foreign Affairs, (Telegram), Shanghai, June 18, 1883" (139) and no. 236: "Mr. Tricou, Special Envoy of France in China, to Mr. Challemel Lacour, Minister of Foreign Affairs, Shang-hai, June 22, 1883" (179), both in *Documents Diplomatiques* 1883, vol. 2.

160. No. 225: "Mr. Tricou, Special Envoy of France in China, to Mr. Challemel Lacour, Minister of Foreign Affairs, (Telegram), Shanghai, July 5, 1883," in *Documents Diplomatiques* 1883, vol. 2, 153–154.

161. No. 218: "A Conversation of Marquis Tseng, Minister of China in Paris, with Mr. Jules Ferry, President of the Council, Minister, Interim Minister of Foreign Affairs, Paris, June 21, 1883," in *Documents Diplomatiques* 1883, vol. 2, 142.

162. No. 221: "Mr. Jules Ferry, President of the Council, Charge, Interim Minister of Foreign Affairs, to Mr. Tricou, Special Envoy of France to China, in Shanghai, (Telegram), June 22, 1883, 9:30 p.m.," in *Documents Diplomatiques* 1883, vol. 2, 149.

163. Norman 1884, 221; Ennis 1936, 48; McAleavy 1968, 211–212; Power 1977, 164.

164. No. 231: "Mr. Charles Brun, Minister of the Navy and Colonies, to Mr. Harmand, Commissioner General to Tonkin, (Telegram), Paris, July 19, 1883," in *Documents Diplomatiques* 1883, vol. 2, 169.

165. For a detailed description, see "Pierre Loti at the bombardment of the forts of Thuan-An (August 18–21, 1883)," in Taboulet 1956, 803–805. See also Norman 1884, 232–233; McAleavy 1968, 213.

166. No. 253: "Mr. Harmand, Commissioner General of the Republic in Tonkin, to the Ministers of the Navy and of Foreign Affairs, in Paris, (Telegram), Tuan-An, August 25, [1883]," in *Documents Diplomatiques* 1883, vol. 2, 201. For the complete text, see Taboulet 1956, 807–809.

167. Power 1977, 190; Munholland 1979, 106.

168. Clodfelter 2008, 257.

6. THE DILEMMA OF INADVERTENT EXPANSION

1. This phrase is from Bosworth 1979.

2. See J. Snyder 1991, 56–58.

3. On the South Manchuria Railway, see Myers 1989.

4. Coox 1985, 1.

5. Hata and Coox 1989, 291.

6. Hata and Coox 1989, 285–286.

7. See Coox 1989.

8. Coox 1985, 27 (table 2.1).

9. Note that this and other names in this chapter are listed according to Japanese tradition, with the family name preceding the given name.

10. Seki 1984, 143. See also Peattie 1975, 21.

11. Peattie 1975, 23–25.

12. Peattie 1975, 37–83; Seki 1984, 148–149.

13. On the comparison between these two individuals, see Yoshihashi 1963, 42–43, 134–143; Peattie 1975, 95; Seki 1984, 139; Hata and Coox 1989, 294.

14. Ishiwara and Itagaki did not act on their own. At least twenty-six officers are believed to have participated in planning for the invasion or knew of it in advance. See Weland 1994, 446.

15. Bix 2001, 207–208.

16. Japan did have a Colonial Ministry, established in 1929, though it was a weak institution with little real influence on foreign or imperial policy. And, in any case, Prime Minister Wakatsuki held the post of colonial minister when the invasion of Manchuria was launched in September 1931. The Ministry of Colonial Affairs would be abandoned after the outbreak of the Pacific War in 1942. See Peattie 1989a, 244.

17. Yoshihashi 1963, 45–56; Ogata 1984, 11–17.

18. Peattie 1975, 106; Coox 1985, 27.

19. Weland 1977, chap. 9.

20. Crowley 1966, 115; Iriye 1989, 731; J. Snyder 1991, 135; Drea 2009, 65.

21. Colegrove 1936, 916–917.

22. O'Dwyer 2017, 4. See also Peattie 1989b, 188–189.

23. The South Manchuria Railway's research division would prove invaluable for Ishiwara and Itagaki's planning for the invasion of Manchuria. See Myers 1989, 125. See also Yoshihashi 1963, 138–139; Seki 1984, 153–154.

24. Crowley 1966, 102; Ogata 1984, 7–9; Hata and Coox 1989, 284; Hattori 2021, 3, 115.

25. "July 30, 1931," in Harada and Saionji 1978, 14–15. See also Yoshihashi 1963, 149; Seki 1984, 173, 176, 202–203; Beasley 1987, 181.

26. "August 27, 1931" (42) and "September 23, 1931" (65–66), both in Harada and Saionji 1978. See also Yoshihashi 1963, 58, 154; Ogata 1984, 58; Seki 1984, 202.

27. Matsusaka 1996, 102n15.

28. Crowley 1966, 114.

29. Hata and Coox 1989, 293.

30. Peattie 1975, 111–112; Ogata 1984, 16; Nish 2002, 76.

31. Nish 1993, 25–27.

32. Crowley 1966, 112; Peattie 1975, 51–52; M. Barnhart 1987, 27, 29.

33. Peattie 1975, 97.

34. The Kwantung Leased Territory totaled 3,461 km^2, and the South Manchuria Railway Zone totaled 233 km^2. See Duus 1996, xiii; Myers 1989, 109.

35. Peattie 1975, 100–101.

36. Yoshihashi 1963, 138; Peattie 1975, 102–106; Coox 1989, 401.

37. Peattie 1975, 106; Seki 1984, 144; Coox 1985, 26–27.

38. Ishiwara discussed this during his testimony at the Tokyo War Crimes Tribunal. See International Military Tribunal for the Far East 1947, 22112–22114. See also Peattie 1975, 106; Coox 1985, 27.

39. Peattie 1975, 112.

40. "August 21, 1931" (39), "August 27, 1931" (40, 42, 43, 47), and "September 14, 1931" (54–55), all in Harada and Saionji 1978. See also Ogata 1984, 57.

41. Seki 1984, 189.

42. Seki 1984, 201.

43. "September 23, 1931," in Harada and Saionji 1978, 65–67.

44. Bix 2001, 231.

45. Seki 1984, 205.

46. Bix 2001, 232. See also Seki 1984, 205.

47. Yoshihashi 1963, 152n4, 156–157.

48. The extent to which Tatekawa may have been aware of the plot is not entirely known. See Yoshihashi 1963, 159; Ogata 1984, 59; Seki 1984, 227.

49. On the differences between Kwantung Army claims and the truth that would ultimately come out after the Pacific War, see Coox 1985, 30–32.

50. Seki 1984, 217, 222; Coox 1985, 30, 32; Nish 1993, 23; 2002, 75.

51. Yoshihashi 1963, 170.

52. "September 23, 1931" (76–78) and "September 28, 1931" (90–91), both in Harada and Saionji 1978. See also Yoshihashi 1963, 8–9; Crowley 1966, 123; Shimada 1984, 246; Hata and Coox 1989, 296; Hattori 2021, 204.

53. Yoshihashi 1963, 6–7.

54. "September 23, 1931," in Harada and Saionji 1978, 76. See also Crowley 1966, 123–124; Ogata 1984, 60–61; Coox 1985, 34.

55. "October 24, 1931," in Harada and Saionji 1978, 125.

56. "September 23, 1931," in Harada and Saionji 1978, 78.

57. Crowley 1966, 111; Kupchan 1994, 301.

58. Yoshihashi 1963, 127; Coox 1989, 422; Nish 2002, 71–72.

59. Crowley 1966, 128; Ogata 1984, 54.

60. Peattie 1975, 98; Ogata 1984, 110.

61. M. Barnhart 1987, 33.

62. On Wakatsuki, see Nish 1993, 46; 2002, 76. On Shidehara, see Crowley 1966, 141. On Minami, see Shimada 1984, 263–264.

63. "September 23, 1931," in Harada and Saionji 1978, 76. See also Yoshihashi 1963, 6–7.

64. Mizoguchi 1989, 10.

65. "October 11, 1931," in Harada and Saionji 1978, 106–107.

66. "October 11, 1931," in Harada and Saionji 1978, 112–113. See also Yoshihashi 1963, 210–211.

67. On Shidehara, see Crowley 1966, 141. On Hirohito, see "October 24, 1931," in Harada and Saionji 1978, 147; Bix 2001, 245. On the General Staff, see Ogata 1984, 131, 177. Such concerns were also shared by the finance minister: "November 17, 1931," in Kido 1984, 15.

68. Peattie 1975, 133; Ogata 1984, 117; Jansen 2000, 584.

69. Coox 1985, 44.

70. Coox 1985, 31.

71. Coox 1985, 32.

72. Yoshihashi 1963, 179–180.

73. Ogata 1984, 111; Shimada 1984, 283; Coox 1985, 41.

74. Young 1998, 106.

75. "October 2, 1931," in Harada and Saionji 1978, 101–102.

76. Bridges 1980; Lozhkina, Shulatov, and Cherevko 2019, 219–225; Tobe 2019, 201–204.

77. Ogata 1984, 179; Hata and Coox 1989, 296.

78. On the United States, see Doc. 6: "Memorandum by the Secretary of State. [Washington,] September 22, 1931" and Doc. 9: "The Secretary of State to the Minister in China (Johnson) [Paraphrase], Washington, September 24, 1931—6 p.m.," both in Fuller 1943. On the United Kingdom, see Nish 1993, 36–37.

79. Beasley 1987, 198.

80. Matsusaka 2001, 384.

81. "November 7, 1931" (13) and "November 17, 1931" (15), both in Kido 1984.

82. Young 1996, 72–79. See also Ogata 1984, 105, 146; Beasley 1987, 193; Nish 1993, 35.

83. Beasley 1987, 190.

NOTES TO PAGES 125-128

84. "July 13, 1931," in Harada and Saionji 1978, 1; Ogata 1984, 48, 56; Seki 1984, 154, 169; Hata and Coox 1989, 292.
85. Yoshihashi 1963, 132–133; "July 30, 1931," in Harada and Saionji 1978, 13.
86. Seki 1984, 170–172, 180–184; Ogata 1984, 38–40.
87. Coox 1985, 58–59; Jansen 2000, 587.
88. Peattie 1975, 123; Ogata 1984, 65; Hata and Coox 1989, 295.
89. Ogata 1984, 67; Shimada 1984, 261.
90. Young 1996, 95.
91. Nish 1993, 39–40.
92. Seki 1984, 178.
93. Crowley 1966, 169; Nish 1993, 74.
94. Nish 2002, 79.
95. On the March 1931 coup plot, see "August 8, 1931," in Harada and Saionji 1978, 22, 24–26, 30–31. On the October 1931 coup plot, see "October 17, 1931," in Kido 1984, 10; "October 24, 1931," in Harada and Saionji 1978, 127.
96. Yoshihashi 1963, 95–102; Ogata 1984, 30–31.
97. "October 2, 1931," in Harada and Saionji 1978, 103.
98. "January 21, 1932" (28), "January 30, 1932" (30), "January 31, 1932" (30–31), "February 10, 1932" (36), "February 19, 1932" (40), and "March 9, 1932" (45–46), all in Kido 1984; "February 29, 1932," in Harada and Saionji 1978, 267. See also Crowley 1966, 82–83; Ogata 1984, 100; Shimada 1984, 279.
99. Coox 1985, 24; Hattori 2021, 201.
100. "August 27, 1931," in Harada and Saionji 1978, 48.
101. "October 24, 1931," in Harada and Saionji 1978, 127; "October 20, 1931," in Kido 1984, 10–11; Ogata 1984, 95; Hattori 2021, 210.
102. "May (3), 1932," in Harada and Saionji 1978, 337–338; "May 15, 1932," in Kido 1984, 52. See also Nish 2002, 85.
103. Emperor Hirohito himself was the target of an assassination attempt in January 1932, though in this case the perpetrator was a Korean independence activist. Among others targeted or killed were the Japanese consul general in Mukden, the Lord Keeper of the Privy Seal, the former finance minister and Bank of Japan governor, and a member of Japan's delegation to the League of Nations. See "October 2, 1931" (97), "October 24, 1931" (130), "November 19, 1931" (176), "January 26, 1932" (223), and "March 10, 1932" (281), all in Harada and Saionji 1978; "January 8, 1932" (24), "February 9, 1932" (36), "March 5, 1932" (44), and "May 15, 1932" (51–52), all in Kido 1984.
104. Shimada 1984, 280. See also "March 3, 1932," in Harada and Saionji 1978, 275.
105. Ishiwara referred to these rumors in his testimony at the Tokyo War Crimes Tribunal. See International Military Tribunal for the Far East 1947, 22117.
106. Peattie 1975, 128. See also Yoshihashi 1963, 210; Ogata 1984, 93.
107. Ogata 1984, 94, 97.
108. Coox 1985, 48.
109. Bix 2001, 236–237. See also "October 24, 1931," in Harada and Saionji 1978, 140.
110. "October 24, 1931," in Harada and Saionji 1978, 117. See also Yoshihashi 1963, 193; "October 24, 1931," in Harada and Saionji 1978, 116.
111. Nish 1993, 47.
112. "December 21, 1931," in Harada and Saionji 1978, 194–195; "December 11, 1931," in Kido 1984, 19.
113. Peattie 1975, 132–133; Iriye 1984, 237–238; Ogata 1984, 138.
114. "February 16, 1932," in Harada and Saionji 1978, 246–247; "February 5, 1932," in Kido 1984, 34. See also Nish 1993, 70.

115. "December 24, 1931," in Harada and Saionji 1978, 199. See also Crowley 1966, 150; "December 12, 1931," in Kido 1984, 20.

116. Bix 2001, 246.

117. Ogata 1984, 150.

118. Beasley 1987, 193.

119. Matsusaka 1996, 105.

120. "March 16, 1932," in Harada and Saionji 1978, 286–287. See also Ogata 1984, 138; Nish 1993, 88; Bix 2001, 249.

121. Peattie 1975, xviii, 139; Coox 1985, 56.

122. Peattie 1975, 122–123.

123. J. MacDonald 1921, 175.

124. Ledeen 1977, 17.

125. Rusinow 1969, 124.

126. Clodfelter 2008, 461–462.

127. MacMillan 2001, chap. 22.

128. Wilson 2023.

129. With Suzak included, the area was approximately 45 percent Slavic and 40 percent Italian. And 36 percent of the population was affiliated with the party advocating annexation to Yugoslavia, 34 percent affiliated with the party advocating annexation to Italy, and 30 percent advocating autonomy and independence. J. MacDonald 1921, 35–37.

130. Ledeen 1977, 40; D. Smith 1997, 282, 291; MacMillan 2001, 280.

131. D. Smith 1997, 282–288; Pearce 2009, 27.

132. J. MacDonald 1921, chap. 4; Rusinow 1969, 125–128; Ledeen 1977, 34.

133. MacMillan 2001, 296.

134. Hughes-Hallett 2013, 402–403.

135. Rusinow 1969, 133.

136. MacMillan 2001, 294–295; Pearce 2009, 25.

137. Ledeen 1977, 7; MacMillan 2001, 294–295.

138. Ledeen 1977, 6, 12; Bonadeo 1995; Pearce 2009, 26–27.

139. Hughes-Hallett 2013, 402.

140. Ledeen 1977, 48.

141. Ledeen 1977, 61; Gumbrecht 1996, 263.

142. Rusinow 1969, 135; Ledeen 1977, 73.

143. MacMillan 2001, 300.

144. Labanca 2021.

145. Labanca 2021.

146. See article 5 in Albert, Lindsay, and Rowe 1894, 27.

147. Labanca 2021.

148. Gooch 2007, 13–15.

149. Ledeen 1977, 65; Hughes-Hallett 2013, 407–408.

150. J. MacDonald 1921, 56; Rusinow 1969, 133; Ledeen 1977, 65–66.

151. Hughes-Hallett 2013, 408.

152. Gumbrecht 1996, 264.

153. Rusinow 1969, 134, 139.

154. Ledeen 1977, 66.

155. J. MacDonald 1921, 95–96.

156. J. MacDonald 1921, 92; Hughes-Hallett 2013, 413.

157. Ledeen 1977, 69–71.

158. Ledeen 1977, 73; Hughes-Hallett 2013, 417.

159. Rusinow 1969, 135–136.

160. J. MacDonald 1921, 103–104; Ledeen 1977, 77.

161. Ledeen 1977, 91–92; Hughes-Hallett 2013, 429.

162. J. MacDonald 1921, 102–103, 122; Ledeen 1977, 79.

163. Ledeen 1977, 77.

164. Ledeen 1977, 51–52, 76–77; MacMillan 2001, 296.

165. On Wilson's position, see Doc. 13: "Notes of a Meeting of the Heads of Delegations of the Five Great Powers Held in M. Clemenceau's Office at the Ministry of War, Monday Afternoon, September 15, 1919, at 4 p.m., Paris, September 15, 1919, 11 a.m." in Fuller 1946a. For the joint memorandum, see US Department of State 1920, 2.

166. Doc. 42: "Secretary's Notes of a Conference Held at 10, Downing Street, London, S. W. 1. on Friday, December 12, 1919, at 11:30 a.m.," in Fuller 1946b.

167. Ledeen 1977, 131.

168. Burgwyn 1997, 14.

169. Ledeen 1977, 15–16, 131; MacMillan 2001, 300.

170. Hughes-Hallett 2013, 426.

171. J. MacDonald 1921, 106; Rusinow 1969, 139.

172. Gumbrecht 1996, 265.

173. MacMillan 2001, 293.

174. Mondini 2006, 452–453. See also Ledeen 1977, 46.

175. MacMillan 2001, 303.

176. Rusinow 1969, 142.

177. Rusinow 1969, 136; Ledeen 1977, 16; MacMillan 2001, 303.

178. Hughes-Hallett 2013, 417.

179. J. MacDonald 1921, 113; MacMillan 2001, 302–303; Hughes-Hallett 2013, 435.

180. Rusinow 1969, 137; Hughes-Hallett 2013, 424.

181. Ledeen 1977, 101–102.

182. J. MacDonald 1921, 121, 151.

183. Peterson 2004.

184. Sforza 1938, 269.

185. Bonadeo 1995, 134; D. Smith 1997, 285–287; Hughes-Hallett 2013, 437–438.

186. Rusinow 1969, 137.

187. Hughes-Hallett 2013, 463.

188. Rusinow 1969, 147; Hughes-Hallett 2013, 471.

189. Rusinow 1969, 149–152; Bonadeo 1995, 140; Hughes-Hallett 2013, 475–480.

190. Hughes-Hallett 2013, 479–480.

191. Gumbrecht 1996.

192. Pearce 2009, 29.

7. INADVERTENT ANNEXATION IN EAST AFRICA

1. Note that because the peripheral actors were a totally private colonial organization in this case, the argument that unauthorized peripheral expansion is a principal-agent problem does not apply, since there is no real delegation of authority in this case.

2. Rich 1992, 188–190. For an interesting take on Bismarck's foreign policy, see Rathbun 2018.

3. W. Smith 1978, 41.

4. W. Smith 1978, 25–27; Perras 2004, 34–35.

5. Meritt 1978, 98; Perras 2004, 38.

6. Wesseling 1996, 140; Perras 2004, 10, 31, 36–37, 51, 91.

7. On Peters's unsuccessful proposals, see Meritt 1978, 98–99; Peters 2001, 15; Perras 2004, 35–36, 48, 51–52.

8. Meritt 1978, 99.

9. Peters would later claim that he was given "confidential hints" that the government was behind him, and some scholars have echoed these claims, arguing he was given a "tentative go-ahead" by the government (see W. Smith 1978, 32; Townsend 1930, 132). But a careful examination of the evidence indicates this was not the case. Peters, it turned out, likely overinterpreted some oblique statements made by a retired government official who was in no way authorized to speak for the government. See Meritt 1978, 100n13.

10. Wesseling 1996, 141; Pakenham 2003, 290; Perras 2004, 51–52.

11. Meritt 1978, 100; Wesseling 1996, 141; Pakenham 2003, 284, 290; Perras 2004, 51–52, 55.

12. Peters 2001, 15.

13. Wehler 1970, 129.

14. Note that the German acquisition of both South-West Africa and Togoland were also cases of inadvertent expansion. See Esterhuyse 1968, 47–48; Knoll 1976, 20, 22, 23, 171n26.

15. Townsend 1930, 132; Freeman-Grenville 1963, 435; Henderson 1965, 125; Meritt 1978, 102–103; W. Smith 1978, 32; Wesseling 1996, 141; Peters 2001, 18–19; Pakenham 2003, 291; Chamberlain 2010, 63.

16. Wesseling 1996, 141; Pakenham 2003, 290; Perras 2004, 56.

17. Wesseling 1996, 141; Perras 2004, 56.

18. Perras 2004, 57.

19. Freeman-Grenville 1963, 435; Meritt 1978, 104; Wesseling 1996, 141–142; Pakenham 2003, 284; Perras 2004, 1, 57–59.

20. Peters 2001, 17, 23–24; Wesseling 1996, 141–142; Pakenham 2003, 291; Perras 2004, 57–58.

21. Meritt 1978, 97; Wesseling 1996, 142; Perras 2004, 1.

22. Wesseling 1996, 142; Peters 2001, 27–29, 31; Pakenham 2003, 291; Perras 2004, 1, 61–62.

23. Peters 2001, 31.

24. Perras 2004, 63n190.

25. Freeman-Grenville 1963, 436; Wesseling 1996, 142.

26. Meritt 1978, 104; Pakenham 2003, 292.

27. Meritt 1978, 105; Perras 2004, 63n191.

28. Meritt 1978, 109.

29. Meritt 1978, 104; W. Smith 1978, 33; Pakenham 2003, 292; Perras 2004, 64.

30. W. Smith 1978, 29–30; Perras 2004, 8, 66; J. Barnhart 2020, 126.

31. P. Kennedy 1980, 169–173; Perras 2004, 42–46.

32. Strandmann 1969, 140.

33. Meritt 1978, 112–113.

34. P. Kennedy 1980, 173, 176–177, 180–181; Lowe 1994, 85–87, 96–99; Perras 2004, 43, 100.

35. P. Kennedy 1980, 180–181.

36. Lowe 1994, 99.

37. P. Kennedy 1980, 181; Pakenham 2003, 292.

38. Perras 2004, 66.

39. Some scholars have argued that Bismarck had "misgivings" and was "reluctant" in accepting East Africa and that the territory was "unwanted" (see Townsend 1930, 133; W. Smith 1978, 32–33, 36–37, 91; S. Press 2017, 217). But Bismarck asked few questions about the territory itself and came to his decision very quickly. See Meritt 1978, 106; Wesseling 1996, 142; Perras 2004, 64–65.

40. Freeman-Grenville 1963, 436; Peters 2001, 35–36.

41. Meritt 1978, 97.

42. Perras 2004, 105.

43. Freeman-Grenville 1963, 436, 442; Peters 2001, 40; Pakenham 2003, 292–293; Perras 2004, 105.

44. Freeman-Grenville 1963, 437; Henderson 1965, 126; Pakenham 2003, 293; Perras 2004, 102–103.

45. Pakenham 2003, 296; Chamberlain 2010, 64.

46. Wesseling 1996, 145; Perras 2004, 112.

47. Freeman-Grenville 1963, 437; Henderson 1965, 126.

48. Wesseling 1996, 149; Pakenham 2003, 312, 344.

49. W. Smith 1978, 35, 76; Wesseling 1996, 146.

50. Perras 2004, 113.

51. Wituland itself had also been acquired by inadvertent expansion. See Townsend 1930, 131.

52. Rich 1992, 246–247; Pakenham 2003, 350.

53. W. Smith 1978, 73; Perras 2004, 68–80, 113.

54. Peters 2001, 22–23, 28–29.

55. Freeman-Grenville 1963, 444; W. Smith 1978, 75; Reuss 1981; Pakenham 2003, 624–625; Perras 2004, 115–116, 118.

56. Perras 2004, 125–126.

57. Collins 1967, 124; Louis 1967, 15; Wesseling 1996, 149.

58. Sanderson 1965, 29; Pakenham 2003, 310; Perras 2004, 132.

59. Langer 1960, 112.

60. Collins 1967, 124.

61. Langer 1960, 112–113; Sanderson 1965, 33–35; Collins 1967, 126–128; Wesseling 1996, 150–151. For an overview of the British expedition, see Pakenham 2003, 316–335.

62. Sanderson 1965, 44; Wesseling 1996, 153; Pakenham 2003, 344; Perras 2004, 134.

63. Peters 1891a, 113.

64. Langer 1960, 116.

65. Townsend 1930, 136; Sanderson 1965, 44; Collins 1967, 129–130; W. Smith 1978, 75; Perras 2004, 133, 135.

66. Perras 2004, 137.

67. Perras 2004, 136.

68. Perras 2004, 137.

69. Perras 2004, 137.

70. Peters 1891b, 6; see also 2001, 64.

71. W. Smith 1978, 77–78; Wesseling 1996, 146–148; Pakenham 2003, 346–349.

72. Freeman-Grenville 1963, 439; Henderson 1965, 128; Louis 1967, 13.

73. Perras 2004, 143–144.

74. Ritchie 1940, 144; Gillard 1960, 639; Louis 1967, 13; P. Kennedy 1980, 201.

75. Perras 2004, 139.

76. Perras 2004, 140.

77. Perras 2004, 140, 143.

78. Huurdeman 2003, 137; Bill Glover, "Cable Timeline: 1850–2018," History of the Atlantic Cable and Undersea Communications, 2022, available at https://atlantic-cable.com/Cables/CableTimeLine/index.htm.

79. Peters 1891b, 29.

80. Peters 1891b, 18.

81. Peters 1891b, 23; Perras 2004, 144–145.

82. Peters 1891b, 27; 2001, 64.

83. Peters 1891b, 26–27; 2001, 64; Pakenham 2003, 351; Perras 2004, 144–145.

84. Peters 1891b, 32.

85. Pakenham 2003, 351.

86. Peters 1891b, 28; 2001, 64.

87. Peters 1891b, 29.

88. Peters 1891b, 28; Perras 2004, 145; Pakenham 2003, 352.

89. Peters 1891b, 32.

90. Sanderson 1965, 45; Collins 1967, 132; Peters 2001, 64; Perras 2004, 146, 148.

91. Peters 1891b, 39; Perras 2004, 147.

92. Peters 1891a, 113; Perras 2004, 144, 147–148.

93. Peters 1891b, 28–29; Pakenham 2003, 352; Perras 2004, 145.

94. Peters 1891b, 77.

95. Peters 1891a, 114; Pakenham 2003, 352; Perras 2004, 153–154.

96. See, for instance, Peters 1891a, 116–121; Pakenham 2003, 352–353; Perras 2004, 154–160, 167.

97. Perras 2004, 160.

98. Peters 1891b, 114.

99. Peters 1891a, 123; 1891b, 360; Wesseling 1996, 153; Pakenham 2003, 353; Perras 2004, 160–161.

100. Peters 1891b, 362; Wesseling 1996, 153; Pakenham 2003, 353; Perras 2004, 161.

101. Peters 1891b, 379–390, 585–586; Perras 2004, 165–166. This treaty has been widely misidentified as a protectorate in the historical literature, such as in Townsend 1930, 137; Langer 1960, 116; Henderson 1965, 130; Wesseling 1996, 149, 153; Pakenham 2003, 356.

102. Perras 2004, 166.

103. Distance estimated using the "Measure Distance" tool in Google Maps, 2023, available at https://www.google.com/maps, as well as "Map of the German Emin Pasha Expedition," in Peters 1891b.

104. See Peters 1891b, 133–136, 145–146, 272–275, 309–310, 481–482, 486, 512–513, 530–531, as well as the accompanying "Map of the German Emin Pasha Expedition."

105. Langer 1960, 119; Sanderson 1965, 53.

106. W. Smith 1978, 76; P. Kennedy 1980, 202–203; Perras 2004, 152.

107. Sanderson 1965, 57–58.

108. Sanderson 1965, 45–46, 49.

109. Perras 2004, 150.

110. Perras 2004, 141.

111. Perras 2004, 149–150.

112. Gillard 1960, 633; Sanderson 1963, 57; 1965, 44.

113. P. Kennedy 1980, 200.

114. Sanderson 1965, 47. See also Townsend 1930, 115, 138; Wesseling 1996, 145, 159.

115. P. Kennedy 1980, 201.

116. P. Kennedy 1980, 201.

117. Sanderson 1965, 47; P. Kennedy 1980, 190–191, 196–197; Pakenham 2003, 350.

118. Langer 1960, 103–106, 108; Sanderson 1965, 42; Collins 1967, 121, 128–129, 139; Louis 1967, 15; P. Kennedy 1980, 200; Wesseling 1996, 153, 156, 158.

119. Townsend 1930, 114; Sanderson 1965, 42; Collins 1967, 120–121; Louis 1967, 16; Wesseling 1996, 153, 156, 158.

120. Louis 1967, 16–17; Wesseling 1996, 145; Pakenham 2003, 344.

121. Sanderson 1965, 44–45.

122. P. Kennedy 1980, 202.

123. Collins 1967, 123.

124. Perras 2004, 139.

125. Sanderson 1965, 45.

126. Collins 1967, 131. See also Sanderson 1963, 52; 1965, 45, 50; Pakenham 2003, 354.

127. Perras 2004, 151. See also Townsend 1930, 115, 123, 138; Wesseling 1996, 159.

128. Pakenham 2003, 349–350.

129. Sanderson 1965, 53; Collins 1967, 133; Wesseling 1996, 158; Pakenham 2003, 355; Chamberlain 2010, 65.

130. Louis 1967, 17. See also Sanderson 1963, 52–53; 1965, 53; Collins 1967, 133; P. Kennedy 1980, 195, 204.

131. Collins 1967, 133–134.

132. Louis 1967, 17.

133. Sanderson 1965, 58.

134. Gillard 1960, 647–648.

135. Sanderson 1965, 54.

136. Gillard 1960, 649; Collins 1967, 150.

137. Langer 1960, 119; Henderson 1965, 131; Collins 1967, 150; P. Kennedy 1980, 205–206; Perras 2004, 168.

138. Wesseling 1996, 159; Perras 2004, 168; Chamberlain 2010, 65.

139. Townsend 1930, 141; Freeman-Grenville 1963, 440–441; Henderson 1965, 131–132; W. Smith 1978, 78; Perras 2004, 127.

140. Wesseling 1996, 159.

141. Peters 1891b, 557; Henderson 1965, 131; Perras 2004, 168.

142. Perras 2004, 172.

143. Peters 1891b, 559.

144. Perras 2004, 171–173.

145. W. Smith 1978, 76–77; Perras 2004, 174.

146. The quote is from Rich 1992, 235. For classic works in the debate over Bismarck's colonial strategy, see Strandmann 1969; Taylor 1970; Wehler 1970.

147. Rich 1992, 247.

CONCLUSION

1. See White 2021.

2. Zacher 2001; Fazal 2007, chap. 7; Goertz, Diehl, and Balas 2016, chap. 5.

3. Territorial Change Data (v5.0). Tir et al. 1998.

4. Altman 2020; see also 2017.

5. Van Evera 1998, 33–34; Lieber 2000, 97–98; K. Adams 2004, 49–50.

6. Brooks 1999.

7. Zacher 2001; Fazal 2007, 44–54.

8. Hathaway and Shapiro 2017, chap. 13.

9. Altman and Lee 2022.

10. Adebajo 2002, 46; Amusan 2013, 272.

11. Brown 1987, 11–16.

12. Herz and Nogueira 2002, 45–46; Mares and Palmer 2012, 78.

13. Marten 2019.

14. Christoph Reuter, "The Truth about the Russian Deaths in Syria," *Der Spiegel International*, March 2, 2018, available at https://www.spiegel.de/international/world/american-fury-the-truth-about-the-russian-deaths-in-syria-a-1196074.html; Thomas Gibbons-Neff, "How a 4-Hour Battle between Russian Mercenaries and US Commandos Unfolded in Syria," *New York Times*, May 24, 2018, available at https://www.nytimes.com/2018/05/24/world/middleeast/american-commandos-russian-mercenaries-syria.html.

15. C. Kennedy and Erickson 2017.

16. Though, see Neil Hauer, "Russia's Mercenary Debacle in Syria: Is the Kremlin Losing Control?" *Foreign Affairs*, February 26, 2018, available at https://www.foreignaffairs.com/articles/syria/2018-02-26/russias-mercenary-debacle-syria.

17. Ellen Nakashima, Karen DeYoung, and Liz Sly, "Putin Ally Said to Be in Touch with Kremlin, Assad before His Mercenaries Attacked US Troops," *Washington Post*, February 22, 2018, available at https://www.washingtonpost.com/world/national-security/putin-ally-said-to-be-in-touch-with-kremlin-assad-before-his-mercenaries-attacked-us-troops/2018/02/22/f4ef050c-1781-11e8-8b08-027a6ccb38eb_story.html.

18. For research on autocratic "audience costs," see J. Weeks 2008; Weiss 2013.

19. Arutunyan 2022, 103–127; Galeotti 2022, 181–184.

20. Emphasis in original. Galeotti 2022, 180.

21. Emphasis in original. Arutunyan 2022, 105.

22. Anna Doglov, "Russia's Igor Strelkov: I Am Responsible for War in Eastern Ukraine," *Moscow Times*, November 21, 2014, available at https://www.themoscowtimes.com/2014/11/21/russias-igor-strelkov-i-am-responsible-for-war-in-eastern-ukraine-a41598.

23. Arutunyan 2022, 129–145.

24. Arutunyan 2022, 140. See also Galeotti 2022, 182.

25. Arutunyan 2022, 169; Galeotti 2022, 188.

26. "Conflict Related Civilian Casualties in Ukraine," United Nations, Ukraine, January 30, 2022, available at https://ukraine.un.org/en/168060-conflict-related-civilian-casualties-ukraine.

27. Keck and Sikkink 1998, 213.

28. Grynaviski 2018, 3.

29. Lake and Powell 1999, 6–7.

30. Richard Betts 2000, 46. See also Edelstein and Krebs 2015.

31. Mintzberg and Waters 1985. See also Popescu 2018.

32. Waltz 2010, 118.

33. Glaser 2010, 31.

34. See, for instance, Posen's (1984) discussion of how leaders and militaries become more cohesive when facing acute external threats. For an important critique of related ideas, see Myrick 2021.

35. Jervis 1976, 319; see also 1968, 475–476.

36. "Remarks by President Biden on Russia's Unprovoked and Unjustified Attack on Ukraine," White House, February 24, 2022, available at https://www.whitehouse.gov/briefing-room/speeches-remarks/2022/02/24/remarks-by-president-biden-on-russias-unprovoked-and-unjustified-attack-on-ukraine/.

37. Robin Wright, "Trump Drops the Mother of All Bombs on Afghanistan," *New Yorker*, April 14, 2017, available at https://www.newyorker.com/news/news-desk/trump-drops-the-mother-of-all-bombs-on-afghanistan; "Xi Jinping's Zero-Covid Policy Has Turned a Health Crisis into a Political One," *The Economist*, December 1, 2022, available at https://www.economist.com/leaders/2022/12/01/xi-jinpings-zero-covid-policy-has-turned-a-health-crisis-into-a-political-one.

References

Adams, Charles Francis, ed. 1875. *Memoirs of John Quincy Adams: Comprising Portions of His Diary from 1795 to 1848*. Vol. 4. Philadelphia: L. B. Lippincott.

Adams, Julia. 1996. "Principals and Agents, Colonialists and Company Men: The Decay of Colonial Control in the Dutch East Indies." *American Sociological Review* 61 (1): 12–28.

Adams, Karen Ruth. 2004. "Attack and Conquer? International Anarchy and the Offense-Defense-Deterrence Balance." *International Security* 28, no. 3 (Winter 2003–04): 45–83.

Adebajo, Adekeye. 2002. *Liberia's Civil War: Nigeria, ECOMOG, and Regional Security in West Africa*. Boulder, CO: Lynne Rienner.

Albert, Charles, S. M. Lindsay, and Leo S. Rowe. 1894. "Supplement: Constitution of the Kingdom of Italy." *Annals of the American Academy of Political and Social Science* 5 (9): 1–44.

Aldrich, Robert. 1996. *Greater France: A History of French Overseas Expansion*. New York: Macmillan.

Aldrich, Robert, and John Connell. 1992. *France's Overseas Frontier: Départements et Territoires D'Outre-Mer*. New York: Cambridge University Press.

Alessio, Dominic, and Wesley B. Renfro. 2016. "The Voldemort of Imperial History: Rethinking Empire and US History." *International Studies Perspectives* 17 (3): 250–266.

Altman, Dan. 2017. "By Fait Accompli, Not Coercion: How States Wrest Territory from Their Adversaries." *International Studies Quarterly* 61 (4): 881–891.

Altman, Dan. 2020. "The Evolution of Territorial Conquest after 1945 and the Limits of the Norm of Territorial Integrity." *International Organization* 74 (3): 490–522.

Altman, Dan, and Melissa M. Lee. 2022. "Why Territorial Disputes Escalate: The Causes of Conquest Attempts since 1945." *International Studies Quarterly* 66 (4): 1–15.

Ammon, Harry. 1971. *James Monroe: The Quest for National Identity*. New York: McGraw-Hill.

Amusan, Lere. 2013. "Nigeria and Its Neighbour in the Age of Climate Change: An Assessment of the Lake Chad Basin Area." In *An Introduction to Political Science in Nigeria*, edited by Adeoye A. Akinsanya and John A. Ayoade, 261–282. Lanham, MD: University Press of America.

Andrew, C. M., and A. S. Kanya-Forstner. 1988. "Centre and Periphery in the Making of the Second French Colonial Empire, 1815–1920." *Journal of Imperial and Commonwealth History* 16 (3): 9–34.

Ansari, Sarah. 2005. "The Sind Blue Books of 1843 and 1844: The Political 'Laundering' of Historical Evidence." *English Historical Review* 120 (485): 35–65.

Arrow, Kenneth J. 1984. "The Economics of Agency." In *Principals and Agents: The Structure of Business*, edited by John W. Pratt and Richard J. Zeckhauser, 37–51. Cambridge, MA: Harvard Business School Press.

Arutunyan, Anna. 2022. *Hybrid Warriors: Proxies, Freelancers and Moscow's Struggle for Ukraine*. London: Hurst.

Avant, Deborah D. 1996. "Are the Reluctant Warriors Out of Control? Why the U.S. Military Is Averse to Responding to Post–Cold War Low-Level Threats." *Security Studies* 6 (2): 51–90.

Barnhart, Joslyn. 2016. "Status Competition and Territorial Aggression: Evidence from the Scramble for Africa." *Security Studies* 25 (3): 385–419.

Barnhart, Joslyn. 2017. "Humiliation and Third-Party Aggression." *World Politics* 69 (3): 532–568.

Barnhart, Joslyn. 2020. *The Consequences of Humiliation: Anger and Status in World Politics*. Ithaca, NY: Cornell University Press.

Barnhart, Michael A. 1987. *Japan Prepares for Total War: The Search for Economic Security, 1919–1941*. Ithaca, NY: Cornell University Press.

Bassett, John Spencer, ed. 1927. *Correspondence of Andrew Jackson*. Vol. 2, *May 1, 1814 to December 31, 1819*. Washington, DC: Carnegie Institution of Washington.

Bassett, John Spencer, ed. 1929. *Correspondence of Andrew Jackson*. Vol. 4, *1829–1832*. Washington, DC: Carnegie Institution of Washington.

Bassett, John Spencer, ed. 1931. *Correspondence of Andrew Jackson*. Vol. 5, *1833–1838*. Washington, DC: Carnegie Institute of Washington.

Beasley, W. G. 1987. *Japanese Imperialism, 1894–1945*. Oxford: Oxford University Press.

Becker, Seymour. 2004. *Russia's Protectorates in Central Asia: Bukhara and Khiva, 1865–1924*. New York: RoutledgeCurzon.

Bell, Kenneth Norman, ed. 1928. *Select Documents on British Colonial Policy, 1830–1860*. Oxford: Clarendon.

Bennett, Andrew, and Jeffrey T. Checkel. 2014. "Process Tracing: From Philosophical Roots to Best Practices." In *Process Tracing: From Metaphor to Analytical Tool*, edited by Andrew Bennett and Jeffrey T. Checkel, 3–38. New York: Cambridge University Press.

Bennett, Andrew, and Colin Elman. 2007. "Case Study Methods in the International Relations Subfield." *Comparative Political Studies* 40 (2): 170–195.

Betts, Raymond. 1978. *Tricouleur: The French Overseas Empire*. London: Gordon and Cremonesi.

Betts, Richard K. 2000. "Is Strategy an Illusion?" *International Security* 25 (2): 5–50.

Billot, Albert. 1888. *L'Affaire du Tonkin: Histoire Diplomatique de l'Établissement de Notre Protectorat sur l'Annam et de Notre Conflit avec la Chine, 1882–1885*. Paris: J. Hetzel.

Bix, Herbert P. 2001. *Hirohito and the Making of Modern Japan*. New York: Perennial.

Bonadeo, Alfredo. 1995. *D'Annunzio and the Great War*. Cranbury, NJ: Associated University Presses.

Bosworth, R. J. B. 1979. *Italy, the Least of the Great Powers: Italian Foreign Policy before the First World War*. Cambridge: Cambridge University Press.

Brambor, Thomas, Agustin Goenaga, Johannes Lindvall, and Jan Teorell. 2020. "The Lay of the Land: Information Capacity and the Modern State." *Comparative Political Studies* 53 (2): 175–213.

Brands, H. W. 2005. *Andrew Jackson: His Life and Times*. New York: Doubleday.

Bregel, Yuri. 2009. "The New Uzbek States: Bukhara, Khiva and Khoqand: c. 1750–1886." In *The Cambridge History of Inner Asia*. Vol. 2, *The Chinggisid Age*, edited by Nicola Di Cosmo, Allen J. Frank, and Peter B. Golden, 392–411. New York: Cambridge University Press.

Brendon, Piers. 2007. *The Decline and Fall of the British Empire, 1781–1997*. New York: Vintage Books.

Bridges, Brian. 1980. "Yoshizawa Kenkichi and the Soviet-Japanese Non-Aggression Pact Proposal." *Modern Asian Studies* 14 (1): 111–127.

Brocheux, Pierre, and Daniel Hémery. 2009. *Indochina: An Ambiguous Colonization, 1858–1954*. Translated by Ly Lan Dill-Klein. Berkeley: University of California Press.

Brooks, Stephen G. 1999. "The Globalization of Production and the Changing Benefits of Conquest." *Journal of Conflict Resolution* 43 (5): 646–670.

Brooks, Stephen G., and William C. Wohlforth. 2016. "The Rise and Fall of the Great Powers in the Twenty-First Century: China's Rise and the Fate of America's Global Position." *International Security* 40, no. 3 (Winter 2015–16): 7–53.

Brown, MacAlister. 1987. "Anatomy of a Border Dispute: Laos and Thailand." *Pacific Focus* 2 (2): 5–30.

Brunschwig, Henri. 1966. *French Colonialism, 1871–1914: Myths and Realities*. London: Pall Mall.

Bueno de Mesquita, Bruce, Alastair Smith, Randolph M. Siverson, and James D. Morrow. 2003. *The Logic of Political Survival*. Cambridge, MA: MIT Press.

Burgwyn, H. James. 1997. *Italian Foreign Policy in the Interwar Period, 1918–1940*. Westport, CT: Praeger.

Buttinger, Joseph. 1958. *The Smaller Dragon: A Political History of Vietnam*. New York: Praeger.

Cady, John F. 1954. *The Roots of French Imperialism in Eastern Asia*. Ithaca, NY: Cornell University Press.

Causes of the Afghan War: Being a Selection of the Papers Laid Before Parliament with a Connecting Narrative and Comment. 1879. London: Chatto & Windus, Piccadilly.

Chamberlain, M. E. 2010. *The Scramble for Africa*. 3rd ed. Harlow, England: Pearson.

Clodfelter, Michael. 2008. *Warfare and Armed Conflicts: A Statistical Encyclopedia of Casualties and Other Figures, 1494–2007*. Jefferson, NC: McFarland.

Coe, Andrew. 2009. *Chop Suey: A Cultural History of Chinese Food in the United States*. New York: Oxford University Press.

Colchester, Lord, ed. 1874. *History of the Indian Administration of Lord Ellenborough, in His Correspondence with the Duke of Wellington: To Which Is Prefixed, by Permission of Her Majesty, Lord Ellenborough's Letters to the Queen during That Period*. London: R. Bentley and Son.

Cole, Donald B. 1993. *The Presidency of Andrew Jackson*. Lawrence, KS: University Press of Kansas.

Colegrove, Kenneth. 1936. "The Japanese Cabinet." *American Political Science Review* 30 (5): 903–923.

Collins, Robert O. 1967. "Origins of the Nile Struggle: Anglo-German Negotiations and the Mackinnon Agreement of 1890." In *Britain and Germany in Africa: Imperial Rivalry and Colonial Rule*, edited by Prosser Gifford and Wm. Roger Louis, 119–152. New Haven, CT: Yale University Press.

Coox, Alvin D. 1985. *Nomonhan: Japan against Russia, 1939*. Vol. 1. Stanford, CA: Stanford University Press.

Coox, Alvin D. 1989. "The Kwantung Army Dimension." In *The Japanese Informal Empire in China, 1895–1937*, edited by Peter Duus, Ramon H. Myers, and Mark R. Peattie, 395–428. Princeton, NJ: Princeton University Press.

Corrado, Sharyl. 2014. "A Land Divided: Sakhalin and the Amur Expedition of G.I. Nevel'skoi, 1848–1855." *Journal of Historical Geography* 45:70–81.

Crowley, James B. 1966. *Japan's Quest for Autonomy: National Security and Foreign Policy, 1930–1938*. Princeton, NJ: Princeton University Press.

Cunningham, Noble E. 1996. *The Presidency of James Monroe*. Lawrence: University Press of Kansas.

Dafoe, Allan, Jonathan Renshon, and Paul Huth. 2014. "Reputation and Status as Motives for War." *Annual Review of Political Science* 17:371–393.

Daily National Intelligencer. 1818. 6 (1729). Washington, DC, July 27, 1818.

Dangerfield, George. 1952. *The Era of Good Feelings.* New York: Harcourt, Brace.

Darwin, John. 1997. "Imperialism and the Victorians: The Dynamics of Territorial Expansion." *English Historical Review* 112 (447): 614–642.

Davis, Bradley Camp. 2017. *Imperial Bandits: Outlaws and Rebels in the China-Vietnam Borderlands.* Seattle: University of Washington Press.

d'Encausse, Hélène Carrère. 1994. "Systematic Conquest." In *Central Asia: 130 Years of Russian Dominance—A Historical Overview,* 3rd ed., edited by Edward Allworth, 131–150. Durham, NC: Duke University Press.

Dickins, Asbury, and John W. Forney, eds. 1861. *American State Papers,* Class V: Military Affairs, Vol. 6, 1836–1837. Washington, DC: Gales and Seaton.

Documents Diplomatiques, Affaires du Tonkin, Première Partie (Vol. 1), *1874–Décembre 1882.* 1883. Paris: Imprimerie Nationale.

Documents Diplomatiques, Affaires du Tonkin, Deuxième Partie (Vol. 2), *Décembre 1882–1883.* 1883. Paris: Imprimerie Nationale.

Downs, George W., and David M. Rocke. 1994. "Conflict, Agency, and Gambling for Resurrection: The Principal-Agent Problem Goes to War." *American Journal of Political Science* 38 (2): 362–380.

Doyle, Michael W. 1986. *Empires.* Ithaca, NY: Cornell University Press.

Drea, Edward J. 2009. *Japan's Imperial Army: Its Rise and Fall, 1853–1945.* Lawrence: University Press of Kansas.

Duckett, Alvin Laroy. 1962. *John Forsyth: Political Tactician.* Athens: University of Georgia Press.

Dutreb, M. 1924. *L'Amiral Dupré et la Conquête du Tonkin.* Paris: E. Leroux.

Duus, Peter. 1996. "Japan's Wartime Empire: Problems and Issues." In *The Japanese Wartime Empire, 1931–1945,* edited by Peter Duus, Ramon H. Myers, and Mark R. Peattie, xi–xlvii. Princeton, NJ: Princeton University Press.

Eastman, Lloyd E. 1967. *Throne and Mandarins: China's Search for a Policy during the Sino-French Controversy, 1880–1885.* Taipei: Rainbow Bridge Book.

Edelstein, David M. 2008. *Occupational Hazards: Success and Failure in Military Occupation.* Ithaca, NY: Cornell University Press.

Edelstein, David M., and Ronald R. Krebs. 2015. "Delusions of Grand Strategy: The Problem with Washington's Planning Obsession." *Foreign Affairs* 94 (6): 109–116.

Eisenhardt, Kathleen M. 1989. "Agency Theory: An Assessment and Review." *Academy of Management Review* 14 (1): 57–74.

Elman, Colin. 1996. "Horses for Courses: Why *Not* Neorealist Theories of Foreign Policy?" *Security Studies* 6 (1): 7–53.

Ennis, Thomas E. 1936. *French Policy and Developments in Indochina.* Chicago: University of Chicago Press.

Esterhuyse, J. H. 1968. *South West Africa, 1880–1894: The Establishment of German Authority in South West Africa.* Cape Town: C. Struik.

Evans, John L. 1999. *Russian Expansion on the Amur, 1848–1860: The Push to the Pacific.* Lewiston, NY: Edwin Mellen.

Fama, Eugene F., and Michael C. Jensen. 1983. "Separation of Ownership and Control." *Journal of Law and Economics* 26 (2): 301–325.

Fazal, Tanisha M. 2007. *State Death: The Politics and Geography of Conquest, Occupation, and Annexation.* Princeton, NJ: Princeton University Press.

Fearon, James D. 1991. "Counterfactuals and Hypothesis Testing in Political Science." *World Politics* 43 (2): 169–195.

Fearon, James D. 2002. "Selection Effects and Deterrence." *International Interactions* 28 (1): 5–29.

Fearon, James D., and David D. Laitin. 2004. "Neotrusteeship and the Problem of Weak States." *International Security* 28 (4): 5–43.

Feaver, Peter D. 2003. *Armed Servants: Agency, Oversight, and Civil-Military Relations.* Cambridge, MA: Harvard University Press.

Fieldhouse, D. K. 1973. *Economics and Empire, 1830–1914.* Ithaca, NY: Cornell University Press.

Finch, Michael P. M. 2013. *A Progressive Occupation? The Gallieni-Lyautey Method and Colonial Pacification in Tonkin and Madagascar, 1885–1900.* Oxford: Oxford University Press.

Freeman-Grenville, G. S. P. 1963. "The German Sphere, 1884–98." In *History of East Africa,* Vol. 1, edited by Roland Oliver and Gervase Mathew, 433–453. Oxford: Clarendon.

Fuller, Joseph V., ed. 1943. *Foreign Relations of the United States, Papers Relating to the Foreign Relations of the United States, Japan, 1931–1941.* Vol. 1. Washington, DC: US Government Printing Office. Available at https://history.state.gov/historical documents/frus1931-41v01/.

Fuller, Joseph V. 1946a. *Papers Relating to the Foreign Relations of the United States, The Paris Peace Conference, 1919.* Vol. 8. Washington, DC: US Government Printing Office. Available at https://history.state.gov/historicaldocuments/frus1919Parisv08.

Fuller, Joseph V. 1946b. *Papers Relating to the Foreign Relations of the United States, The Paris Peace Conference, 1919.* Vol. 9. Washington, DC: US Government Printing Office. Available at https://history.state.gov/historicaldocuments/frus1919Parisv09.

Galbraith, John S. 1960. "The 'Turbulent Frontier' as a Factor in British Expansion." *Comparative Studies in Society and History* 2 (2): 150–168.

Galbraith, John S. 1963. *Reluctant Empire: British Policy on the South African Frontier, 1834–1854.* Berkeley: University of California Press.

Galeotti, Mark. 2022. *Putin's Wars: From Chechnya to Ukraine.* Oxford: Osprey.

Gallagher, John, and Ronald Robinson. 1953. "The Imperialism of Free Trade." *Economic History Review* 6 (1): 1–15.

Garrison, George P., ed. 1908. *Diplomatic Correspondence of the Republic of Texas.* Vol. 2, Pt. 1. Washington, DC: US Government Printing Office.

Gash, Norman. 1972. *Sir Robert Peel: The Life of Sir Robert Peel after 1830.* Totowa, NJ: Rowman and Littlefield.

Geddes, Barbara. 1990. "How the Cases You Choose Affect the Answers You Get: Selection Bias in Comparative Politics." *Political Analysis* 2:131–150.

George, Alexander L., and Andrew Bennett. 2005. *Case Studies and Theory Development in the Social Sciences.* Cambridge, MA: MIT Press.

Gerring, John. 2001. *Social Science Methodology: A Critical Framework.* New York: Cambridge University Press.

Ghosn, Faten, Glenn Palmer, and Stuart Bremer. 2004. "The MID3 Data Set, 1993–2001: Procedures, Coding Rules, and Description." *Conflict Management and Peace Science* 21 (2): 133–154.

Gibler, Douglas M. 2009. *International Military Alliances, 1648–2008.* Washington, DC: CQ Press.

Gillard, D. R. 1960. "Salisbury's African Policy and the Heligoland Offer of 1890." *English Historical Review* 75 (297): 631–653.

Gilpin, Robert. 1981. *War and Change in World Politics.* New York: Cambridge University Press.

Gladstone, W. E. 1876. "Russian Policy and Deeds in Turkistan." *Contemporary Review* 28:873–891.

Glaser, Charles L. 2010. *Rational Theory of International Politics: The Logic of Competition and Cooperation.* Princeton, NJ: Princeton University Press.

Goertz, Gary, and Paul F. Diehl. 1992. *Territorial Changes and International Conflict*. New York: Routledge.

Goertz, Gary, Paul F. Diehl, and Alexandru Balas. 2016. *The Puzzle of Peace: The Evolution of Peace in the International System*. New York: Oxford University Press.

Gooch, John. 2007. *Mussolini and His Generals: The Armed Forces and Fascist Foreign Policy*. New York: Cambridge University Press.

Gorenberg, Gershom. 2006. *The Accidental Empire: Israel and the Birth of the Settlements, 1967–1977*. New York: Times Books.

Gourou, Pierre. 1936. *Les Paysans du Delta Tonkinois: Étude de Géographie Humaine*. Paris: Les Éditions d'art et d'histoire.

Greenhalgh, Elizabeth. 2014. *The French Army and the First World War*. Cambridge: Cambridge University Press.

Grynaviski, Eric. 2018. *America's Middlemen: Power at the Edge of Empire*. New York: Cambridge University Press.

Gumbrecht, Hans Ulrich. 1996. "*I redentori della vittoria*: On Fiume's Place in the Genealogy of Fascism." *Journal of Contemporary History* 31 (2): 253–272.

Haley, James L. 2002. *Sam Houston*. Norman: University of Oklahoma Press.

Hamilton, Stanislaus Murray, ed. 1902. *The Writings of James Monroe: Including a Collection of His Public and Private Papers and Correspondence Now for the First Time Printed*. Vol. 6, *1817–1823*. New York: G. P. Putnam's Sons.

Harada, Kumao, and Kinmochi Saionji. 1978. *The Saionji-Harada Memoirs, 1931–1940*. Washington, DC: University Publications of America.

Hassner, Ron E. 2007. "The Path to Intractability: Time and the Entrenchment of Territorial Disputes." *International Security* 31, no. 3 (Winter 2006–07): 107–138.

Hata, Ikuhiko, and Alvin D. Coox. 1989. "Continental Expansion, 1905–1941." In *The Cambridge History of Japan*, Vol. 6, *The Twentieth Century*, edited by Peter Duus, 271–314. New York: Cambridge University Press.

Hathaway, Oona A., and Scott J. Shapiro. 2017. *The Internationalists: How a Radical Plan to Outlaw War Remade the World*. New York: Simon and Schuster.

Hattori, Ryuji. 2021. *Japan at War and Peace: Shidehara Kijūrō and the Making of Modern Diplomacy*. Canberra: Australian National University Press.

Hawkins, Darren G., David A. Lake, Daniel L. Nelson, and Michael Tierney. 2006. "Delegation under Anarchy: States, International Organizations, and Principal-Agent Theory." In *Delegation and Agency in International Organizations*, edited by Darren G. Hawkins, David A. Lake, Daniel L. Nelson, and Michael Tierney, 3–38. New York: Cambridge University Press.

Headrick, Daniel R. 1981. *The Tools of Empire: Technology and European Imperialism in the Nineteenth Century*. New York: Oxford University Press.

Hemphill, W. Edwin, ed. 1963. *The Papers of John C. Calhoun*. Vol. 2, *1817–1818*. Columbia: University of South Carolina Press.

Hemphill, W. Edwin, ed. 1967. *The Papers of John C. Calhoun*. Vol. 3, *1818–1819*. Columbia: University of South Carolina Press.

Henderson, W. O. 1965. "German East Africa, 1884–1918." In *History of East Africa*, Vol. 2, edited by Vincent Harlow, E. M. Chilver, and Alison Smith, 123–162. Oxford: Clarendon.

Herring, George C. 2008. *From Colony to Superpower: U.S. Foreign Relations since 1776*. New York: Oxford University Press.

Herz, Monica, and João Pontes Nogueira. 2002. *Ecuador vs. Peru: Peacemaking amid Rivalry*. Boulder, CO: Lynne Rienner.

Hobson, J. A. 1902. *Imperialism: A Study*. London: James Nisbett.

Holmstrom, Bengt. 1979. "Moral Hazard and Observability." *Bell Journal of Economics* 10 (1): 74–91

Hopkins, James F., ed. 1961. *The Papers of Henry Clay*. Vol. 2, *The Rising Statesman, 1815–1820*. Lexington: University of Kentucky Press.

Howe, Daniel Walker. 2007. *What Hath God Wrought: The Transformation of America, 1815–1848*. New York: Oxford University Press.

Hsü, Immanuel C. Y. 1965. *The Ili Crisis: A Study of Sino-Russian Diplomacy, 1871–1881*. Oxford: Clarendon.

Hughes-Hallett, Lucy. 2013. *Gabriele D'Annunzio: Poet, Seducer, and Preacher of War*. New York: Knopf.

Huttenback, Robert A. 1962. *British Relations with Sind, 1799–1843: An Anatomy of Imperialism*. Berkeley: University of California Press.

Huttenback, Robert A. 1993. "The Annexation of Sind (1843)." In *The Politics of the British Annexation of India, 1757–1857*, edited by Michael H. Fischer, 224–248. Oxford: Oxford University Press.

Huurdeman, Anton A. 2003. *The Worldwide History of Telecommunications*. Hoboken, NJ: John Wiley and Sons.

Hyam, Ronald. 1999. "The Primacy of Geopolitics: The Dynamics of British Imperial Policy, 1763–1963." *Journal of Imperial and Commonwealth History* 27 (2): 27–52.

International Military Tribunal for the Far East. 1947. Transcript of Proceedings (May 14), 22112–22114. Available at https://www.legal-tools.org/doc/bf54e7/.

Iriye, Akira. 1984. "Introduction." In *Japan Erupts: The London Naval Conference and the Manchurian Incident, 1928–1932*, edited by James William Morley, 233–240. New York: Columbia University Press.

Iriye, Akira. 1989. "Japan's Drive to Great-Power Status." In *The Cambridge History of Japan*, Vol. 5, *The Nineteenth Century*, edited by Marius B. Jansen, 721–782. New York: Cambridge University Press.

James, Lawrence. 1997. *Raj: The Making and Unmaking of British India*. London: Little, Brown.

Jansen, Marius B. 2000. *The Making of Modern Japan*. Cambridge, MA: Harvard University Press.

Jelavich, Charles, and Barbara Jelavich, eds. 1959. *Russia in the East, 1876–1880: The Russo-Turkish War and the Kuldja Crisis as Seen through the Letters of A.G. Jomini to N.K. Giers*. Leiden: E. J. Brill.

Jensen, Michael C., and William H. Meckling. 1976. "Theory of the Firm: Managerial Behavior, Agency Costs and Ownership Structure." *Journal of Financial Economics* 3 (4): 305–360.

Jervis, Robert. 1968. "Hypotheses on Misperception." *World Politics* 20 (3): 454–479.

Jervis, Robert. 1976. *Perception and Misperception in International Politics*. Princeton, NJ: Princeton University Press.

Jervis, Robert. 1998. *System Effects: Complexity in Political and Social Life*. Princeton, NJ: Princeton University Press.

Journal officiel de la République française. Débats parlementaires. Sénat: Compte redu in-extenso. March 14, 1883.

Kanya-Forstner, A. S. 1969. *The Conquest of the Western Sudan: A Study in French Military Imperialism*. Cambridge: Cambridge University Press.

Keck, Margaret E., and Kathryn Sikkink. 1998. *Activists beyond Borders: Advocacy Networks in International Politics*. Ithaca, NY: Cornell University Press.

Kennedy, Conor M., and Andrew S. Erickson. 2017. "China's Third Sea Force, the People's Armed Forces Maritime Militia: Tethered to the PLA." *CMSI China Maritime Report* 1:1–22.

Kennedy, Paul M. 1971. "Imperial Cable Communications and Strategy, 1870–1914." *English Historical Review* 86 (341): 728–752.

Kennedy, Paul M. 1980. *The Rise of Anglo-German Antagonism, 1860–1914*. Boston: Allen and Unwin.

Kido, Koichi. 1984. *The Diary of Marquis Kido, 1931–45: Selected Translations into English*. Frederick: University Publications of America.

King, Gary, Robert Keohane, and Sidney Verba. 1994. *Designing Social Inquiry: Scientific Inference in Qualitative Research*. Princeton, NJ: Princeton University Press.

Kiser, Edgar. 1999. "Comparing Varieties of Agency Theory in Economics, Political Science, and Sociology: An Illustration from State Policy Implementation." *Sociological Theory* 17 (2): 146–170.

Klein, Martin A. 1998. *Slavery and Colonial Rule in French West Africa*. New York: Cambridge University Press.

Klunder, Willard Carl. 1996. *Lewis Cass and the Politics of Moderation*. Kent, OH: Kent State University Press.

Knoll, Arthur J. 1976. *Togo under Imperial Germany, 1884–1914: A Case Study in Colonial Rule*. Stanford, CA: Stanford University Press.

Knoll, Arthur J., and Hermann J. Hiery, eds. 2010. *The German Colonial Experience: Select Documents on German Rule in Africa, China, and the Pacific, 1884–1914*. Lanham, MD: University Press of America.

Kohen, Marcelo G. 2015. "Conquest." In *The Max Planck Encyclopedia of Public International Law*, edited by Rüdiger Wolfrum. New York: Oxford University Press.

Krakowski, Edouard. 1932. *La Naissance de la IIIᵉ République: Challemel-Lacour, le Philosophe et l'Homme d'État*. Paris: Victor Attinger.

Krause, Peter, and Ehud Eiran. 2018. "How Human Boundaries Become State Borders: Radical Flanks and Territorial Control in the Modern Era." *Comparative Politics* 50 (4): 479–499.

Kupchan, Charles A. 1994. *The Vulnerability of Empire*. Ithaca, NY: Cornell University Press.

Labanca, Nicola. 2021. "Italy: The Military in Politics." In *Oxford Research Encyclopedia of Politics*, edited by William R. Thompson. New York: Oxford University Press.

Labs, Eric J. 1997. "Beyond Victory: Offensive Realism and the Expansion of War Aims." *Security Studies* 6 (4): 1–49.

Laffey, Ella S. 1975. "French Adventurers and Chinese Bandits in Tonkin: The Garnier Affairs in Its Local Context." *Journal of Southeast Asian Studies* 6 (1): 38–51.

Laffey, Ella S. 1979. "Social Dissidence and Government Suppression on the Sino-Vietnam Frontier: The Black Flag Army in Tonkin." *Ch'ing-Shih Wen-T'i* 4 (2): 113–125.

Lake, David A. 1992. "Powerful Pacifists: Democratic States and War." *American Political Science Review* 86 (1): 24–37.

Lake, David A., and Robert Powell. 1999. "International Relations: A Strategic Choice Approach." In *Strategic Choice and International Relations*, edited by David A. Lake and Robert Powell, 3–38. Princeton, NJ: Princeton University Press.

Landes, David S. 1961. "Some Thoughts on the Nature of Economic Imperialism." *Journal of Economic History* 21 (4): 496–512.

Langer, William L. 1960. *The Diplomacy of Imperialism, 1890–1902*. 2nd ed. New York: Alfred A. Knopf.

Lattimore, Owen. 1950. *Pivot of Asia: Sinkiang and the Inner Asian Frontiers of China and Russia*. Boston: Atlantic-Little, Brown.

Ledeen, Michael A. 1977. *The First Duce: D'Annunzio at Fiume*. Baltimore, MD: Johns Hopkins University Press.

Leeds, Brett Ashley, Jeffrey M. Ritter, Sara McLaughlin Mitchell, and Andrew G. Long. 2002. "Alliance Treaty Obligations and Provisions, 1815–1944." *International Interactions* 28 (3): 237–260.

Lenin, V. I. 1987. "Imperialism, the Highest Stage of Capitalism." In *Essential Works of Lenin*, edited by Henry M. Christman, 177–270. New York: Dover.

Levy, Jack S. 2008a. "Case Studies: Types, Designs, and Logics of Inference." *Conflict Management and Peace Science* 25, no. 1 (2008): 1–18.

Levy, Jack S. 2008b. "Counterfactuals and Case Studies." In *The Oxford Handbook of Political Methodology*, edited by Janet M. Box-Steffensmeier, Henry E. Brady, and David Collier, 627–644. New York: Oxford University Press.

Liberman, Peter. 1998. *Does Conquest Pay? The Exploitation of Occupied Industrial Societies*. Princeton, NJ: Princeton University Press.

Lieber, Keir A. 2000. "Grasping the Technological Peace: The Offense-Defense Balance and International Security." *International Security* 25 (1): 71–104.

Lobinov-Rostovsky, Andrei. 1951. *Russia and Asia*. Ann Arbor, MI: George Wahr.

Louis, Wm. Roger. 1967. "Great Britain and German Expansion in Africa, 1884–1919." In *Britain and Germany in Africa: Imperial Rivalry and Colonial Rule*, edited by Prosser Gifford and Wm. Roger Louis, 3–46. New Haven, CT: Yale University Press.

Lowe, John. 1994. *The Great Powers, Imperialism, and the German Problem, 1865–1925*. New York: Routledge.

Lowrie, Walter, and Matthew St. Clair Clarke, eds. 1832. *American State Papers*, Class V: Military Affairs, Vol. 1, 1789–1819. Washington, DC: Gales and Seaton.

Lowrie, Walter, and Walter S. Franklin, eds. 1834. *American State Papers*, Class I: Foreign Relations, Vol. 4, 1815–1822. Washington, DC: Gales and Seaton.

Lozhkina, Anastasia S., Yaroslav A. Shulatov, and Kirill E. Cherevko. 2019. "Soviet-Japanese Relations after the Manchurian Incident, 1931–1932." In *A History of Russo-Japanese Relations: Over Two Centuries of Cooperation and Competition*, edited by Dmitry V. Streltsov and Shimotomai Nobuo, 218–240. Leiden: Brill.

Lustick, Ian S. 1996. "History, Historiography, and Political Science: Multiple Historical Records and the Problem of Selection Bias." *American Political Science Review* 90 (3): 605–618.

Lyall, Jason. 2021. *Divided Armies: Inequality and Battlefield Performance in Modern War*. Princeton, NJ: Princeton University Press.

Lynn-Jones, Sean M. 1998. "Realism and America's Rise." *International Security* 23 (2): 157–182.

Maass, Richard W. 2020. *Picky Eagle: How Democracy and Xenophobia Limited U.S. Territorial Expansion*. Ithaca, NY: Cornell University Press.

MacDonald, J. N. 1921. *A Political Escapade: The Story of Fiume and D'Annunzio*. London: John Murray.

MacDonald, Paul K. 2004. "Peripheral Pulls: Great Power Expansion and Lessons for the 'American Empire.'" Unpublished manuscript, International Studies Association, Montreal, Canada.

MacDonald, Paul K. 2020. "The Governor's Dilemma in Colonial Empires." In *The Governor's Dilemma: Indirect Governance beyond Principals and Agents*, edited by Kenneth W. Abbott, Philipp Genschel, Duncan Snidal, and Bernhard Zangl, 39–58. New York: Oxford University Press.

MacDonald, Paul K., and Joseph M. Parent. 2021. "The Status of Status in World Politics." *World Politics* 73 (2): 358–391.

MacKenzie, David. 1967. "Kaufman of Turkestan: An Assessment of His Administration." *Slavic Review* 26, no. 2 (June 1967): 265–285.

MacKenzie, David. 1969. "Expansion in Central Asia: St. Petersburg vs. the Turkestan Generals." *Canadian Slavic Studies* 3 (2): 286–311.

MacKenzie, David. 1974a. *The Lion of Tashkent: The Career of General M. G. Cherniaev.* Athens: University of Georgia Press.

MacKenzie, David. 1974b. "Turkestan's Significance to Russia (1850–1917)." *Russia Review* 33 (2): 167–188.

MacKenzie, David. 1988. "The Conquest and Administration of Turkestan, 1860–85." In *Russian Colonial Expansion to 1917*, edited by Michael Rywkin, 208–234. New York: Mansell.

MacMillan, Margaret. 2001. *Paris 1919: Six Months That Changed the World.* New York: Random House.

Manning, William R., ed. 1937. *Diplomatic Correspondence of the United States, Inter-American Affairs, 1831–1860.* Vol. 8, *Mexico, 1831–1848 (Mid-Year).* Washington, DC: Carnegie Endowment for International Peace.

Manning, William R., ed. 1939. *Diplomatic Correspondence of the United States, Inter-American Affairs, 1831–1860.* Vol. 12, *Texas and Venezuela.* Washington, DC: Carnegie Endowment for International Peace.

March, Patrick G. 1996. *Eastern Destiny: Russia in Asia and the North Pacific.* Westport, CT: Praeger.

Mares, David R., and David Scott Palmer. 2012. *Power, Institutions, and Leadership in War and Peace: Lessons from Peru and Ecuador, 1995–1998.* Austin: University of Texas Press.

Marten, Kimberly. 2019. "Russia's Use of Semi-State Security Forces: The Case of the Wagner Group." *Post-Soviet Affairs* 35 (3): 181–204.

Masson, André, ed. 1933. *Correspondence Politique du Commandant Rivière au Tonkin, Avril 1882–Mai 1883.* Paris: D'Art et d'Histoire.

Matsusaka, Y. Tak. 1996. "Managing Occupied Manchuria, 1931–1934." In *The Japanese Wartime Empire, 1931–1945*, edited by Peter Duus, Ramon H. Myers, and Mark R. Peattie, 97–135. Princeton, NJ: Princeton University Press.

Matsusaka, Yoshihisa Tak. 2001. *The Making of Japanese Manchuria, 1904–1932.* Cambridge, MA: Harvard University Press.

Maurceley, Charles Baude de. 1884. *Le Commandant Rivière et l'expédition du Tonkin.* Paris: P. Ollendorff.

McAdam, Doug, Sidney Tarrow, and Charles Tilly. 2001. *Dynamics of Contention.* New York: Cambridge University Press.

McAfee, R. Preston, Hugo M. Mialon, and Sue H. Mialon. 2010. "Do Sunk Costs Matter?" *Economic Inquiry* 48 (2): 323–336.

McAleavy, Henry. 1968. *Black Flags in Vietnam: The Story of a Chinese Intervention.* London: George Allen and Unwin.

McIntyre, W. David. 1967. *The Imperial Frontier in the Tropics, 1867–75: A Study in British Colonial Policy in West Africa, Malaya and the South Pacific in the Age of Gladstone and Disraeli.* New York: St. Martin's.

McLeod, Mark W. 1991. *The Vietnamese Response to French Intervention, 1862–1874.* New York: Praeger.

Meacham, Jon. 2008. *American Lion: Andrew Jackson in the White House.* New York: Random House.

Mearsheimer, John J. 2014. *The Tragedy of Great Power Politics.* Rev. ed. New York: W. W. Norton.

Meinig, D. W. 1993. *The Shaping of America: A Geographical Perspective on 500 Years of History.* Vol. 2, *Continental America, 1800–1867.* New Haven, CT: Yale University Press.

Meinig, D. W. 1998. *The Shaping of America: A Geographical Perspective on 500 Years of History*. Vol. 3, *Transcontinental America, 1850–1915*. New Haven, CT: Yale University Press.

Mercer, Jonathan. 1996. *Reputation and International Politics*. Ithaca, NY: Cornell University Press.

Meritt, H. P. 1978. "Bismarck and the German Interest in East Africa, 1884–1885." *Historical Journal* 21 (1): 97–116.

Miller, Charles A. 2019. "Sunk Costs and Political Decision Making." In *Oxford Research Encyclopedia of Politics*, edited by William R. Thompson. New York: Oxford University Press.

Miller, Gary J. 2005. "The Political Evolution of Principal-Agent Models." *Annual Review of Political Science* 8:203–225.

Mintzberg, Henry, and James A. Waters. 1985. "Of Strategies, Deliberate and Emergent." *Strategic Management Journal* 6 (3): 257–272.

Mizoguchi, Toshiyuki. 1989. "The Changing Pattern of Sino-Japanese Trade, 1884–1937." In *The Japanese Informal Empire in China, 1895–1937*, edited by Peter Duus, Ramon H. Myers, and Mark R. Peattie, 10–30. Princeton, NJ: Princeton University Press.

Moe, Terry M. 1984. "The New Economics of Organization." *American Journal of Political Science* 28 (4): 739–777.

Mondini, Marco. 2006. "Between Subversion and Coup d'État: Military Power and Politics after the Great War (1919–1922)," *Journal of Modern Italian Studies* 11 (4): 445–464.

Moon, Penderel. 1989. *The British Conquest and Dominion of India*. London: Gerald Duckworth.

Morris, Peter. 1975. "The Russians in Central Asia, 1870–1887." *Slavonic and European Review* 53 (133): 521–538.

Morrison, Alexander. 2014a. "Russia, Khoqand, and the Search for a 'Natural' Frontier, 1863–1865." *Ab Imperio* 2:166–192.

Morrison, Alexander. 2014b. "'Nechto erotischeskoe', 'Courir après l'ombre'? Logistical Imperatives and the Fall of Tashkent." *Central Asian Survey* 33 (2): 153–169.

Morrison, Alexander. 2021. *The Russian Conquest of Central Asia: A Study in Imperial Expansion, 1814–1914*. Cambridge: Cambridge University Press.

Moser, Harold D., David R. Hoth, and George H. Hoemann, eds. 1994. *The Papers of Andrew Jackson*. Vol. 4, *1816–1820*. Knoxville: University of Tennessee Press.

Muller, Julius W., ed. 1917. *Presidential Messages and State Papers*. Vol. 4. New York: Review of Reviews.

Munholland, Kim. 1979. "Admiral Jauréguiberry and the French Scramble for Tonkin, 1879–83." *French Historical Studies* 11 (1): 81–107.

Musgrave, Paul, and Daniel H. Nexon. 2018. "Defending Hierarchy from the Moon to the Indian Ocean: Symbolic Capital and Political Dominance in Early Modern China and the Cold War." *International Organization* 72 (3): 591–626.

Myers, Ramon H. 1989. "Japanese Imperialism in Manchuria: The South Manchuria Railway Company, 1906–1933." In *The Japanese Informal Empire in China, 1895–1937*, edited by Peter Duus, Ramon H. Myers, and Mark R. Peattie, 101–132. Princeton, NJ: Princeton University Press.

Myrick, Rachel. 2021. "Do External Threats Unite or Divide? Security Crises, Rivalries, and Polarization in American Foreign Policy." *International Organization* 75 (4): 921–958.

Nexon, Daniel H., and Thomas Wright. 2007. "What's at Stake in the American Empire Debate." *American Political Science Review* 101 (2): 253–271.

Nish, Ian. 1993. *Japan's Struggle with Internationalism: Japan, China and the League of Nations, 1931–33*. London: Kegan Paul International.

Nish, Ian. 2002. *Japanese Foreign Policy in the Interwar Period*. Westport, CT: Praeger.

Niven, John. 1988. *John C. Calhoun and the Price of Union: A Biography*. Baton Rouge: Louisiana State University Press.

Norman, C. B. 1884. *Tonkin, or France in the Far East*. London: Chapman and Hall.

Nugent, Walter. 2008. *Habits of Empire: A History of American Expansion*. New York: Vintage Books.

O'Dwyer, Emer. 2017. "Japanese Empire in Manchuria." In *Oxford Research Encyclopedia of Asian History*, edited by David Ludden. New York: Oxford University Press.

Ogata, Sadako N. 1984. *Defiance in Manchuria: The Making of Japanese Foreign Policy, 1931–1932*. Westport, CT: Greenwood.

Osborne, Milton. 1995. "Francis Garnier (1839–1873): Explorer of the Mekong River." In *Explorers of South-East Asia: Six Lives*, edited by Victor T. King, 51–107. Kuala Lumpur: Oxford University Press.

Osborne, Milton. 1996. *River Road to China: The Search for the Source of the Mekong, 1866–73*. New York: Atlantic Monthly.

Owsley Jr., Frank L. 1985. "Ambrister and Arbuthnot: Adventurers or Martyrs of British Honor?" *Journal of the Early Republic* 5 (3): 289–308.

Paine, S. C. M. 1996. *Imperial Rivals: China, Russia, and Their Disputed Frontier*. New York: M. E. Sharpe.

Pakenham, Thomas. 2003. *The Scramble for Africa: White Man's Conquest of the Dark Continent from 1876 to 1912*. New York: Perennial.

Papers Relating to the Foreign Relations of the United States, Transmitted to Congress, with the Annual Message of the President, December 7, 1874. 1874. Washington, DC: US Government Printing Office.

Parker, Charles Stuart, ed. 1899. *Sir Robert Peel: From His Private Papers*. Vol. 3. 2nd ed. London: John Murray.

Pearce, Robert. 2009. "D'Annunzio, Fiume, and Fascism." *History Review* 64:24–29.

Peattie, Mark R. 1975. *Ishiwara Kanji and Japan's Confrontation with the West*. Princeton, NJ: Princeton University Press.

Peattie, Mark R. 1989a. "The Japanese Colonial Empire, 1895–1945." In *The Cambridge History of Japan*, Vol. 6, *The Twentieth Century*, edited by Peter Duus, 215–270. New York: Cambridge University Press.

Peattie, Mark R. 1989b. "Japanese Treaty Port Settlements in China, 1895–1937." In *The Japanese Informal Empire in China, 1895–1937*, edited by Peter Duus, Ramon H. Myers, and Mark R. Peattie, 166–209. Princeton, NJ: Princeton University Press.

Perkins, Bradford. 1964. *Castlereagh and Adams: England and the United States, 1812–1823*. Berkeley: University of California Press.

Perras, Arne. 2004. *Carl Peters and German Imperialism, 1856–1918: A Political Biography*. Oxford: Oxford University Press.

Peters, Carl. 1891a. "From the Mouth of the Tana to the Source-Region of the Nile." *Scottish Geographical Magazine* 7 (3): 113–123.

Peters, Carl. 1891b. *New Light on Dark Africa: Being the Narrative of the German Emin Pasha Expedition*. Translated by H. W. Dulcken. London: Ward, Lock.

Peters, Carl. 2001. *How German East Africa Was Founded*. Translated by Philip O'Connor. Belfast: Athol Books.

Peterson, Thomas E. 2004. "Schismogenesis and National Character: The D'Annunzio-Mussolini Correspondence." *Italica* 81 (1): 44–64.

Pierce, Richard A. 1960. *Russian Central Asia, 1867–1917: A Study in Colonial Rule*. Berkeley: University of California Press.

Pletcher, David M. 1973. *The Diplomacy of Annexation: Texas, Oregon, and the Mexican War*. Columbia: University of Missouri Press.

Pollack, Oliver B. 1978. "A Mid-Victorian Coverup: The Case of the 'Combustible Commodore' and the Second Anglo-Burmese War, 1851–1852." *Albion: A Quarterly Journal Concerned with British Studies* 10 (2): 171–183.

Popescu, Ionut C. 2018. "Grand Strategy vs. Emergent Strategy in the Conduct of Foreign Policy." *Journal of Strategic Studies* 41 (3): 438–460.

Porch, Douglas. 1982. *The Conquest of Morocco*. New York: Alfred A. Knopf.

Porch, Douglas. 1984. *The Conquest of the Sahara*. New York: Farrar, Straus, and Giroux.

Posen, Barry R. 1984. *The Sources of Military Doctrine: France, Britain, and Germany between the World Wars*. Ithaca, NY: Cornell University Press.

Power Jr., Thomas F. 1977. *Jules Ferry and the Renaissance of French Imperialism*. New York: Octagon Books.

Press, Daryl G. 2005. *Calculating Credibility: How Leaders Assess Military Threats*. Ithaca, NY: Cornell University Press.

Press, Steven. 2017. *Rogue Empires: Contracts and Conmen in Europe's Scramble for Africa*. Cambridge, MA: Harvard University Press.

Quinn, Frederick. 2000. *The French Overseas Empire*. Westport, CT: Praeger.

Rathbun, Brian. 2018. "The Rarity of Realpolitik: What Bismarck's Rationality Reveals about International Politics." *International Security* 43 (1): 7–55.

Remini, Robert V. 1977. *Andrew Jackson and the Course of American Empire, 1767–1821*. New York: Harper and Row.

Remini, Robert V. 1981. *Andrew Jackson and the Course of American Freedom, 1822–1832*. Vol. 2. New York: Harper and Row.

Remini, Robert V. 1984. *Andrew Jackson and the Course of American Democracy, 1833–1845*. Vol. 3. New York: Harper and Row.

Reuss, Martin. 1981. "The Disgrace and Fall of Carl Peters: Morality, Politics, and Staatsräson in the Time of Wilhelm II." *Central European History* 14 (2): 110–141.

Rich, Norman. 1992. *Great Power Diplomacy, 1814–1914*. Boston: McGraw-Hill.

Ritchie, Eric Moore. 1940. *The Unfinished War: The Drama of Anglo-German Conflict in Africa in Relation to the Future of the British Empire*. London: Eyre and Spottiswoode.

Roberts, Stephen H. 1963. *The History of French Colonial Policy, 1870–1925*. London: Frank Cass.

Robinson, Ronald. 1972. "Non-European Foundations of European Imperialism: Sketch for a Theory of Collaboration." In *Studies in the Theory of Imperialism*, edited by Roger Owen and Robert B. Sutcliffe, 117–142. London: Longman.

Robiquet, Paul, ed. 1897. *Discours et Opinion de Jules Ferry: Publiés avec Commentaires et Notes*, Vol. 5: *Discours sur la Politique Extérieure et Coloniale*. Paris: Armand Colin.

Rush, Richard. 1833. *A Residence at the Court of London, 1817–1819*. London: Richard Bentley.

Rusinow, Dennison I. 1969. *Italy's Austrian Heritage, 1919–1946*. Oxford: Oxford University Press.

Sadaheo, Jeff. 2007. *Russian Colonial Society in Tashkent, 1865–1923*. Bloomington: Indiana University Press.

Sanderson, G. N. 1963. "The Anglo-German Agreement of 1890 and the Upper Nile." *English Historical Review* 78 (306): 49–72.

Sanderson, G. N. 1965. *England, Europe, and the Upper Nile, 1882–1899: A Study in the Partition of Africa*. Edinburgh: Edinburgh University Press.

Saray, Mehmet. 1982. "The Russian Conquest of Central Asia." *Central Asian Survey* 1 (2–3): 1–30.

Sarkees, Meredith Reid, and Frank Wayman. 2010. *Resort to War: 1816–2007*. Washington, DC: CQ Press.

Schuyler, Eugene. 1876. *Turkistan: Notes of a Journey in Russian Turkistan, Khokand, Bukhara, and Kuldja*. Vol. 1. New York: Scribner, Armstrong.

Schweller, Randall. 1994. "Bandwagoning for Profit: Bringing the Revisionist State Back In." *International Security* 19 (1): 72–107.

Schweller, Randall. 2006. *Unanswered Threats: Political Constraints on the Balance of Power*. Princeton, NJ: Princeton University Press.

Seeley, John Robert. 1883. *The Expansion of England: Two Courses of Lectures*. London: MacMillan.

Seki, Hiroharu. 1984. "The Manchurian Incident, 1931." Translated by Marius B. Jansen. In *Japan Erupts: The London Naval Conference and the Manchurian Incident, 1928–1932*, edited by James William Morley, 139–230. New York: Columbia University Press.

Serebrennikov, A. G., ed. 1914. *Turkestanskii krai: Sbornik Materialov Dlya Istorii ego Zavoevaniya*, 1864, Pt. 1. Tashkent: Tip. Shtaba Turkestanskago Voen. Okruga.

Sergeev, Evgeny. 2013. *The Great Game, 1856–1907: Russo-British Relations in Central and East Asia*. Washington, DC: Woodrow Wilson Center.

Seton-Watson, Hugh. 1967. *The Russian Empire, 1801–1917*. London: Oxford University Press.

Sforza, Count Carlo. 1938. "D'Annunzio, Inventor of Fascism." *Books Abroad* 12 (3): 269–271.

Shapiro, Susan P. 2005. "Agency Theory." *Annual Review of Sociology* 31:263–284.

Shimada, Toshihiko. 1984. "The Extension of Hostilities, 1931–1932." Translated by Akira Iriye. In *Japan Erupts: The London Naval Conference and the Manchurian Incident, 1928–1932*, edited by James William Morley, 241–335. New York: Columbia University Press.

Singer, J. David, Stuart Bremer, and John Stuckey. 1972. "Capability Distribution, Uncertainty, and Major Power War, 1820–1965." In *Peace, War, and Numbers*, edited by Bruce Russett, 19–48. Beverly Hills: Sage.

Smith, Denis Mack. 1997. *Modern Italy: A Political History*. Ann Arbor: University of Michigan Press.

Smith, Woodruff D. 1978. *The German Colonial Empire*. Chapel Hill: University of North Carolina Press.

Snyder, Glenn H. 1996. "Process Variables in Neorealist Theory." *Security Studies* 5 (3): 167–192.

Snyder, Jack. 1984. *Ideology of the Offensive: Military Decision Making and the Disasters of 1914*. Ithaca, NY: Cornell University Press.

Snyder, Jack. 1991. *Myths of Empire: Domestic Politics and International Ambition*. Ithaca, NY: Cornell University Press.

Snyder, Jack. 2014. "Better Now Than Later: The Paradox of 1914 as Everyone's Favored Year for War." *International Security* 39 (1): 71–94.

Statistical Yearbook of Viet Nam, 2019. 2019. Hanoi: Statistical.

Stern, Jacques. 1944. *The French Colonies: Past and Future*. Translated by Norbert Guterman. New York: Didier.

Stewart, R. M. J. 1982. "Raffles of Singapore: The Man and the Legacy." *Asian Affairs* 13 (1): 16–27.

Strachan, Hew. 2004. *The First World War in Africa*. New York: Oxford University Press.

Strandmann, Hartmut Pogge von. 1969. "Domestic Origins of Germany's Colonial Expansion under Bismarck." *Past and Present* 42:140–159.

Sutch, Richard, and Susan B. Carter, ed. 2020. *Historical Statistics of the United States*. Millennial ed. New York: Cambridge University Press. Available at https://hsus.cambridge.org/HSUSWeb/HSUSEntryServlet.

Taboulet, Georges. 1956. *La Geste Française en Indochine*. Vol. 2. Paris: Adrien-Maissonneuve.

Taliaferro, Jeffrey W. 2004. *Balancing Risks: Great Power Intervention on the Periphery*. Ithaca, NY: Cornell University Press.

Tang, Shiping. 2005. "Reputation, Cult of Reputation, and International Conflict." *Security Studies* 14 (1): 34–62.

Tarar, Ahmer. 2016. "A Strategic Logic of the Military Fait Accompli." *International Studies Quarterly* 60 (4): 742–752.

Taylor, A. J. P. 1970. *Germany's First Bid for Colonies, 1884–1885: A Move in Bismarck's European Policy*. New York: W. W. Norton.

Thaler, Richard. 1980. "Toward a Positive Theory of Consumer Choice." *Journal of Economic Behavior and Organization* 1 (1): 39–60.

Thompson, Virginia. 1937. *French Indo-China*. New York: MacMillan.

Thomson, Janice E. 1996. *Mercenaries, Pirates, and Sovereigns: State-Building and Extraterritorial Violence in Early Modern Europe*. Princeton, NJ: Princeton University Press.

Tir, Jaroslav, Philip Schafer, Paul F. Diehl, and Gary Goertz. 1998. "Territorial Changes, 1816–1996: Procedures and Data." *Conflict Management and Peace Science* 16 (1): 89–97.

Tobe, Ryōchi. 2019. "Japan's Policy toward the Soviet Union, 1931–1941: The Japanese-Soviet Non-aggression Pact." In *A History of Russo-Japanese Relations: Over Two Centuries of Cooperation and Competition*, edited by Dmitry V. Streltsov and Shimotomai Nobuo, 201–217. Leiden: Brill.

Townsend, Mary Evelyn. 1930. *The Rise and Fall of Germany's Colonial Empire, 1884–1918*. New York: MacMillan.

Turnbull, C. M. 2009. *A History of Modern Singapore, 1819–2005*. Singapore: National University of Singapore Press.

US Department of State, Division of Foreign Intelligence. 1920. *The Adriatic Question: Papers Relating to the Italian-Jugoslav Boundary*. Series M, No. 167. Washington, DC: US Government Printing Office.

Van Der Oye, David Schimmelpenninck. 2006. "Russian Foreign Policy: 1815–1917." In *The Cambridge History of Russia*, Vol. 2, *Imperial Russia, 1689–1917*, edited by Dominic Lieven, 554–574. New York: Cambridge University Press.

Van Evera, Stephen. 1984. "The Cult of the Offensive and the Origins of the First World War." *International Security* 9 (1): 58–107.

Van Evera, Stephen. 1998. "Offense, Defense, and the Causes of War." *International Security* 22 (4): 5–43.

Van Evera, Stephen. 1999. *The Causes of War: Power and the Roots of Conflict*. Ithaca, NY: Cornell University Press.

Walter, Barbara F. 2003. "Explaining the Intractability of Territorial Conflict." *International Studies Review* 5 (4): 137–153.

Waltz, Kenneth N. 2010. *Theory of International Politics*. Long Grove, IL: Waveland.

Weeks, Jessica L. 2008. "Autocratic Audience Costs: Regime Type and Signaling Resolve." *International Organization* 62 (1): 35–64.

Weeks, William Earl. 1992. *John Quincy Adams and American Global Empire*. Lexington: University Press of Kentucky.

Weeks, William Earl. 1996. *Building the Continental Empire: American Expansion from the Revolution to the Civil War*. Chicago: Ivan R. Dee.

Weeks, William Earl. 2013. *The New Cambridge History of American Foreign Relations*. Vol. 1, *Dimensions of the Early American Empire, 1754–1865*. New York: Cambridge University Press.

Wehler, Hans-Ulrich. 1970. "Bismarck's Imperialism, 1862–1890." *Past and Present* 48:119–155.

Weisiger, Alex. 2014. "Victory without Peace: Conquest, Insurgency, and War Termination." *Conflict Management and Peace Science* 31 (4): 357–382.

Weiss, Jessica Chen. 2013. "Authoritarian Signaling, Mass Audiences, and Nationalist Protest in China." *International Organization* 67 (1): 1–35.

Weland, James E. 1977. "The Japanese Army in Manchuria: Covert Operations and the Roots of Kwantung Army Insubordination." PhD diss., University of Arizona.

Weland, James. 1994. "Misguided Intelligence: Japanese Military Officers in the Manchurian Incident, September 1931." *Journal of Military History* 58 (3): 445–460.

Wendt, Alexander. 2004. "The State as a Person in International Theory." *Review of International Studies* 30 (2): 289–316.

Wesseling, H. L. 1996. *Divide and Rule: The Partition of Africa, 1880–1914*. Translated by Arnold J. Pomerans. Westport, CT: Praeger.

White, Peter. 2021. "Generals in the Cabinet: Military Participation in Government and International Conflict Initiation." *International Studies Quarterly* 65 (2): 551–561.

Wieczynski, Joseph L., ed. 1980. *The Modern Encyclopedia of Russian and Soviet History*, Vol. 16. Gulf Breeze, FL: Academic International Press.

Wieczynski, Joseph L., ed. 1981. *The Modern Encyclopedia of Russian and Soviet History*, Vol. 20. Gulf Breeze, FL: Academic International Press.

Wieczynski, Joseph L., ed. 1983. *The Modern Encyclopedia of Russian and Soviet History*, Vol. 33. Gulf Breeze, FL: Academic International Press.

Wilson, Woodrow. 2023. "Wilson's 'Fourteen Points,' January 8, 1918." University of Virginia Miller Center Presidential Speeches. Available at https://millercenter.org/the-presidency/presidential-speeches/january-8-1918-wilsons-fourteen-points.

Wood, Gordon S. 2009. *Empire of Liberty: A History of the Early Republic, 1789–1815*. New York: Oxford University Press.

Yoshihashi, Takehiko. 1963. *Conspiracy at Mukden: The Rise of the Japanese Military*. New Haven, CT: Yale University Press.

Young, Louise. 1996. "Imagined Empire: The Cultural Construction of Manchukuo." In *The Japanese Wartime Empire, 1931–1945*, edited by Peter Duus, Ramon H. Myers, and Mark R. Peattie, 71–96. Princeton, NJ: Princeton University Press.

Young, Louise. 1998. *Japan's Total Empire: Manchuria and the Culture of Wartime Imperialism*. Berkeley: University of California Press.

Zacher, Mark W. 2001. "The Territorial Integrity Norm: International Boundaries and the Use of Force." *International Organization* 55 (2): 215–250.

Zakaria, Fareed. 1998. *From Wealth to Power: The Unusual Origins of America's World Role*. Princeton, NJ: Princeton University Press.

Zakharova, Larisa. 2006. "The Reign of Alexander II: A Watershed?" In *The Cambridge History of Russia*, Vol. 2, *Imperial Russia, 1689–1917*, edited by Dominic Lieven, 593–616. New York: Cambridge University Press.

Index

Page numbers in italics refer to figures and tables.